A CRITICAL INTRODUCTION TO THE POEMS OF THOMAS HARDY

Trevor Johnson

MACMILLAN

821
8
HAR
Joh

First published 1991

Published by
MACMILLAN EDUCATION LTD
Houndmills, Basingstoke, Hampshire RG21 2XS
and London
Companies and representatives
throughout the world

Printed in Hong Kong

British Library Cataloguing in Publication Data
Johnson, Trevor, *1929–*
A critical introduction to the poems of Thomas Hardy.
1. Poetry in English. Hardy, Thomas, 1840–1928
I. Title
821.8

ISBN 0–333–49577–2
ISBN 0–333–49578–0 pbk

14/10/92

Contents

For my wife, Margaret, without whom I should never finish anything, and my daughters, Sarah and Kate.

Acknowledgements

The author and publishers are indebted to *The Folio Society* for their permission to use the wood-engraved portrait of Thomas Hardy by Jacques Hnizdovsky which adorns the front cover and to the Librarian and Fellows of Magdalene College, Cambridge for their permission to reproduce Hardy's manuscript of *During Wind and Rain*, which forms the frontispiece.

The text used for Hardy's poems is that of Dr James Gibson's *Thomas Hardy: The Complete Poems* (Macmillan, 1976) and I also owe a great deal to his *Variorum Complete Poems*. To the late J. O. Bailey's and to Frank Pinion's handbooks to Hardy's verse I am often indebted, while no one who writes on Hardy can afford to neglect Michael Millgate's definitive biography.

It would be invidious to single out individuals among the many critics from whose work I have profited over the years, but I take this occasion to thank the many generations of English students at Mather and at the City of Manchester Colleges, from whose insights into Hardy's poems this book will derive a good deal of any value it may have.

Finally, to those who may have read my previous articles and essays on Hardy's poetry, and who recognise occasional fragments from them embedded in this book, I hope they will forgive me if, where I felt I could not improve on what I had already said of a poem, I have let it stand here.

TREVOR JOHNSON

Note on abbreviations
Throughout the text I have employed the following abbreviations:
(1) *Life* (or *The Life*) for *The Life of Thomas Hardy* by F. E. Hardy (Macmillan, 1962).
(2) MS for [Hardy's] holograph manuscript, i.e. of the poems in question.
Other abbreviations are dealt with in the sections where they occur.

During Wind & Rain

They sing their dearest songs —
He, she, all of them — yea,
Treble & tenor & bass,
   And one to play;
With the candles mooning each face , ...
   Ah, no; the years O!
How the sick leaves reel down in throngs!

They clear the creeping moss —
Elders & juniors — yea,
Making the pathways neat
   And the garden gay;
And they build a shady seat . . . .
   Ah, no; the years O!
See, The webbed white storm-birds wing across‡

They are blithely breakfasting all —
Men & maidens — yea,
Under the summer tree,
   With a glimpse of the bay,
While pet birds come to the knee . . . .
   Ah, no; the years O!
The rotten rose is ript from the wall.

                    They

They change to a high new house,
He, she, all of them — yea,
Clocks & carpets & chairs
    On the lawn all day,
And brightest things that are theirs.....
    Ah, no; the years O!
Down their chiselled names the rain-drop ploughs.

During Wind and Rain (441/ALL/*). The MS shows Hardy's clear, strong handwriting. Hardy's emendations to the text given here are discussed in the detailed analysis of the poem on pp. 167–9. Reproduced by permission of the Master and Fellows, Magdalene College, Cambridge.

1

Introduction

Thomas Hardy was born in 1840, so that the 150th anniversary of his birth, for which this book was written, seems an appropriate time to offer an introduction to his verse for those – conscripts and volunteers alike – who are approaching it for the first time, probably by way of a selection from his large and diverse output. I believe that Hardy would have approved my intention at least, since he made it a condition of his Will that his *Collected Poems* should continue to be sold at a price 'within the means of poorer readers'. With nearly a dozen selections and three complete editions of his verse in print he must enjoy one of the largest audiences of any poet, past or present, and only a perverse critic would now deny him a place among the titans of English poetry. Moreover, unlike the verse of his contemporaries G. M. Hopkins and W. B. Yeats, his poetry is seldom verbally obscure or technically abstruse. Yet, though usually quite straightforward both in *what* he says and in *how* he says it, what his poems *impart* to us – a poem being much more than a statement – can all too readily be missed by those unaccustomed to his highly individual voice. Because, as one of his most perceptive early critics, Arthur McDowall, observed, 'He seems often bent on showing us how much poetry can do without and still be poetry', it is not difficult to suppose that some of the most profound, technically accomplished, challenging, ironic and resonant verse of this century is hardly poetry at all, or, as some influential critics formerly contended, only very infrequently and, as it were, accidentally so.

I hope to show that this is false; even so it is only by according him that blend of imaginative sympathy and meticulous attention to the words on the page which all great poetry demands that the full rewards of his work can be won. And then indeed, in the words of one of his own favourite poems, Wordsworth's *Tintern Abbey*, we can expect to be 'hearing

1

oftentimes//The still, sad music of humanity'. So much for my aims; now for the approach I have chosen to take.

Chapter 2 is a succinct biography, concentrating on those aspects of Hardy's long life which bear most directly on his verse. Chapter 3 attempts a broad overview of Hardy's poetry and his thoughts on it and poetry in general. Four critical chapters follow and these set a problem which those who approach Hardy via the *Complete Poems* run into headlong. For whereas scarcely any poets have made a formal arrangement of their complete works, we can nearly always study their verse in something close to its chronological order of composition. It is not so with Hardy, for whom accident and his own blend of reticence and indifference combine to complicate matters into an impasse easier to express than to resolve.

Hardy had written verse, on and off, for thirty years before – with trival exceptions – it first saw print in 1898. Because he also revised early drafts extensively, sometimes resurrecting poems 'from an old note' as he put it, he was often unable or unwilling to date them, and even where some do carry an early date it is probable that they were extensively refashioned later. Moreover, he was always an assiduous and meticulous reviser of his verse, even when it had been printed. He had, says the *Life*, 'an artistic inability to rest content [with his poems] until he had brought the expression as near the thought as language would permit'. This perfectionist attitude leaves us with very little juvenilia and so, though it would be an exaggeration to say that Hardy's work shows *no* development, yet the poems in his first and last volumes exhibit far fewer differences in style and subject than the thirty years between them would lead us to expect.

The associated difficulty is one Hardy identified in his *Apology* to *Late Lyrics and Earlier* (1922) when he acknowledged that each of his – ultimately eight – separate volumes was 'a miscellany of various character'. He goes on to regret 'the juxtaposition of un-related, even discordant effusions'. (He might, still more justifiably, have regretted the frequent separation of poems with strong affinities.) His none-too-confident hope that his readers will be 'finely-touched spirits who can define [his intentions] without half a whisper' is qualified by the qualm that less 'intuitive' ones may 'miss the writer's aim' because of this haphazard lack of order. Even when he made his own selections from his poetry his twofold division into *Lyrics* and *Narratives* begs as many questions as it answers, for, as he conceded in his *Select Poems of William Barnes*, it is a virtual impossibility to define the word 'lyric' satisfactorily.

All but two of his fifteen or so successors in compiling selections from his verse have followed his principle of categorisation, but have both modified and amplified it, urging the overriding necessity for readers to encounter the poems in an order which will throw up affinities and avoid fortuitous separations or discordancies. Because, like them, I wish to avoid what Hardy called the 'accidents of inconsequence' and help readers to what he termed 'right note-catching', I have assigned to each critical chapter what appear to me to be an arguably homogenous group of poems, sub-dividing as seems reasonable.

My method – I do not say it is the only or necessarily the best one – is to group by *subject*. Thus Chapter 4 is confined to poems about people, 5 to poems about things (i.e. seasons, places, weather, animals, plants, etc.) 6 to poems about ideas, and 7–8 – less consistently but I think justifiably – to love poems. It will in fact be found that, to a considerable extent, my arrangements tally with Hardy's in his individual volumes, where his intention is detectable, and as he invariably grouped love poems (twice using sub-titles to emphasise the fact) I have done the same. Of course there are some disputable placings, some overlap between categories, some poems that defy categorisation. Still, I hope my readers will come to see the system as having practical advantages which outweigh its defects. To have adopted the arrangement of any one selection would plainly have been arbitrary and restrictive.

I naturally hope my readers will come to own and explore the *Complete Poems* of which the late Philip Larkin said he would not discard a single one, thus echoing Dylan Thomas's remark, 'You've got to read the whole damn lot!' But it would be silly to pretend that Hardy's poetry is always and everywhere equally good – he certainly would have found such a notion laughable – and since the best remains the best, no matter how many people have said so, that is where I start from. By attending closely to the words on the page, and always bearing in mind his dictum that 'The mission of poetry is to record impressions, not convictions', I hope to avoid deserving his mordant dig at those 'reviewers who judge the poetic landscape by a nocturnal exploration with a flash-lantern.'

KEY TO THE USE OF THIS BOOK WITH SELECTIONS FROM HARDY'S VERSE

Two devices should ensure that a reader can easily refer to the full text of any poem under detailed discussion. The coding system explained below will show, at a glance, whether or not the poem in question is in the reader's chosen selection. Second, with all detailed analyses the full text is printed here if it does not appear in ALL the selections listed below. Two examples will clarify the system. The coded information immediately follows the *first* appearance of a poem's title in brackets and is always repeated at the point (if it is not the same point) where full discussion occurs.

Examples (a) *Afterwards* (247/ALL/H/*) and (b) *The Ruined Maid* (218/C/D/W/*)

In both (a) and (b) the number following the title is the serial number assigned to the poem for ease of reference in *The Complete Poems of Thomas Hardy*, edited by James Gibson (Macmillan, 1976). The standard single-volume edition, it prints the eight volumes of Hardy's verse in order of issue, adding a further 27 'uncollected poems and fragments'. It is from this edition (subsequently abbreviated to CP) that the text is taken. The same numeration is used in Gibson's *Variorum CP* (see the Further Reading List).

In (a) the word ALL indicates that *all* the first four listed selections include the poem. H indicates that Hardy himself included it in his own *Chosen Poems* (1929), an enlargement of his earlier *Selected Poems* (1916) up to *Human Shows* (1925). The final symbol, an asterisk (used to avoid confusion with H = Hardy) indicates inclusion in *The Oxford Authors: Thomas Hardy* [Poems], edited by Samuel Hynes (OUP, 1984).

In (b) the coding following the CP number shows which selections include *The Ruined Maid*. Because this is not in ALL the chosen selections whereas I have elected to give it a full analysis, its text is, in this instance, printed here prior to the analysis. But many poems are more briefly considered which only appear in some selections. Every selection (except Hardy's) has an alphabetical *Index of Titles* by which poems mentioned may be located. What I judge to be the five most generally useful selections are, together with Hardy's, set out below, with their codings. They vary considerably in price and scope. All are available in paperback, all have introductions, and all are annotated in varying degrees.

C = Creighton   *Poems by Thomas Hardy A New Selection*, by T. R. M. Creighton (Macmillan, 1974; 2nd edn, 1979). Open University set text.

D = Davies   *Selected Poems of Thomas Hardy*, edited by Walford Davies (Dent, Everyman Classics series, 1984).

G = Gibson   *Chosen Poems of Thomas Hardy*, selected and edited by James Gibson (Macmillan, Student's Hardy series, 1975).

W = Wright   *Thomas Hardy, Selected Poems*, edited with an introduction by David Wright (Penguin Books, 1978).

H = Hardy   *Chosen Poems of Thomas Hardy* [i.e. by himself] (Macmillan, 1929). Of great interest but long out of print and now scarce, though a paperback reprint was done in the 1970s in the USA.

* = Hynes   *The Oxford Authors: Thomas Hardy*, edited by Samuel Hynes (OUP, 1984). N.B. I have coded this copious selection separately because, unlike all the others, it prints the poems it includes in the order of the *Complete Poems* instead of arranging them thematically.

2

Hardy's Life

> The most prosaic man becomes a poem when you stand by his grave at his funeral and think of him.
>
> Hardy's *Notebook* for 29 May 1871

Thomas Hardy himself was not a prosaic man by any means; nevertheless his long life was much less outwardly remarkable than those of many authors. Shelley, for example, the first poet to win his devotion, and Browning, whom he knew personally and admired, both cut much more exciting capers on the stage of the nineteenth century than he did. Naturally this need not imply that his biography is devoid of interest, but his extended double career – starting with fiction and ending with poetry it stretched over some sixty years – means that I shall have to be selective as well as succinct. Where a choice must be made I shall incline to what bears upon his verse, giving very short shrift to his prose. Even so, much will have to be omitted. After all, when Hardy was born on 2 June at Higher Bockhampton in Dorset, Queen Victoria, soon to marry Prince Albert, had only reigned for three years. Who would then have guessed that this frail child of a country stonemason, set aside at birth as still-born and only revived by the sharp-eyed midwife, would live to see the old Queen's grandson on the throne for seventeen years, and entertain the Prince of Wales to tea at his home in Dorchester?

Though Hardy's own maturity coincided with the high noon of Victorian affluence and confidence, he lived to see the ostensibly indestructible fabric of British wealth and empire first crack under the strain of the Boer War and the political upheavals of Edward VII's reign, and then crumble into ruin in the inferno of World War I, which also ended Hardy's hope that mankind was slowly improving. The generation before his birth had witnessed Napoleon's conquest of Europe and England's lonely defiance (the theme of several of his poems

6

and stories). The generation after his death was to see Hitler's megalomania set off World War II, after which the world Hardy knew was lost to sight forever under the pall of Hiroshima.

When Hardy died in 1928, his plans to issue an eighth volume of poems, (drily entitled *Winter Words*) on his eighty-eighth birthday, were far advanced. T. S. Eliot's *The Waste Land* had been on sale for six years then, and Hardy was one of the very few who had read it and made extracts and notes upon it for his common-place book. This testifies to his voracious and catholic appetite for reading. 'That, and that alone' he said, 'was unchanging in [me]'.

One lyric in *Winter Words* tells us a good deal about Hardy's perception of his own personality as a writer. *I Am the One* (818/C/*) begins

> I am the one whom ring-doves see
> Through chinks in boughs
> When they do not rouse
> In sudden dread,
> But stay in cooing, as if they said:
> 'Oh; it's only he.'

It was as such an observer, quiet, sharp eyed and detached, that Hardy chose to portray himself, a man pondering on rather than participating in life, musing on mutability, on 'What bond-servants of Chance//We are all'. *Ditty* (18/D). He had an acute sense of the difference between things as they are and things as they ought to be, an awareness that forms the catalyst for both comic and tragic writing. He saw Man as neither hero nor villain but, like his great tragic creation Michael Henchard (in *The Mayor of Casterbridge*),

> Placed on this isthmus of a middle state,
> A being darkly wise and rudely great.
> Pope, *An Essay on Man*

Accordingly, he had no time for those whom he sardonically christened the 'stout upstanders' who, in face of all evidence, maintain that

> . . . All's well with us: ruers have nought to rue!

and contend

> Our times are blessed times, they cry: Life shapes it as is
> most meet,
> And nothing is much the matter; there are many smiles to a
> tear,
>
> *In Tenebris II* (137/C/D/W/H/*)

For Hardy the truth of the human condition, however disagreeable, was always to be confronted and proclaimed. His outspokenness, at times brutal, was often a salient, frequently a
bitterly resented, feature of his verse. Yet to label him cynic or
pessimist is to discount his all-embracing compassion for living
creatures, animals as well as humans, though this never slips
into easy sentimentality. In his haunting *To an Unborn Pauper
Child* (91/C/D/G/H/*) he asks whether, given the choice, such a
child would elect to be born at all. Next, birth being inevitable,
he expresses his desire to help one against whom Fate has so
cruelly loaded the dice and even allows himself to 'dream' the
child may ' . . . find//Joys seldom yet attained by humankind.'
But, finally, unsparingly, he returns upon himself to admit:

> I am weak as thou, and bare,
> No man may change the common lot to rare.

It is an excoriating simplicity, reminiscent of Shakespeare's
King Lear contemplating humanity as 'Poor naked wretches',
and this immediately felt truthfulness and universality is a
hallmark of Hardy's meditative poetry.

In Hardy, as the critic Middleton Murry remarked in an
obituary tribute, 'The truth once recognised is never suffered
for a moment to be hidden or mollified.' To a mind of his
sombre cast, ultimately unconvinced of any benevolent power's
concern for our world, schemes for the attainment of heaven on
earth had little appeal. Though he did believe, as what he called
a 'meliorist', that mankind could, with much effort and some
luck, better itself by slow degrees; and though he was a lifelong
Liberal in politics, he rarely made his work a platform for any

cause. Like Keats, he distrusted 'Poetry which has a palpable design upon us.'

Never, like such contemporaries as Shaw, Chesterton, Belloc and Arnold Bennett, a public figure, involved in political or religious debate, he did not lavish his creative energies on journalism or even on glowing correspondence. Virtually all his work is imaginative; creative rather than critical. 'Criticism is so easy', he once said, 'and art so hard'. He was indeed a reticent person; a very private man, like William Shakespeare, of whom it has been said that the known facts of his life could be handily written on a postcard. We know a great deal more than that about Hardy, but not as much as we should like. His shyness and secretiveness prompted him to destroy many letters in his last years; his widow presided over sizeable bonfires of documents after his death. It was entirely characteristic of him that when, in his eighties, he set about his autobiography with the help of his wife Florence, he drafted it in the third person, and then arranged for it to appear as *her* work in its entirety, a piece of disinformation that went undetected for more than a decade. In fact, only the concluding chapters are Florence's work. Accordingly, the *Life* omits, or glosses over much that Hardy thought it painful or profitless to record. Nevertheless, it remains the prime source for Hardy's opinions and his early years. All unattributed quotations in this chapter are taken from the *Life*.

So much is by way of general background; in what follows I have tried to divide Hardy's long life and literary career into periods which display some internal coherence. Each section takes its title from one of Hardy's poems.

(i) *The Self-Unseeing* (135/ALL/H/*)

Here is the ancient floor,
Footworn and hollowed and thin,
Here was the former door
Where the dead feet walked in.

She sat here in her chair,
Smiling into the fire;
He who played stood there,
Bowing it higher and higher.

> Childlike, I danced in a dream;
> Blessings emblazoned that day;
> Everything glowed with a gleam;
> Yet we were looking away!

This extraordinarily poignant and lucid small lyric (written between 1892 and 1901), besides displaying Hardy's gift for expressing an idea both simple and universal, conveys to us, indirectly, much of what we most need to know about Hardy's early life. Impressions made in childhood are generally indelible; and it would be hard to think of any writer for whom those years were more important as the seedbed of a later creative flowering. Indeed, a significant number of Hardy's best poems derive more or less directly from childhood experiences like *The Self-Unseeing*.

His birthplace, which he is revisiting in the poem, was built for his grandfather, the first Thomas in a line of three, by Hardy's great-grandfather John. Hardy's paternal ancestors had, he said, been master-masons 'from time immemorial' and, whether or not he was connected with Nelson's flag-captain and the Thomas Hardye who founded the Dorchester Grammar School, his deep and ancient roots in his home county, what he once called his 'parochialism', were of incalculable importance to his poems. Many bear witness to Hardy as local historian, ferreter in old papers and churches, collector of gossip and folk myth. Indeed, the cottage itself was the subject of Hardy's earliest surviving poem *Domicilium* (1/D/G/W/*) as his grandmother Mary recalled it from when she first came to live there in 1801. Then it stood quite alone, and

> . . . heathcroppers [i.e. wild ponies]
> Lived on the hills and were our only friends
> So wild it was when first we settled there.

Its position, on the border between the bleak grandeur of the heathlands of *The Return of the Native* and the gentler, more fertile farmlands of *Far from the Madding Crowd* is a metaphor for Hardy's own blend of tragedy and pastoral comedy, but, when Hardy's mother and father took it over in 1839 other houses had joined it to form a hamlet. As Hardy's father expanded his business and family he enlarged and altered it, hence the 'former door'. The neighbours, like the Hardys, were hospitable (see *The House of Hospitalities* 156/C/D/W/H/*). Relations, friends and workmen made the floor 'footworn and hollow and thin'.

'She' is, of course, Hardy's mother, Jemima, born Jemima Hand. Her drunken, feckless father died young and left her mother to bring up seven children on the pittance of 'parish relief'. No wonder she was tough, resilient, down to earth and ambitious that her offspring should have the advantages fate had denied her. She instilled in all her children a rock-like family solidarity which they never lost and strong traces of her steely will and resentment of patronage can be seen in her firstborn son. Yet there was another side to her. She was an 'omnivorous reader' though no hand with a pen. She had a sense of fun, once dressing herself and Hardy in ragged old clothes to call on and scare relations, and, when in old age she trudged over miles of icy roads to see him and he grumblingly asked why she had taken such risks, she replied 'To enjoy the beauties of nature, of course, and why shouldn't I?' One would have expected this rather formidable personality to have been the dominant influence in Hardy's upbringing as, no doubt, she was, but his father was a man of marked individuality too.

Hardy's father was a fine craftsman and perhaps more successful in business than his son later supposed – the family were never hard up, were indeed quite well off in relative terms. He may have been something of a philanderer. Jemima was certainly three months pregnant at the time she married him, though that would not have raised many eyebrows in rural Dorset at the time perhaps. But more deeply rooted than either avocation was his love of music. It was 'He who played' and he passed on this passionate attachment to his son. He become ' . . . a child of ecstatic temperament, extraordinarily sensitive to music,' who learnt to play the violin when quite young. For Hardy music, classical, popular and folk alike, was a potent influence all his life, as many poems testify. In some he uses the folk-song idiom, in others the stanza patterns – the so-called 'common metres' – of hymns and ballads. In others again a tune – for example, the *Minuet* of Mozart's *E-Flat Symphony* – is the catalyst of the poem. He went on dancing too, until he was over 70. For Hardy then, whose initially fragile health and precocious intelligence secured him plenty of attention, childhood was a stable and happy time. So this poem's solitary unusual word, *emblazoned*, with its suggestion of clear, unfading, heraldic colour effectively highlights the unemphatic but heart-felt *blessings*, and *everything glowed with a gleam*, while no doubt literally true of the furniture, also suggests one of those serene, sunlit interiors typical of the Dutch painters whom Hardy admired. The last line returns with quiet regret and gentle irony to the point made by the title. So clear is the picture, so unerringly selective are Hardy's powers of seeing and saying, that it is as if a small window in time were opened for us to see him there, a snapshot in words which makes formal biography look clumsy. This blend of nostalgia and regret with a re-creation of timeless and self-absorbed delight is also highly characteristic of the mood of Hardy's poetry, while the glance backward is one of his commonest techniques for giving immediacy to the present.

Similar glances illuminate his parents' first encounter (*A Church Romance* 211/ALL/H/*), his father's character (*On One Who Lived and Died Where He was Born* 621/W/*), his mother when he was a small boy (*The Roman Road* 218/C/G/W/H/*) and as a widow (*She Hears the Storm* 228/C/D/W/H/*) with *Bereft* (157/C/D/W/*). One of the most touching is *Logs on the Hearth* (433/C/D/W/*) which Hardy subtitled *A Memory of a Sister*. With his elder sister Mary, to whom it refers, Hardy enjoyed a particularly warm and enduring affinity. She was born only a year after him and was akin in temperament, similarly bookish and inclined to be dreamy and easy going. Both took after their father, in whom a reflective, melancholy streak was also evident. 'He had not the tradesman's soul,' said his son, 'he liked going alone into the woods or on the heath . . . lying on a bank of thyme or camomile, with the grasshoppers leaping over him.'

His younger siblings, Henry and Kate, born respectively ten and sixteen years after him, were much more like their mother, with whom this relaxed attitude to life did not go down at all well. Their arrival also put some stress on the family's finances and may well have militated against Hardy's prolonging his education past sixteen. But Jemima, who had several traits in common with Clym Yeobright's imperious mother (in *The*

Return of the Native) bequeathed him many valuable qualities. He had enough of her own inflexibility of purpose to resent it and rebel when her plans for his future did not coincide with his, which stood him in good stead during his struggles to establish himself as a writer. She once told him that she envisaged Fate as a 'figure standing in our way, . . . arm uplifted to knock us back from any pleasant prospect we indulge in as probable,' a view he came to share. But most importantly, she first encouraged him to read, then gave him books and finally procured him the best education she could find. In doing so she removed him from the village school and from what she probably thought was the rather stifling patronage of the local squire's wife, Mrs Martin. But Hardy had deep feelings for his patroness ' . . . almost those of a lover,' as he recalled, and thus received a stinging foretaste of the Victorian class structure which erected a thorny hedge of prejudice and snobbery between people who might otherwise have found themselves friends or even lovers. This, too, gives a cutting edge to some of his verse, especially such sharply satirical pieces as, for example, *The Conformers* (181/W) and *The Christening* (214/*), to name only two.

He now began to walk the two or three miles to Dorchester, of which his novel *The Mayor of Casterbridge* gives (as he said when the Freedom of the Borough was conferred on him in 1910) 'a sort of essence'. He attended the school kept by a Mr Isaac Last, an able teacher whom he always recalled with gratitude, made rapid progress, waxed in health and vigour, and presently undertook Latin and French as 'extras'. He also devoured every kind of book he could lay his hands on, from Dr Johnson's moral fable *Rasselas* with its dry deflation of human vanity and self-deception, to *The Boy's Own Book* which he saved up for and bought out of coppers earned by playing the fiddle at dances. Yet, small as it was, Dorchester seemed a metropolis to upland shepherds who regarded the railway as a 'marvel' and Hardy always kept in touch with this unchanging rural world, drawing a deep satisfaction from its combination of beauty and utility, as poem after poem testifies; too many to need exemplifying.

Some of his experiences were obviously seminal. He witnessed two public hangings, attended one of the last harvest suppers where the old ballads were sung before they were 'slain at a stroke' by the 'London comic songs' brought in by the advent of the railway, and accompanied his father to parties at which they played their violins for the dancing, despite Jemima's strong disapproval. Some seventy years later he recalled the aftermath of one such outing, as they walked home at 3 a.m. one winter night.

> It was bitterly cold and the moon glistened bright on the encrusted snow, amid which we saw, motionless in the snow, what appeared to be a white human figure without a head. I . . . was for passing the ghastly sight quickly, but my father went up to the object, which proved to be a very tall thin man in a long white smock-frock, leaning against the bank in a drunken stupor, his head hanging forward so low that at a distance he had seemed to have no head at all. Seeing the danger of leaving the man where he might be frozen to death, he awoke him after much exertion, and we supported him home to his cottage, and pushed him through the door, our ears being greeted as we left by a stream of abuse from the man's wife, which was also vented upon her unfortunate husband, whom she promptly knocked down. My father remarked that it might have been as well to leave him where he was, to take his chance of being frozen to death.

That whole incident, atmospheric, slightly macabre, grotesquely comic, and clinched by his father's dour postscript, must have been both shocking and imaginatively formative. It perhaps laid the foundation of that peculiarly Hardeian perception that the road to tragedy may be paved with generous intentions, as in the black comedy of *The Curate's Kindness* (159/C/D/W/*). A not infrequently savage irony pervades many other poems besides.

But another incident which is actually recreated in *Childhood Among the Ferns* (846/C/D/G/*) displays something of equal significance as a theme, the melancholy, meditative habit of mind which colours so much of the verse.

> I was lying on my back in the sun, thinking how useless I was, and covered my face with my straw hat. The sun's rays streamed through the interstices of the straw, the lining

having disappeared. Reflecting on my experience of the world, I came to the conclusion that I did not want to grow up . . . to be a man, or to possess things, but to remain as I was, in the same spot, and to know no more people than I already knew (about half a dozen).'

Despite the wry parenthesis, this passage and the poem both exemplify that intense attachment to his family, and to 'the soil of one particular spot' coupled with a feeling of lonely withdrawal, of exile almost, from humanity, which mark so many of his poems.

Yet if, up to the age of sixteen, there were a few shadows on his life, Hardy, small, slightly built, and, as he admits, immature, was liked by most people who knew him and regarded as both intelligent and promising. Though somewhat shy, 'disliking to be touched' and still under his mother's thumb, he enjoyed the friendship of his schoolfellows, the warmth and stability of his family circle. These were his most cloudless years. The poem with which I began finds a curious pre-echo in two lines from the Jacobean dramatist Tourneur. In an aside he remarks

>   Joye's a Subtil Elfe,
>   I think Man's happiest when he forgets himselfe.

– a state of mind which Hardy, sensitive, thin-skinned, idealistic and impatient of smug panaceas was seldom to experience again.

(ii) The Sun on the Bookcase 1856–71

This is the title of a poem in which Hardy pictures a 'student' – plainly himself – who is recalled by the sunset reddening his books to the realisation that he has 'wasted' a whole day in dreams of romance and high endeavour. Throughout this period Hardy was notionally studying architecture but in reality was studying both art in the widest sense and life in a context much wider than hitherto. It was a period of much promise, considerable achievement, and towering hopes; indeed, he later christened it 'the buoyant time'. But it was also, and less happily, a period when his doubts about the religion in which he had been brought up steadily crystallised into flat disbelief, a state of mind painfully explored in his poem *The Impercipient* (44/ALL/*) among many others. Of his two best male friends one went abroad, and the other committed suicide. He fell deeply in love, twice at least, and – since from a fifth to a quarter of his poems deal with this aspect of the human predicament – examples need not be cited here of how this affected his verse. He also experienced the unhappiness, first of physical, later of intellectual, separation from his family. Though here love continued, understanding was gradually lost. Finally, he abandoned architecture to become a 'working novelist'.

By the age of sixteen (old in those days to be still at school) Hardy had probably formed some private 'dream' of going to Oxford or Cambridge. His schoolmaster, Mr Last, had given him a Latin New Testament as a prize, which clearly suggests that he saw Hardy as unusually gifted. But his family chose the less adventurous (and much less costly) alternative of apprenticing him to John Hicks, a Dorchester architect in good standing, for whom Hardy's father had worked. Hicks, impressed by the boy's quick-wittedness when he met him on site one day, offered to take him as a pupil, and Jemima, always an opportunist, haggled him down from £100 to £40 for cash in advance (though that would still represent well over £1000 at today's values).

In Hicks's office Hardy found an atmosphere both congenial and broadly educative. His employer was a cultured man, his fellow students were well educated and argumentative, especially on theological issues. So Hardy not only became a first-class draughtsman, later travelling all over Wessex on the new railways to measure and estimate for church repairs and 'restoration', but he also set himself to learn New Testament Greek, to hold his own in argument. He met the Reverend William Barnes, who kept his Classical and Mathematical School next door and was a university in himself. A philological authority of international repute, folklorist, linguist and a most gifted teacher, he was also a fine poet. Hardy read his dialect verse as it appeared in local newspapers, and no doubt attended his locally famous readings in the Dorset vernacular of which he was a past master. Barnes was also, with his Cambridge MA and numerous books to his credit, a remarkable example of what self-education could achieve from a background less promising than Hardy's own. Hardy later came to know him well enough to edit an anthology of his poems. He wrote a moving elegy on his death, *The Last Signal* (412/ALL/*). In his obituary notice Hardy observed of Barnes that:

> . . . the poetical side of his nature . . . was but faintly ruled by the practical at any time, that his place attachment was strong almost to a fault, and that his cosmopolitan interests, though lively, were always subordinate to those local hobbies and solicitudes whence came alike his special powers and his limitations.
>
> *The Athenaeum*, 16 October 1886

I quote this because, however unintentionally, it tells us as much about Hardy's predilections, both as man and writer, as it does of Barnes's.

If the already patriarchal Barnes was a rather awe-inspiring figure to the gauche, somewhat gawky, adolescent Hardy, Horace Moule, one of the seven brilliant sons of the Vicar of Fordington (near Dorchester) was to become his mentor and close friend. It would be hard to overestimate his influence on his impressionable young disciple, into which a good deal of hero worship no doubt entered to begin with. For Moule had already published work to his name when Hardy came to know him well and was in some demand as a reviewer. It was he who spurred Hardy on to tackle classical Greek, he who lent him books, some of them controversial, on topics like geology and the new criticism of the Bible. He was an inspiring teacher, eloquent and challenging; day-to-day conversation with him must have been a heady brew for Hardy to swallow. His restlessness, his melancholia, and his alcoholism were not yet apparent. Later they culminated in suicide and Hardy was desolated. But, for Hardy, experiencing this interplay of mind, no doubt, 'Bliss was it in that dawn to be alive.' Though this is to look rather ahead there is no question but that Moule's tragedy darkened Hardy's views of life. Promise unfulfilled is a recurrent theme in his work and there is, in his poem *Standing* *by the Mantelpiece* (874/W/C/*) a most poignant, if ambiguous, farewell to the one man Hardy may be said to have loved unreservedly.

Hardy's studies progressed, though Moule dissuaded him at this time from aiming at a university place. He became an Assistant Architect, taking on wider responsibilities, including some designing, for Hicks. He began to try his hand at writing, though nothing of his juvenilia (apart from *Domicilium*/1) has survived. He continued to read omnivorously, getting up at cockcrow to do so, and then walking the three miles to work in busy Dorchester every day. Though stronger, he was no taller, his spare, wiry frame having settled into the shape it was to retain for the rest of his life. He was leading, as he said, ' . . . a life twisted of three strands . . . which enabled me, like a conjuror at the fair, to keep in the air the three balls of architecture, scholarship and dance-fiddling.' Yet every night and every weekend he went back to the small world of his creative origins, a world with which he was never to lose touch altogether, a world whose 'seclusion and immutability', as he once put it, gives its characteristic stamp to much of his finest work. So many of his poems relate, directly or obliquely, to this rural environment, that it may be invidious to give examples. Still, *Winter Night in Woodland* (703/G/W/*) and *Shortening Days at the Homestead* (791/ALL/*) which refer to the Bockhampton neighbourhood, are excellent examples of a particular kind of poetry – we might call it poetry of *place* – in which only his predecessor John Clare and his much younger contemporary, Edward Thomas, have equalled him for precision and insight into the natural world and man's place in it.

But, at 23, as for many other young men, London beckoned. If the prospect of professional advancement offered a plausible argument to convince his mother and father he should go, there cannot be much doubt that Hardy also saw the capital as a city, in Robert Browning's phrase, 'crowded with culture'. The year before he set out had seen a profusion of work in prose and poetry published, much of it still read today. Cannily, if rather touchingly, he boarded his train with a return ticket in his pocket, and, after some ups and downs, landed a good job with Arthur (later Sir Arthur) Blomfield, one of the up-and-coming men in the vanguard of the Gothic revivalists, who were busily flooding England with their own versions of the masterworks of the Middle Ages. If some of this architecture was both exuberant and imaginative, much more was derivative and uninspired, while the 'restoration' which Hardy was mostly occupied with, often meant the virtual destruction or wholesale uglification of ancient churches in the interests of a stylistic uniformity quite foreign to the spirit of English architecture. All this was something Hardy later came to regret his share in. He had already learnt by observing his father's traditional craftsmanship to detect skimped or shoddy work. Now he came to detest 'ornament' applied as 'decoration' instead of springing naturally out of function. His deep acquaintance with medieval masonry became a potent influence on his verse. Of course, it provided him with subjects; *A Cathedral Façade at Midnight* (669/C/D/W/*) and *Architectural Masks* (130/D) are two good examples. But, more crucially, it helped form his theory and his method in poetry. He tells us, in *The Life* that he discovered 'a close and curious parallel' between the two arts. 'In architecture,' he contends, 'cunning irregularity is of enormous worth' and he 'carried into his verse . . . the Gothic art principle . . . of spontaneity, . . . – resulting in the 'unforeseen' character of his metres and stanzas'. As we shall see, this is of the first importance for a study of his verse.

He enjoyed some success in his profession, winning a couple of prizes for essays and designs, but he did not limit himself to the drawing board. He sang in the office choir, went to the opera, to Phelps's cheap and lively productions of Shakespeare, spent hours methodically studying the Old Masters in the National Gallery, and continued to buy books and read voraciously. During the years 1866–7 he embarked on a poetry-reading voyage, 'not reading a word of prose except . . . newspapers,' and not by any means confining himself to well-known authors; Wyatt, Donne and Crabbe among others were poets whom he admired and studied during the 1860s.

Some of his own early poems date from 1863–7 when he was lodging at Westbourne Park Villas. In more than a few we can already hear an original and challenging new voice. The magazine editors to whom he submitted them did not, he felt, 'know good poetry from bad', so he abandoned the attempt. But he did find publication, and pay, for a short comic piece in

Chambers' Journal called *How I Built Myself a House* which no
doubt suggested the possibility of earning a living by writing.
He was not so romantic as to think that poetry would pay the
rent, then or ever.

London had a darker face too, and Hardy could not have
missed, even had he wished, the evidence of extreme poverty
and depravity all around him as he traversed its streets. The
early satirical poem *The Ruined Maid* (128/C/D/W/*), a brilliant
piece of 'black comedy', and the sombre vignette *An East End
Curate* (679/H) both grew out of this side of his experience. It
was in London that he courted Eliza Nicholls, to whom he may
possibly have been informally engaged for some time. She came
from Dorset too, but the engagement – if it existed – fell
through and Hardy was left, emotionally, at a loose end,
experiencing bouts of depression which, together with the slow
waning of his religious belief, the weakened health induced by
his sedentary life and London's then notoriously insanitary
atmosphere, were probably major causes of the dark mood
which suffuses so many of his poems dating from this
time – poems like *Hap* (4/C/D/W/H/*) and *Her Dilemma* (12/C/
D), for example, and colours with a grey melancholy *Neutral
Tones* (9/ALL/H/*). For a variety of reasons then, he was not
sorry to return home and pick up the work which his old
employer, Hicks and his successor Crickmay, were happy to
offer someone who had worked for an architect as well known
as Blomfield. To his family, and especially his mother, Hardy's
return may have smacked of defeat, but in the event it was to
prove the catalyst of a new career as a novelist and the agency
of, first, a frustrated love affair, and then of his journeying to
Cornwall on Crickmay's orders, where he was to meet, fall in
love with, and ultimately marry, his first wife Emma Lavinia.

(iii) Show me again the time 1870–74

This line, the first of a poem entitled *Lines. To a Movement in
Mozart's E-Flat Symphony* (388/D/W) encapsulates Hardy's own
passionate retrospective vision of these years, brought to life in
so many of his best poems. But, before considering those
events, which are of an altogether crucial importance for an

understanding of Hardy's love poetry, I shall deal, very briefly indeed, with his career as a novelist in its entirety. I am content to condense ruthlessly for two reasons. The first is that during the years when he climbed to fame and a not inconsiderable fortune by way of prose fiction he was necessarily debarred from writing much poetry. Though he never entirely abandoned his first love, the pressure of work, often against the clock to meet serial deadlines, the irritating need to first bowdlerise his novels and then restore the 'offending' passages for publication in book form, the increasing demands made upon him for short stories (besides fifteen novels he produced over forty other tales of differing length, not to mention a dramatic version of *Tess* and a fair number of miscellaneous pieces), the incessant proof-correcting for new editions as demand grew; all this cannot but have reduced the amount of his creative energy left for poetry to a very tiny share indeed. It is likely that when he did contrive to begin a poem he was often unable to take it beyond a first draft. The second reason is that, naturally enough, most general biographies dwell heavily upon this aspect of his career and Michael Millgate, in particular, has covered the ground brilliantly in his *Thomas Hardy: His Career as a Novelist*.

It seems probable that Hardy had been mulling over the notion of a novel for some time. Released from the physical and mental pressures of London, he began to write the never-to-be-published manuscript of *The Poor Man and the Lady*. In July 1868 he sent it off to Alexander Macmillan. He declined to publish it, softening the blow by telling Hardy he had real promise. He gave him some shrewd advice and introduced him to Chapman and Hall's literary adviser, George Meredith, whose work as poet and novelist Hardy admired. However, Meredith's well-meant suggestions sent Hardy down a blind alley; in attempting to follow them he produced the 'sensational' *Desperate Remedies* (1871), the cost of which he shared with his new-found publisher, Tinsley. It was critically and financially unsuccessful, Hardy lost some of his hard-won capital, and his choice of career hung in the balance. But Tinsley did not lack shrewdness; he published the delightful pastoral romance *Under the Greenwood Tree* in 1872 and commissioned Hardy to write a full-length novel for serialisation in *Tinsley's Magazine*. This became the tragi-comic *A Pair of Blue Eyes* (1873) which Tennyson much admired, and which prompted the distinguished poet Coventry Patmore to write, 'I regretted . . . that such almost unequalled beauty and power should not have assured themselves the immortality which would have been impressed upon them by the form of verse.'

However, by that time, *Under the Greenwood Tree* had excited the interest of Leslie Stephen, editor of *The Cornhill*, the most influential literary periodical of its day. He invited Hardy to write a serial for him which became *Far from the Madding Crowd* (1874), first of the great novels 'of character and environment' as Hardy was later to define them. It was an enormous success, with critics and public alike. Thereafter, Hardy, though he had his ups and downs, never lacked readers or publishers.

His last two famous novels, *Tess of the D'Urbervilles* and *Jude the Obscure* appeared, respectively, in 1891 and 1895. Each precipitated a furore about its supposedly 'immoral' tendencies, though each in spite of (or perhaps partly because of) the controversy, sold in large numbers. This hullabaloo was Hardy's stated reason for abandoning prose, but the advent of the 'royalties' system had given him an assured income, and he had been putting his first volume of poetry together for at least two years before *Jude* was published. So, when *Wessex Poems* appeared in 1898, it really marked the fulfilment of a long-cherished ambition rather than an angry response – however excusable – to stupidity and crass misrepresentation. But, having leapt over nearly thiry years, it is time to pick up the threads of Hardy's life from around 1867.

Back home at Bockhampton he met his sixteen-year-old cousin, Tryphena Sparks (the unusual Christian name means 'child of love') from nearby Puddletown. He must have formerly known her quite well when she was still a child. But now she was a pupil-teacher, working for a college place at a nearby school, and Hardy fell in love with her, something which no one who has seen her portrait, taken at eighteen, will find surprising. Though not conventionally pretty, she was, with her sloe-black eyes, dark hair and generous mouth, decidedly attractive. She was also intelligent and capable, later winning a Queen's Scholarship to Stockwell College from which she passed out to become immediately Mistress-in-Charge of the

Girls (500 of them) at a huge school in Plymouth. Mary, Hardy's
sister and confidante, had herself qualified as a teacher in 1863
and was away at her post in Denchworth (Berkshire) with her
sister Kate. If there was anyone in the family circle able to
understand and enthuse about Hardy's authorial ambitions it
was likely to be Tryphena. She came from the same background
as he did, and was similarly climbing up the educational ladder.
Country girls grew up, perforce, pretty quickly then; she would
not have been a child at sixteen. There were only three miles of
footpath over the heath between their homes and each was
known to the other's family. Assignations would have been
easy to contrive even if their respective parents had reservations about the affair. It is certain they met frequently, highly
probable that Hardy gave her a ring (perhaps not for public
display). The engagement seems to have been ended by Tryphena, maybe after a period when they were no longer in close
contact, and she ultimately married a Plymouth businessman,
Charles Gale. So much is more or less common ground among
biographers. Where they differ sharply is over the theory that
Tryphena conceived a child by Hardy only for the lovers to
discover, traumatically, that she was really his niece and so
barred (under the Church's consanguinity laws) from marrying
him. In the absence of hard evidence the exact nature of their
relationship must remain speculative. Still, I see no reason to
throw out all the bathwater with the baby, so to speak. There is
good ground for saying that they were once in love, and that
she had mattered deeply to Hardy. That he remembered her
with affection and mourned her death (he was later to visit her
grave) are facts attested by the poem *Thoughts of Phena at News
of Her Death* (38/C/D/W/H/*) which is more closely considered
later. It is enough to point out here that Hardy calls her his
' . . . lost prize . . . whom I knew when her dreams were
upbrimming with light//And with laughter her eyes.' There can
be little doubt that several other early poems refer to their time
together, nor that the character of Sue (in *Jude*) has some marked
affinities with what we know of her, however questionable it
may be to view Tryphena as the inspiration of *most* of Hardy's
literary output.

In February 1870, chance, as so often in his novels, took a
hand in Hardy's life. When Crickmay, his new employer, had

taken over Hicks's business, he tended to make use of Hardy's expertise in church restoration to look after that side of his inherited work. He had on his hands one gravely dilapidated old church for survey and recommendations in the remotest part of North Cornwall, and Hardy set out by starlight on 3 March to reach the rectory of St Juliot in the late evening by pony trap, after travelling all day. There he was greeted by Emma Lavinia Gifford, the sister-in-law of the rector who was in bed with gout, with his wife looking after him. She was – as she tells us in her vivid, artless, and often very moving *Some Recollections* (set down in an exercise book and only printed in full all but forty years after her death) ' . . . immediately arrested by his familiar appearance, as if I had seen him in a dream – his slightly different accent, his soft voice: also I noticed a blue paper sticking out of his pocket.' The paper, it was later to emerge, had a poem on it. The meeting, with what flowed from it of something approaching ecstasy to be succeeded by slow disillusion and 'deep division', was as fateful as that between young Stephen Smith and the wayward Elfride in *A Pair of Blue Eyes*, which is scarcely surprising as the opening sequences of that novel are thinly veiled autobiography, despite Hardy's disclaimers. With the novel, Hardy's own account in *The Life*, Emma's memories, and – above all – the many poems, including some of the greatest elegies in the English language, that Hardy wrote about a time when, for him, 'Time was away and somewhere else', all available to draw on, it would be impertinent to do more than trace the events that were to lead to marriage, a marriage enjoyed or endured for thirty-eight years, until Emma's unexpected and sudden death in 1912.

At this time, though she looked younger, she was actually only a few months short of Hardy's own thirty years. She was certainly pretty, if in a rather chocolate-box fashion, with luxuriant red-gold hair and fine eyes. She was enthusiastic, impetuous, even perhaps a trifle febrile in manner, and, with her sister none too happily married to a man thirty-five years her senior, she can hardly be blamed for extending a warm welcome to this eligible male visitor. In an inaccessible hamlet Emma can have had almost no company of her own age and social class; she would have had to be exceptionally disinterested not to see in Hardy the possibility of escape from perpetual dependent spinsterhood. Moreover, she genuinely liked poetry and music, they sang together by candlelight and read Tennyson's *Idylls of the King* aloud in the garden. They traced the lovely valley of the Valency rivulet to the sea, and, when Hardy was not sketching and surveying the church – probably in her company – she showed him the wild, romantic country nearby. Of this, no more beautiful evocation exists than the sentence Hardy wrote for his 1895 Preface to *A Pair of Blue Eyes*.

> The place is pre-eminently (for one person at least) the region of dream and mystery. The ghostly birds, the pall-like sea, the frothy wind, the eternal soliloquy of the waters, the bloom of dark purple cast that seems to exhale from the shoreward precipices, in themselves lend to the scene an atmosphere like the twilight of a night vision.

They walked, picnicked and sketched – another shared interest – inland and along the coast to the ruins of Camelot. Emma often rode her pony, cantering recklessly over the dangerous terrain ' . . . as if she would fall//But she never did.' wrote Hardy in fond retrospect. On her side there was the initial attraction of the mysterious scrap of paper. Hardy no doubt soon told her of his literary hopes; indeed, Emma was to write out the whole of the fair copy of *Desperate Remedies* for him subsequently. For his part her gaiety, the childlike enthusiasm which she never lost, her spontaneity, were all qualities new to him in women no doubt. And day-to-day proximity, with the virtually total absence of any other young women at all, must have sharpened her physical attractiveness a good deal. By degrees they fell in love, and at the end of his first visit (several more were to follow), though nothing was said directly, a delicate hint was given and taken. They strolled in the garden after Hardy had announced his imminent departure, and

> Even then the scale might have been turned
>   Against love by a feather,
> – But crimson one cheek of hers burned
>   As we came in together.
> *At the Word 'Farewell'* (360/C/D/W/H/*)

As with all Hardy's poems on this theme, we are made aware of the precariousness of love. But the 'scale' dropped towards him, and, after he had, most assiduously, supervised the virtual rebuilding of the church (in which there are now memorial tablets to him and to Emma) they came to an understanding and, with the success of *Far from the Madding Crowd*, felt secure enough to marry. Emma ends *Some Recollections* with her wedding,

> The day we were married was a perfect September day – the 17th 1874 – not brilliant sunshine, but wearing a soft, sunny luminousness, just as it should be.

It is a charming sentence to be sure but, like Emma's syntax, the auguries were not uniformly good. Both families were absent from the wedding which took place in the unromantic hinterland of Paddington (London). Though Emma's uncle, Dr E. H. Gifford, later to become an eminent churchman, conducted the ceremony, both sets of parents and siblings signified a stony disapproval by what must have been a wounding absence. That the lovers had the courage to defy family opinion says a good deal for their strength of feeling, if rather less for their diplomacy. Hardy had received a stinging rebuff from Emma's father who accused him of being a presumptuous upstart of peasant origins with the effrontery to seek the hand of a 'gentleman's daughter'. Emma was never to establish any kind of intimacy with Hardy's parents, particularly Jemima who plainly thought she had 'set her cap' at Hardy from the outset as an escape route from prolonged spinsterhood. But none of her other children ever married, so her attitude to Emma was not likely to have been welcoming anyway. After the marriage the couple had, for some years, no permanent home, but when the three-volume edition of *Far from the Madding Crowd* sold over 2000 copies in two months they could happily reflect that the gamble had come off; Hardy had 'arrived' on the literary scene. From then on his was a name to reckon with.

(iv) 'The running of Time's far glass' 1874–1912

This line is from a poem entitled *Near Lanivet* 1872 (366/C/D/W/ H/*). It relates to an incident which occurred during the St Juliot period, and the words 'From an old note' have been deleted from Hardy's manuscript. I shall consider the poem more fully later, but for the moment it is enough to say that the *glass* is an hour-glass and it is the sands of (future) Time that are running out. The image, like the whole poem, is foreboding and, given that the poem was drafted at the time, also prophetic. For Emma is seen in it as doomed to be 'crucified' . . . in spirit' and it is certainly true that hers was not to be, beyond its first few years, a happy marriage. It was far from being an unmitigated disaster either, but it did fall a long way short of what the lovers, 'Sweeping like summertide wind on our ways,' (*A Two-Years Idyll* 587/D/W/*) experienced together, mostly in the pleasant country town of Sturminster Newton, between 1876–8, the period Hardy summed up in the title of the poem just cited. But, as the poem goes on to relate, the 'idyll' did not last; it proved 'A preface without any book//A trumpet uplipped with no call.' Life together was to become something 'Commonplace, scrawled//Dully on days that go past . . . '. On 18 March 1878 Hardy wrote in his *Journal* 'End of Sturminster Newton idyll.' Later – we cannot tell how much later – he added a sad postscript, 'Our happiest time.' Another poem *Overlooking the River Stour* (424/D/W/*) provides a poignant footnote to this period.

Hardy and Emma decided to try living in London and leased a house in the unpoetical district of Tooting. The experiment failed. Hardy became seriously ill and spent months housebound and bedridden. He muses on this near approach of death in the grim poem *A Wasted Illness* (122/C/D). He says (in one of the few direct references to his domestic discord in *The Life*) that 'their troubles began' there, that 'they seemed to begin to feel that "there had past away a glory from the earth"'. Their stated reasons for the move – Emma's desire for a wider social circle, Hardy's to extend his acquaintance in the literary world of the capital – probably stemmed from their realisation, never to be overtly acknowledged, that they were to have no children. Since they both seem to have enjoyed excellent relations with their young cousins this was unfortunate, but perhaps the decision to move back to Dorchester was, for Emma, a great misfortune because it brought her within close range of the veiled hostility of Hardy's mother, and cast Hardy in the unwelcome role of buffer state.

Just outside Dorchester Hardy bought land, and himself designed and had built a solid, unpretentious brick house called 'Max Gate' (after the nearby Mack's Gate). Once settled in, a routine was established which was to endure for the rest of their lives, and hardly to change even after Emma's death and Hardy's second marriage. It was not an entirely humdrum existence, of course. Weekends away as guests, longer stays in London during 'the Season' for visits to the theatre, the opera, art galleries and 'society' dinners formed intervals in a life that, for Hardy himself, consisted largely of unremitting daily toil at his desk, where he wrote in his bold clear script several of the greatest Victorian novels and much other fiction besides, corrected proofs, corresponded with editors, put forward suggestions to publishers (he had a shrewd grasp of the economics of the book trade) and, as the century drew towards its end, increasingly turned his hand to poetry again.

Outwardly no doubt it seemed a life of growing reputation, solid achievement and domestic stability. But there was a pattern of storm beneath the tranquil surface. Over three decades the Hardys' private life slowly worsened into a sour coexistence, mitigated by the fact that they often only met over dinner, or when they had guests. Although it does not directly refer to his own predicament, Hardy's *The Conformers* (181/W) sums it up with bitter precision:

> When we abide alone,
> No leapings each to each,
> But syllables in frigid tone
>   Of household speech.

Since, in 1918, Lytton Strachey published his *Eminent Victorians*, it has tended to become a matter of routine expectation that the famous should be equipped with as large a size in clay feet as seems feasible. Hardy was certainly no saint; creative geniuses rarely are. Nevertheless the breakdown of his and Emma's marriage is more a matter for pity than for judgemental hindsight. As De la Rochefoucauld, whose caustic *Maxims* Hardy admired, put it, 'If we were faultless ourselves, we should not take so much pleasure in commenting on the faults of others.' (Maxim 31).

But we cannot leave it there, because the marriage was to be the catalyst of much of Hardy's finest poetry, in terms both of subject matter and of emotional temper, so that some attempt, not to adjudicate morally, but to account for its failure, must be made here. We may begin by sympathising with Emma, who liked company (see *Lament* 283/C/W/*). She, in what Hardy admitted was a 'lonely and cottage-like existence', did not possess, like him, a partial anodyne for loneliness and depression in work. Their relative prosperity, bringing servants in its train, deprived her even of pleasure in small domestic tasks. She was not a good manager, either. For Hardy, his writing, from being a happily shared interest, changed by degrees into an escape hatch and finally something like a dugout in their marital strife. In this, as he later confessed in the poem *Lonely Days* (614/D/*) Hardy was culpable of neglect. He wrote, 'versifying' from a Diary of Emma's now lost, 'Lonely her fate was,// . . . //None there to share it,//No one to tell://Long she'd to bear it,//And bore it well.' Other poems, among them *Had You Wept* (313/D/W/*), *The Last Performance* (430/W/*) and *Lost Love* (259/C/D/W/H/*) all make it plain that, when it was too late, Hardy understood Emma's isolation and the part he had played in it.

Nevertheless, the weight of the evidence – and there is plenty of verbal testimony – unquestionably points towards the conclusion that Hardy had a lot to put up with, too much perhaps for anyone to bear without resentment. Emma's family, most notably in her father, contained some decidedly unstable personalities. Even if we do not attach too much weight to the alleged opinion of a Commissioner in Lunacy that she was, in her last years, perhaps 'certifiable' there is no question that she was a neurotic. She sincerely believed herself to be Hardy's superior in birth, breeding and education (all points on which he was, not surprisingly, touchy) and lost few chances to stress these matters in company. She had an obsessive conviction that Hardy and his friends paid far too little acknowledgement to her share in his literary achievement (except for odd suggestions and some copying out this was, in fact, negligible). Eventually she persuaded herself, and also disseminated the idea among any who would listen, that she had virtually *written* some of the fiction. It is true that Emma did possess, as her *Some*

Recollections testifies, a genuine, if small-scale talent for writing. Even so, the weird 'effusions' she published in her later years would never have seen print but for her husband's literary eminence.

Emma's own relations found her insufferable at times, so that it is not surprising to find the ill-feeling between her and the Bockhampton Hardys worsening. If they were 'peasants' to her, she was 'poor gentry' to them, despite Mary Hardy's gentle diplomacy. Caught in the crossfire there was little Hardy could do. He endured his wife's verbal onslaughts with something of his own rustics' stoicism, he accompanied and supported her in public, never writing or saying anything overtly critical about her, though she had no such reservations about him.

It is sad that those qualities Hardy had found so enchanting in Cornwall, Emma's rapt enthusiasm, her fragile prettiness, her apparent openness to new ideas should, with time, have turned into their opposites, but the saddest part of this sad story is the fact that Hardy's novels – once a bond between them (Emma wrote but never published a novel herself) – should, with their sombre agnosticism, have come to seem almost literally devil inspired to her. For Emma had embraced a particularly illiberal and fundamentalist variety of Protestantism. The more determinedly Hardy set himself to challenge what he once defined as 'inert, crystallised opinion – hard as a rock – which the vast body of men have vested interests in supporting,' the more unbridgeable became the intellectual rift between them. Hardy's verse, often more overtly sceptical about revealed religion than his prose, must have made matters worse still.

There were happier interludes; they enjoyed cycling together. Emma, as *The Prospect* (735/W/*) records, enjoyed entertaining. Both were fond of pets, as many poems reveal, notably the moving elegy for their cat Snowdove, *Last Words to a Dumb Friend* (619/C/G/W/*). But the final verdict must be that Hardy's disillusioned view of marriage arose from his having learned through experience the bitter truth summed up in W. B. Yeats's lines,

> Maybe the bride-bed brings despair,
> For each an imagined image brings
> And finds a real image there . . .

Hardy was shy, hyper-sensitive to criticism of his work, and surprisingly – in view of his fame – diffident about its ultimate value. He sent stamped addressed envelopes with his verse contributions to periodicals when there was hardly an editor in the English speaking world who would not have given his eye-teeth for any scrap of verse from his pen. He badly needed what Emma could no longer provide – a sensitive, sympathetic feminine ear. However well aware we may be that the wine of love sometimes turns vinegary, few of us are ready to go on drinking it neat for ever, out of a sense of duty. Hardy's remarkable loyalty to Emma – he certainly never took a mistress – did not stretch quite so far as to renounce all female company and he came to form friendships, via his literary acquaintances, with a number of attractive and accomplished women. Perhaps they made use of him to further their own literary ambitions, but they did, while keeping him dextrously at arm's length, provide him with some warmth, some banter and some sparkle. On his side it may have amounted to a little more. One poignant lyric, *A Thunderstorm in Town* (255/C/D/W/ *) tells of a moment when he and Mrs Arthur Henniker (with whom he collaborated in a book) were caught in a hansom cab during a downpour in London. The storm ceased,

> . . . and out she sprang to her door:
> I should have kissed her if the rain
> Had lasted a minute more.

But this is only another instance of 'the road not taken', always a recurrent motif in his verse; see, for example *Faintheart in a Railway Train* (516/ALL/*).

By the turn of the century Hardy had abandoned fiction for poetry. He was able to afford secretarial assistance and from around 1907 Florence Emily Dugdale was acting as secretary and typist to both Hardy and Emma, spending much time at Max Gate. Emma took to her strongly at first, but eventually drove her into a corner by demanding she should take sides in a resurgence of the perennial dispute about the Bockhampton Hardys' attitude to her. Florence dodged this confrontation, shrewdly, and contrived subsequently to avoid meeting her employers together, as far as possible. She was a perceptive observer, wisely remarking of the dispute in question that it was one ' . . . where everyone was partly, and no one wholly, to blame.' Never robust, she had not stood up well to the strain of teaching, but she was intelligent and well informed on literary conventions, having earned some money by freelance journalism herself. Not conventionally good looking, she was slim and dark, but with strikingly large, luminous eyes. By degrees, no doubt, Hardy was drawn to her and she to him, but if the feeling was acknowledged at all, it was, perforce, platonic, and probably unspoken too. One fine poem, *After the Visit* (250/C/D/W/H/*) tells of this time, obliquely and delicately.

For most of the first decade of the twentieth century Hardy was engaged in researching and writing *The Dynasts*, his three-volume *magnum opus*, a poetic drama surveying, *sub specie æternitatis*, the Napoleonic Wars, a few fragments from which, notably *The Eve of Waterloo* (932/G/H/*), may be found in *The Complete Poems* (with his implicit authority, since he included them in his *Chosen Poems*). This caused an interval in the publication of his shorter poems, but in 1909 *Time's Laughingstocks*, a title so quintessentially Hardeian that it comes as a surprise to find it is from Tennyson's *The Princess*, came out, including a section entitled *More Love Lyrics*, hardly one of which could plausibly be connected with Emma, albeit most are very early in date. It must, for Emma, have been a period of

> . . . heavy years she would remember
> When circumstance held her in thrall.

as Hardy wrote retrospectively in *The Marble Tablet* (617/D/W). But no one foresaw, although she had been intermittently unwell for two or three years, that she would die, suddenly and unexpectedly, quite early in the morning of 27 November 1912, only three days after her seventy-second birthday. Earlier in the month she had refused to see a doctor, despite severe back pains and loss of appetite. Even when, the day before, she had agreed to see the local GP she refused to be examined, so that he could only prescribe for her debility. So Hardy felt, after discussing it with her, that he might go to a rehearsal (of a play made from one of his novels) that night in Dorchester. He was never to speak to her again, since, arriving home late, he did not want to disturb her. First thing in the morning he asked

Emma's maid how she was, and was told she seemed quite well, but by eight o'clock she had become alarmingly worse and Hardy found her in a coma. She was dead before the doctor arrived and Hardy was shattered. To a friend he wrote, soon afterwards,

> In spite of the differences between us, which it would be affectation to deny, and certain painful delusions she suffered from at times, my life is intensely sad to me without her.

And now an upwelling of remorse not wholly justified, a grief long held in check, a love felt to be irrecoverably lost, broke in Hardy's mind to release a clear stream of the most moving elegiac love poems of this or any other century, recapturing – as if Time had never cracked it with his cold finger – that crystal world of joy and desire which the lovers had known in their first years together. The *Poems of 1912–13* (277–97) and the quite numerous other lyrics which belong with them (many of which will be considered in detail in Chapter 8) close an epoch of Hardy's long life as surely as if a great door had swung to.

(v) 'Nay rush not. Time serves. We are going.' 1912–28

This line from *An Ancient to Ancients* (660/C/D/W/*) is Hardy's dry advice to young poets in a hurry. He had married Florence in 1914, and with her his home life, which for years had been rather muddled and distraught, became calm and orderly. Yet, even in his seventies, he was far from content to rest upon his laurels, which from 1910 included the Order of Merit and – what probably pleased him still more – the title of Freeman of the Borough of Dorchester, the awarding of which prompted him to a speech full of local pride, though not devoid of sly humour too. Like Dr Samuel Johnson he now enjoyed 'folding his legs and having his talk out', but his advice to young writers – 'Never let a day go by without writing something.' – was based on his own invariable practice.

Almost alone among the established poets he did not see the First World War as glorious. After an initial burst of patriotism he was thrown into despair by the pointless holocaust in France. He lost his cousin's son Frank George, who was to have been his heir, at Gallipoli in 1915. Earlier, Florence wrote that he 'seemed to have aged ten years in a month [i.e. from the outbreak of war]. He visited German and British wounded lying only a few hundred yards apart in Dorchester hospitals and was moved to tears by the haunting similarities in their dialectal speech, as one poem, *The Pity of It* (498/W/*) bears witness. Another, *Often When Warring* (503/W) describes a soldier's action in giving water, in the thick of battle, to a wounded enemy, as ' . . . triumphing in the act//Over the throes of artificial rage.'

In 1913 he had revisited St Juliot and Cornwall having read – after her death – Emma's memoir of their romance, *Some Recollections*, and probably his own *A Pair of Blue Eyes* too. There and then or soon aftewards, he wrote the marvellous series of elegiac poems already mentioned which were published in a volume inappropriately entitled (by the publisher) *Satires of Circumstance* (after a series of acrid vignettes which had initially appeared in 1911 and came early in the new volume). Three more volumes of verse were to come, as well as the strange little play, *The Queen of Cornwall*, a version of the Tristram and Iseult legend.

Now in his eighties, he was still alert and courteous, interested in everything. He owned a wireless set, enjoyed motoring about the country, and was visited by several of the young writers who had survived the war. Siegfried Sassoon, Edmund Blunden and Lawrence of Arabia, who became a great friend, were among them. The poet Walter de la Mare was shown round Stinsford churchyard and then listened to Hardy's reading of his own poem *Voices from Things Growing in a Country Churchyard* (580/C/D/W/*). That visit was almost certainly the genesis of De la Mare's haunting fantasy *Ding Dong Bell*. But there was no direct debt. Rather it was his attitude to the craft of poetry which attracted these young men, as it was still to do with an even younger generation; W. H. Auden, C. Day Lewis, Dylan Thomas and Philip Larkin among them. What made so strong an appeal was his refusal to edit experience, his determination to show 'the grandeur underlying the sorriest things, the sorriness underlying the grandest things', Hardy's own formulation of the mission of poetry. Perhaps a poem by Robert Graves, another visitor, (though it is not *about* Hardy but entitled *A Country Mansion*) contains the best metaphor of Hardy's creative longevity,

> A smell of mould from loft to cellar
> Yet sap still brisk in the oak
> Of the great beams: if ever they use a saw
> It will stain, as cutting a branch from a green tree.

And Hardy's ninth decade brought a further harvest of poems, sweet and tart as apples from an ancient tree until, after listening to Florence reading poems including De la Mare's *The Traveller* which tells how – after the Traveller had gone – 'The silence surged softly backwards', he died quietly, as he had lived. No doubt he would have been intrigued, probably he would have been moved to ironical comment, by his State Funeral, replete with politicians and poets, at Westminster Abbey. But the small ceremony at Stinsford, where his heart was interred, with his first wife and by the family graves, would have pleased him more. Home, after all, is where the heart is.

3

Hardy's Poetry: a general survey

> . . . The characteristic of all great poetry – the general perfectly reduced to the particular.
>
> Hardy in conversation with Elliott Felkin in 1919

Hardy always thought of himself as a poet first and foremost. He was not above making disparaging remarks about the fiction which brought him his bread and butter, dismissing it once as a 'mechanical trade'. He wrote poetry intermittently for seventy years or so although virtually none of it saw print until he was nearly sixty. The *Complete Poems* contains 947 poems and the late Philip Larkin boldly asserted that it was ' . . . many times over the best body of poetic work this century has so far to show', backing his judgement by including 28, his largest single allocation, in his *Oxford Book of Twentieth Century Verse*. Dame Helen Gardner, in her *New Oxford Book of Verse* also chose 22, thereby placing Hardy on a level with the very greatest English poets of the last five centuries. The most recent large conspectual anthology, John Wain's *Oxford Library of English Poetry* (1987) gives Hardy similar prominence. There are three complete editions of his verse and more than twenty selections have been made from it. So much cannot be said of any of his contemporaries, or more than a few of his predecessors.

Yet all this represents an astonishing shift in opinion from 1898 when *Wessex Poems* was saluted as including 'the most astounding balderdash that ever found its way into a book of verse', while the view propounded by F. R. Leavis, and echoed by R. P. Blackmur among others, that Hardy had by what might be called happy accident produced a mere handful of great poems, was widely current until quite recently. Although, as Hardy drily observed, part of the initial reaction could be ascribed to 'his having taken the liberty to adopt another vehicle of expression than prose-fiction without consulting [the critics]', there were other reasons, not altogether insubstantial, why even well-disposed readers found a good deal to puzzle and provoke them in Hardy's verse. If time has dispersed some of the obstacles, others remain in place. Partly by examining them and partly by taking into account Hardy's own pronoun-cements about what he was trying to do in his poetry, we may find our way towards a standpoint from which more detailed consideration of individual poems may begin.

To begin with, as even his denigrators have always admitted, Hardy's is a singular genius; his verse has a stern, stubborn individuality which, for all its evident integrity, can be forbidd-ing. It is difficult to imitate and has rarely been successfully parodied. Though seldom obscure, it is both exceptionally varied and exceptionally idiosyncratic in form, while it displays as wide a range of subjects as any English poet's work before or since. But just about the last epithet anyone would be likely to apply to it is *charming*, and it is very seldom that Hardy offers us anything as immediately winning as *Weathers* (512/ALL/H/*) which over a dozen composers have set to music and which appears in innumerable school anthologies, often as the sole example of Hardy's work! It begins

> This is the weather the cuckoo likes,
>   And so do I;
> When showers betumble the chestnut spikes,
>   And nestlings fly:
> And the little brown nightingale bills his best,
> And they sit outside at 'The Travellers' Rest',
> And maids come forth sprig-muslin drest,
> And citizens dream of the south and west,
>   And so do I.

What could be more engaging than the lilting rhythms (the stanza form is indeed Elizabethan in origin), the sharp-eyed observation of springtime – 'showers *betumble* the chestnut *spikes*' – the shared enjoyment of life's simpler pleasures, even the impudent, six-times-repeated initial *And*, which we have all been taught never to begin a sentence with? Nothing, except perhaps the Shakespeare of *Love's Labours Lost* who, in one of the play's concluding lyrics, also brings on the cuckoo to tell of spring

When shepherds pipe on oaten straws,
And merry larks are ploughmens clocks
When turtles tread and rooks and daws,
And maidens bleach their summer smocks:

Shakespeare was country bred too; the acute vision, the gaiety, the sparkling imagery, the easy mastery of form they also share. Yet neither stanza can be called typical of its author, though we may well wish that both had written more in this vein.

The truth is that much of Hardy's characteristic strength, and something of his characteristic weakness too, derives from his steady refusal to write one kind of poetry – the kind well exemplified by the first verse of *Weathers* – to the exclusion of another. For just as Shakespeare goes on to tell of *Winter* (notice the *Ands*),

When icicles hang by the wall,
And Dick the shepherd blows his nail:
And Tom bears logs into the hall,
And milk comes frozen home in pail
When blood is nipt and ways be foul,

so Hardy, in verse 2 of *Weathers*, goes on,

This is the weather the shepherd shuns,
    And so do I;
When beeches drip in browns and duns,
    And thresh and ply;
And hill-hid tides throb, throe on throe,
And meadow rivulets overflow,
And drops on gate-bars hang in a row,
And rooks in families homeward go,
    And so do I.

The catalogue of winter's discomforts – the sodden landscape, the icy winds, the black, lumbering birds – makes a bleak contrast with the first stanza, which is, of course, much more agreeable to contemplate. But, as Coleridge, with whose critical opinions Hardy was well acquainted, once said, one of the most widespread errors is the confusion of what is 'agreeable' with what is 'beautiful'. So, in his *Apology* to *Late Lyrics and Earlier* Hardy quotes Wordsworth's Preface to *The Lyrical Ballads* (jointly written by him and Coleridge) to the effect that most readers assume that 'by the act of writing in verse' poets undertake to confine themselves to ' . . . certain [i.e. pleasing and innocuous] classes of ideas and expressions.' Such readers think poetry is meant to cheer us up, and would take Browning at his breeziest (in, say, 'God's in his Heaven,//All's right with the world!') as a touchstone of what poetry's mission should be. To them Hardy might well seem a crusty old curmudgeon, glumly intent on the mirier back-alleys of human existence, though such a view would have to be based upon superficial reading, something Hardy often complained of. But Hardy is not so much concerned with subject matter as with attitudes. He cites next in his *Apology* two phrases from one of his favourite poems, Wordsworth's *Ode: Intimations of Immortality from Recollections of Early Childhood*. He says, and this is absolutely crucial to his poetic creed, that

> It must be obvious to open intelligences that . . . disallowance of 'obstinate questionings' and 'blank misgivings' (11. 146 & 149 of the *Ode*) tends to a paralysed intellectual sta-lemate . . . the present author's alleged . . . 'pessimism' is, in truth, only such 'questionings' in the exploration of reality.

Hardy thereupon quotes from his own *In Tenebris II* (137/C/D/ W/H/*) the line

> If a way to the Better there be, it exacts a full look at the Worst.

Since 1945 it is easier for us to agree with him, no doubt.

Hardy's references to Coleridge, Wordsworth, to the German poet Heine, and his contention that ' . . . the real function of poetry [is] the application of ideas to life' (which is Hardy's précis of remarks made by Matthew Arnold, whom he thought the best critic of his time, *on* Wordsworth,) all show how firmly he took his stand within the English poetic tradition. Yet many, both at the outset of his poetic career and since, have seen him as an iconoclast, someone who 'dispensed with tradition in his most ambitious verse' as J. C. Ransom disparagingly put it in an influential essay. Hardy certainly did not think he had done any such thing; indeed, in conversation with the young Robert Graves, then much in thrall to *vers libre* theories, he firmly observed, 'All we can do is to write on the old themes and in the old styles and try to do a little better than those who went before us.' He was playing down his own innovations somewhat perhaps but there can be no possible doubt that he saw himself as working within that great continuum of English poets and their poems which we usually refer to as 'the tradition'.

But there has always been a diversity of views about the nature and the purposes of poetry, and the side Hardy took in this debate is made clear in his Journal for 29 May 1887. He quotes from the minor eighteenth-century poet Thomson these lines

> Thrice happy he who on the sunless side
> Of a romantic mountain,
> Sits coolly calm; while all the world without
> Unsatisfied and sick, tosses at noon . . .

and comments 'Instance of a WRONG (i.e. *selfish*) philosophy in poetry.' Now although Hardy thought this wrong, the vast preponderance of Victorian readers, not to mention most critics and many poets, would have thought Thomson's idea – which is basically that poetry is a form of *escape* – absolutely right.

There is no shortage of evidence. F. T. Palgrave's *Golden Treasury* of 1861 was easily the most influential, as it was also the best-selling Victorian anthology. Hardy bought it when it first appeared or soon after. It was really a manifesto for Tennyson's view of poetry, however, for Tennyson made the final choice of the poems in it, and there can be little doubt he also determined the general tenor of the *Preface*. Here we learn that 'poetry gives pleasures more golden than gold, leading us in *higher and healthier ways* than those of the world.' (My italics). There is much more to the same purpose and the editors remorselessly carry this principle into practice. Presumably because (as they unblushingly inform us) ' . . . more thought than mastery of expression' was a disqualification, three poets whom Hardy particularly admired get very short shrift. Donne – the *only* poet whose influence Hardy specifically acknowledged – is totally excluded, while Sir Thomas Wyatt and George Herbert get just one poem each. Significantly, the Romantics as a group get more space than all the other poets, apart from Shakespeare, put together, albeit the mediocre Thomas Campbell's allocation of eleven is the same as Keats's. This is because they exhibit 'a bloom of feeling . . . unattained and perhaps unattainable by their predecessors.' A little earlier the very influential poet and essayist R. W. Emerson had announced in America that 'The poet cannot descend into the turbid present without injury to his rarest gifts . . . nothing is of any value [in poetry] except the transcendental.' Tennyson was one of his admirers, not surprisingly.

F. W. Bateson mordantly summed up this attitude to poetry as 'The quickest way out of Manchester' and nothing could be further removed from Hardy's theory and practice. Railway station waiting-rooms and third-class carriages, insects flying into his lamp, the skeleton of an old parasol, a second-hand suit, a pat of butter, lines from a Borough Minute Book, even a pair of new boots, in his old age a passing motor car: all are, for him, equally the stuff of poetry. Indeed he frequently starts with something tangible, and often not conventionally 'poetic' at all. Two notes from his Journals make his position plain. In 1877 he observed, 'There is enough beauty in what is left in life, after all the false romance has been extracted, to make a sweet pattern . . . the art lies in making defects [in Nature] the basis of a hitherto unperceived beauty . . . latent in them.' More succinctly, he noted in 1888, 'To find beauty in ugliness is the province of the poet.'

Keats, whom he revered and studied closely (even suggesting an emendation in the text of his poems) would have agreed. In his early verse, which Victorian readers admired most warmly, he could write

> Give me a golden pen and let me lean
> On heap'd-up flowers in regions far and clear . . .

But he defines the poet's mission very differently in *The Fall of Hyperion*. There he says that 'The poet and the dreamer are distinct//Sheer opposites . . . ' and when he asks how the 'throne' of the highest poetry may be attained,

> 'None can usurp this height,' returned that shade,
> But those to whom the miseries of the world
> *Are* misery and will not let them rest . . .

For Hardy then, though he could and did admire poetry which revealed, like Keat's *Ode to a Nightingale*,

> Charm'd magic casements, opening on the foam
> Of perilous seas, in faery lands forlorn.

it was also necessary to open a few windows on life as lived in Mixen Lane (the dreadful slum depicted in his novel *The Mayor of Casterbridge*.)

The matter a poet chooses to depict is one thing; the method he employs to depict it another. Even if we concede that the strictures on Hardy's subjects were insubstantial, deriving from a simplistic notion of the purpose of poetry, we still have to face the fact that Hardy's treatment, his poetic style, has come in for a great deal of adverse comment, some of it from readers not unsympathetic to his aims. It may be as well to confess at once that this is where a blanket denial will not wash. Hardy *did* write some of the weakest lines (and a few of the more inept poems) that any major English poet has produced, and it is not enough to use, as some have, his 'playfulness' in exculpation. One can say, as some recent critics have said, that even Hardy at his worst is instantly recognisable as Hardy; one may even come to enjoy some of his eccentricities. But the fact that we grow fond of our pet mongrel does not turn it into a dog with a pedigree, capable of winning at Cruft's.

Some examples may substantiate my point. Hardy had a remarkable vocabulary but his sudden shifts from one *level* to another do not always come off. When he drops out of a dignified into a mundane diction, as in *The Levelled Churchyard* (127/C/*)

> We late-lamented, resting here
> Are mixed to human jam . . .

the impact, albeit meant to shock, is merely ludicrous, like Harry Graham's *Ruthless Rhymes for Heartless Homes*. Brilliantly as he exploited and often extended the resources of metre he could stray into forms out of key with the mood of the poem. Thus a lyric of sad reflection, *The Dawn After the Dance* (182/C) inappropriately moves to a jingling, cantering rhythm throughout,

> I would be candid willingly, but dawn draws on so
>   chillingly
> As to render further cheerlessness intolerable now . . .

Gilbert might have written it for Sullivan to set to music.

Then there are the occasions where it seems that Hardy simply cuts prose up into more or less regular lengths. Who, for example, would care to mark the line divisions in this fragment from *In the Servants' Quarters* (316/C/W.*): 'Man you too, aren't you one of these rough followers of the criminal; all hanging about to hear how he is going to bear examination in the hall?'? Also he has lines which seem asthmatic from the strain of getting everything in, like this one from *At Madame Tussaud's in Victorian Years* (437/W)

> Yet, gamuts that graced forty year's flight were not a small
>   thing!

But these slips and fumbles do not amount to more than a minute proportion of Hardy's output. All his life he was fascinated by the technicalities of verse. A devoted experimentalist, he employed more distinctive stanza forms than any other English poet, sometimes writing 'skeleton' outlines in order to ' try out' new patterns. An occasional over-reaching is the price we have to pay for his many triumphs in harmonising the movement of his verse with the mood he wishes to convey. His *The Fallow Deer at the Lonely House* (551/C/D/G/H/*) perfectly exemplifies this gift in its second verse.

> We do not discern those eyes
>   Watching in the snow;
> Lit by lamps of rosy dyes
> We do not discern those eyes
> Wondering, aglow
> Four-footed, tip-toe.

Only a pedant would grumble that 'eyes' cannot be 'four-footed'. (All Hardy and Emma can see of the deer from inside the lighted room is their eyes.) The 'otherness' of the animal world outside, the blend of fear and curiosity – the deer poised to flee at the least sound or movement – is not only conveyed by the unerring choice of epithet for the closing four words, but also by the short lines in which the natural stressing of the words induces a tense, hesitant quality, best brought out by reading the poem aloud.

Perhaps a poem which displays good and bad side by side may be helpful. It is hard to imagine solitude better rendered than in *The Wanderer* (553/*)

> Sometimes outside the fence
>   Feet swing past,
> Clock-like, and then go hence,
>   Till at last
> There is a silence, dense
>   Deep and vast.

Here the rhythm is itself 'clock-like'; the emptiness of the night suggested by the strong pause after 'silence' with the double rhyme and heavy stresses on the concluding adjectives, 'dense', 'deep' and 'vast' (which are by no means synonymous). This poem also supplies instances of Hardy's original, sometimes odd, but always arresting use of language. Initially he describes the stars, conventionally enough, as 'The lights by which I sup//Glimmeringly . . . ' (a tramp is speaking). But he goes on to say, 'They wag as though they were//Panting for joy'. Well, do stars *wag*? Not, it must be admitted, in poetry before Hardy. Yet, as a matter of observable fact, they do, or appear to do so, however much 'Twinkle, twinkle, little star' obstructs this perception for most of us. Like Alice's Humpty Dumpty, Hardy was determined to be 'master' where words were concerned, which was not invariably a wise resolution. *The Wanderer* also reveals a much less persuasive Hardy. When his benighted narrator complains that there is

> . . . no beseeming abode
> I can try

> For shelter, so abroad
> I must lie.

one feels that even a house-agent would wince at 'beseeming abode', even a schoolboy conscript feel that 'abode' isn't the ideal rhyme for 'abroad'!

Words, considered as things in themselves, were a minor passion of Hardy's. He prized his copy of the all-inclusive *New English Dictionary*, in the later volumes of which several words are exemplified largely from his works! And some of the words he employed do seem to have been exhumed from defunct dictionaries: *influent, largened, thuswise, meseemed, asile, typic, roomage, joyance, cohue* all come from a random dip into his *Complete Poems*. Though always an easy target for quibblers, the actual incidence of such words is very slight, and even when taken out of context, few need glossing. Still, archaic words are one thing, Hardy's own coinages quite another and a much more important aspect of his art. His most characteristic device is the compound epithet; hardly a page goes by without one or two. They are not invariably convincing. The lines from *Copying Architecture in an Old Minster* (369/W/C/*), 'Maybe they have met for a parle on some plan//To better ail-stricken mankind', not only suffer from the intrusively gallic 'parle' (i.e. parley) but 'ail-stricken' surely *sounds* far too much like the sequel to an Anglo-Saxon feast. However, Hardy's occasional linguistic misadventures are a small price to pay for what G. M. Young memorably called 'his ancient music . . . this gnarled and wintry phrasing'. Nor is it always 'wintry' either. It can bestow on us such glowing turns of phrase as 'the foam-fingered sea', the 'Isle by the Race//Many-caverned, bald, wrinkled of face', 'mothy curfew-tide' and 'air-blue', and such delicate insights as 'cobweb-time', 'wind-thridded' and 'ripple-gleam'. I could continue but I do not wish to imply that Hardy's use of more conventional language is less effective. He can bring out lines as Miltonic in their assurance as these from a sonnet, *The Schreckhorn, with Thoughts of Leslie Stephen* (264/ALL/H)

> And the eternal essence of his mind
> Enter this silent adamantine shape,

Hardy has phrases like 'Oblivion's swallowing sea', in *The-To-Be-Forgotten* (110/C/*) which Shakespeare somehow omitted from his plays; he can write openings as lyrical as Herrick's; 'She was as fair as early day// Shining on meads unmown', though *The Satin Shoes* (334) does not long continue in this vein. With equal felicity, he can pick his verse bare of all but the very simplest words, as in *I Found Her Out There* (281/C/D/W/H/*)

> I found her out there
> On a slope few see,
> That falls westwardly
> To the salt-edged air,
> Where the ocean breaks
> On the purple strand,
> And the hurricane shakes
> The solid land.

Here the purity and restraint of the language need no comment, but it is worth noticing the dextrous use of sibilants (in all but the initial line) to prevent the clipped lines becoming abrupt. And, to take a single word, how much of the force of 'hurricane' derives from the framework of plain English around it, and how evocative of the smell and 'feel' of the sea is the solitary compound 'salt-edged' (a brilliant emendation for 'sharp-edged'). Indeed, all the *Poems of 1912–13* abound in miraculously apt phrasing, while frequently the most striking effects arise from Hardy's insistence on the *exact* word, at whatever risk of its being unexpected, for what he wishes to convey. For example, in *Beeny Cliff* (291/ALL/H/*) he writes, 'Still in all its chasmal beauty bulks old Beeny to the sky', a line which, in 'chasmal' and 'bulks', contains two words few other poets would have employed. Yet these unfamiliar, even disconcerting, words, seen in context – the crucial stipulation – acquire inevitability. No others, however many alternatives are explored, quite fit. In this once much-vexed matter of his vocabulary then, Hardy is so often bang on target that a few ill-directed shafts seem insignificant. Furthermore, what at first glance may appear inept, can, on reflection and re-reading, become peculiarly apt. Most poets would be content with the line, from *The Wind's Prophecy* (440/C/D/W/*) as Hardy originally drafted it, 'Where the sun *rises*, mist-imbued' with its striking compound epithet. But Hardy, in search of a more sudden, startling quality for his sunrise, changed the commonplace verb 'rises' for 'ups it'. Sometimes, as perhaps here, one may argue whether the game was worth the candle, but Hardy always knew what he was about, and nearly always achieves his aim. His occasionally obsessive concern for verbal precision was indeed a facet of his general attitude to poetry and truth. He had little time for Pope's thesis, in his *An Essay on Criticism*, that in poetry,

> True wit is Nature to advantage dressed
> What oft was thought, but ne'er so well expressed.

There all the emphasis is on the skill with which the poet presents what he has to say: what the poem is *about* – its theme or subject – will be, Pope implies, of little importance as against its treatment. Hardy took the opposite view, siding with Wordsworth who exhorted the poet always to 'look steadily at his subject' and Matthew Arnold who echoes this in his insistence that poetry should 'strive . . . to see the thing [i.e. the subject] as in itself it really is.' Put bluntly, it is *what* the poet says that matters most. Hardy often expressed his distaste for what he called 'poetic veneer' and dismissed it tartly as 'the art of saying nothing in mellifluous polysyllables'. To his friend Edmund Gosse he confided, 'For as long as I can remember my instinctive feeling has been to avoid the jewelled line in poetry as being effeminate.' He cites another friend's – Leslie Stephen's – dictum with warm approval, 'The ultimate aim of the poet should be to touch our hearts by showing his own, and not to exhibit his learning, his fine taste, or his skill.' Bearing all this in mind it is not at all surprising to find that Hardy's own definition was, 'The secret of poetry lies in seeing into the heart of a thing, which . . . is realism in fact', a position he always defended vigorously, contending that there was such a thing as 'too much style' and arguing, in 1901, that,

> There is a latent music in the sincere utterance of deep emotion, however expressed, which fills the place of the actual word-music in rhythmic phraseology on thinner emot-

ive subjects . . . some verses . . . apparently infringe all
rules, and yet bring unreasoned convictions that they are
poetry.

He also grounded his convictions on his experience as an
architect, pointing out that the 'great Gothic Cathedrals' often
display this 'art of cunning irregularity', from which he claimed
to have derived the 'principle of spontaneity' and carried it into
his verse.

Now there may very well be a smack of rationalisation about
all this; most of us, after all, are attracted to those theories which
square with our own practice. But there were good reasons
why, beginning to write poetry abortively in the 1860s, and
returning to it in the 1890s, Hardy should have rejected that
reliance on ' . . . finish . . . clarity and unity' which Tennyson
and Palgrave set up as criteria for admission to the pages of *The
Golden Treasury*. Tennyson himself was, after all, the greatest
exponent of the 'jewelled line' in English, becoming Poet
Laureate in 1850. He had an impeccable ear and an endless
supply of melodious phrases. Such *tours de force* as

> The moan of doves in immemorial elms,
> And murmuring of innumerable bees.

from *The Princess* (1853) were on everyone's lips in the later
nineteenth century. Tennyson came to dominate the poetic
landscape; a poet both great and various, it was impossible to
ignore him. Hardy certainly did not ignore him, on the contrary
he greatly admired him, just as Tennyson admired Hardy's
novel *A Pair of Blue Eyes*. But, from the outset of his career
Hardy was determined to 'go and do otherwise'. He could, of
course, sometimes overdo his distrust of the Tennysonian line.
No doubt Tennyson would have admired the opening of *In
Front of the Landscape* (246/C/W/H/*) with its vivid picture of

> . . . a headland of hoary aspect
> Gnawed by the tide,
> Frilled by the nimb of the morning . . .

The tactile verb 'gnawed', the strikingly visual 'frilled by the nimb' are very much in his own line. But what would he have made of the 'faces' later on,

> Some as with slow-born tears that brinily trundled [down them]

This has impact; it is, if you think about it both apt and accurate, but it deliberately disperses all the expected associations of 'tears' as, say, crystals, dew-drops or pearls. On balance, in this poem, it works. But sometimes Hardy so cudgels the reader with his insistence on truth to fact as to knock the stuffing out of the poem. Thus, he starts a lyric in the Elizabethan manner, *The Memorial Brass 186–?* (452/W)

> 'Why do you weep there, O sweet lady,
> Why do you weep before that brass?–

and then immediately informs us, parenthetically, superfluously and to the optimum deflationary effect that,

> (I'm a mere student sketching the mediaeval.)

Not content with this display of the 'art of sinking' he reverts to his opening mode with

> Is some late death lined there, alas?–

only, driven by the exigencies of rhyme, to wrench the last line into

> Your father's? . . . Well, all pay the debt that paid he!'

The next line, and this is very rare in Hardy, is actually impossible to scan.

> 'Young man, O must I tell!–My husbands.' *And under*

The italicised words simply cannot be made to fit the metre. The poem – an ironic anecdote of a kind to which Hardy was over-addicted anyway – may well have been meant to shock, but not, one feels, in quite this way!

But mis-hits do not play a large part in Hardy's 943 poems. Far more often than not he was right in his aims; far more often than not he demonstrably achieves them. Even Tennyson has no line more opulent than the one that opens *Beeny Cliff* (291/ALL/H/*),

O the opal and the sapphire of that wandering western sea

Here the use of jewels for the sea-colours; opal for the evanescent sunlit water, sapphire for the blue-black shadow below the cliff, the long roll of the line with its strong alliteration (O/opal, sapphire/sea, wandering/western) binding it together – Hardy is always first-class on the sea – combine to produce an unrivalled warmth and brilliance of effect. The unusual epithet 'wandering' (which Tennyson himself had used of the sea in *In Memoriam*) is also felicitous.

But the next line is a test case. It runs

And the woman riding high above with bright hair
      flapping free

Now the word 'flapping' is decidedly not the one that most Victorian poets would have chosen. Its associations are predominantly with washing on the line, or perhaps ungainly birds. Either 'flowing' or 'floating' would be far more glamorous and Hardy must have been especially tempted by 'floating' since, in *Some Recollections*, Emma, in telling of this very incident, had herself written of 'my hair floating in the wind'. But he remembered even better than she did, with an astonishing clarity and precision which he knew well to be one of his greatest assets as a poet. When he was 75 he noted, 'I have a faculty (possibly not uncommon) for burying an emotion in my heart or brain for forty years, and exhuming it at the end of that time as fresh as when interred.' This is something more than nostalgic recall; it is an ability to recreate, to re-explore the past as if it were still the present. In many of Hardy's finest poems Time is the enemy against which memory is the only shield. But if, for whatever reason, memory is distorted, to comfort, to ennoble or even in quest of the melodious, then the cause of truth and poetry is betrayed, and Time will have triumphed. So in *I Found Her Out There* (281/C/D/W/H/*) Emma is pictured gazing out at 'Dundagel's famed head'

> As a wind-tugged tress
> Flapped her cheek like a flail.

That, on the wild Atlantic coast of North Cornwall, is what happens. On those high cliffs the wind is never steady; it blows in unpredictable swirls and gusts (nearly causing the hero's death in *A Pair of Blue Eyes*) so that long, heavy, ringleted hair doesn't 'flow' or 'float' but does, in fact, flap! It may seem niggling to insist upon so apparently trivial a matter, but if, as Coleridge said, poetry is 'the best words in the best order' then no amount of care in choosing the best is too much. Moreover, the antagonism of Time and Memory are among the essential ingredients of Hardy's poetic art, from which his tireless quest for truth to the actual experience naturally stems. If we want poetry tailored to what readers are accustomed to, to what 'looks' or 'sounds' most beguiling, we must go elsewhere for it.

'Real poets', wrote the countryman John Clare in the year of Hardy's birth, 'must be truly honest men,//Tied to no mongrel laws on flattery's page.' Clare's supremely authentic pictures of the rural world were bowdlerised by his publisher who was horrified by such scenes as that of a field-mouse disturbed by reapers, bolting out 'With all her young ones hanging from her teats'. Similarly, Wilfrid Owen's terrible visions of war derive from his belief that ' . . . true poets must be truthful' and that 'the poetry is in the pity'. It is with men like these that Hardy belongs; those who refuse to pick over their experience and amend or select from it on any ground whatever, especially that of what is or is not pleasing to the conventionally minded reader. Hardy set himself to struggle against the expectations of a public addicted to *Golden Treasury* verse. That his struggles are sometimes ungainly, his vocabulary eccentric, his subject matter dreary and his irony somewhat too predictable cannot be denied. But we should not look for perfect balance in a rebellious intellect, and, even at his worst, Hardy's work was a salutary corrective. For, though it took W. B. Yeats half a lifetime to discover that, in poetry, 'there's more enterprise in walking naked' Hardy, one might say, had never done anything else. This is the quality Hardy shared with Wordsworth and it is perfectly summed up by Matthew Arnold in his essay on the older poet. '[Wordsworth's] expression may often be called bald . . . but it is bald as the bare mountain tops are bald, with a baldness full of grandeur'.

If, in conclusion, I say very little about Hardy's 'thought' it is because I think it is seldom feasible or desirable to siphon it off from the poems in which it is suspended. Many ingenious and some ingenuous attempts have been made to pigeon-hole Hardy's ideas. He has been labelled 'Nietzchean', 'Schopen-hauerian', 'monistic materialist', 'determinist' and 'scientific humanist' at various times, which to me suggests some inhe-rent elusiveness in the subject of the labels. Hardy was unusually well read in both ancient and modern philosophy, subscribing to the esoteric journal *Mind*. He even found room in his late, light-hearted *Drinking Song* (896/C/*) – a potted verse-history of philosophy – for Einstein 'with a notion . . . //That there's no time, no space, no motion'. Browning's once-vaunted 'philosophy' he unkindly dismissed as 'worthy of a dissenting grocer,' and he bemoaned the fact that 'in their later writings [Wordsworth and Tennyson] . . . fall into the error of recording their convictions' (as opposed to their 'impressions'). In 1917 an article about his work prompted him to this riposte:

> Many critics treat my works of art as if they were a scientific system of philosophy, although I have repeatedly stated that the views in them are *seemings*, provisional impressions only, used for artistic purposes . . . '.

This summing-up is perfectly compatible with the fact that a good few of Hardy's poems exhibit very similar 'impressions'. Mere repetition does not validate an idea; only the vital force of the poem expressing it can hope to do that, and often only then just for the moment of reading. Hardy would have thought it absurd to say, as Shelley did, that 'Poets are the . . . unacknow-ledged legislators of the world', much as he admired Shelley's poetry.

Nevertheless, to say that Hardy was not and did not wish to

seem a systematic thinker is not to deny him many valuable insights into the human condition. His attitude to his own poetry may strike us as modest, even humble. He told his second wife that 'He had written his poems entirely because he liked doing them, without any ulterior thought; because he wanted to say the things they contained . . . ', and, though he could drive a hard bargain where his novels were concerned, he actually offered to pay for the publication of *Wessex Poems* in 1898 and made it a condition of his will that his *Collected Poems* should be sold at a price within reach of the 'poorer reader', a condition still honoured today by Macmillan.

Remarkably, one might even say paradoxically, this modest estimate of his own importance goes with what is arguably one of the most protean talents of any English poet; there is almost nothing in the range of human experience from which Hardy cannot fashion a poem. It is this openness, this immense receptivity, which he never lost, that enables him so often to surprise us – even in run-of-the-mill poems – with some new perception, some sudden apprehension of the force and value of life, and led Edward Thomas to say (reviewing *Time's Laughingstocks*), 'This book contains ninety-nine reasons for not living. Yet it is not a book of despair. It is a book of sincerity.' Thomas saw more clearly than most of his contemporaries that it was just this sincerity which prevented Hardy from systematising life, which he saw as inherently mysterious, according to any set of preconceptions whatever. As Middleton Murry put it, memorably, in an essay on Hardy's poetry, 'The great poet remembers both rose and thorn, and it is beyond his power to remember them otherwise than as together.' Hardy's was an austere concept of the poet's task; always to tell the whole truth, never to edit experience, never to accept facile answers. But he left a distinctive legacy to his successors, many of whom, Edward Thomas, Siegfried Sassoon, W. H. Auden, C. Day Lewis, Dylan Thomas and Philip Larkin among them, have warmly acknowledged their debt to him. In October 1919 Sassoon came to Max Gate and presented Hardy with a unique tribute which moved him very deeply. It was a beautifully bound manuscript volume in which 43 poets, including the Laureate Bridges, Kipling, Yeats, De la Mare, D. H. Lawrence, Robert Graves, Edmund Blunden and Sassoon himself had each inscribed one of their own poems. Typically, Hardy wrote to thank each of them in his own hand and individually. The poems were not written about Hardy, of course, though subsequently several good ones have been, notably by De la Mare, Sassoon, Blunden and Day Lewis. Yet none is quite as appropriate as the lines written by Wordsworth in his *A Poet's Epitaph*, with which I end this chapter.

> In common things that round us lie
> Some random truths he can impart,–
> The harvest of a quiet eye
> That broods and sleeps on his own heart.
>   From *Lyrical Ballads with Other Poems*, 1800

4

Poems about People

Speaking generally there is more autobiography in a hundred
lines of the poetry than in all the novels.

Life, p. 392

In the broad sense Havelock Ellis used when he wrote of
Tolstoy 'Every artist is his own biographer', Hardy's remark is
doubtless true. Setting aside the manifestly fictitious narratives,
anecdotes and ballads, virtually all of Hardy's poems tell us
something of his intellectual, spiritual or emotional pilgrimage
through life. But a narrower definition of autobiography is
needed to make this section manageable and, since the love
poetry has a chapter to itself, I shall begin with that small, but
highly significant, group of poems which treat directly of what
might be called Hardy's family history. Not that they are simply
word-portraits: all include Hardy's comments or reflections. But
family memories and associations were a kind of piety to Hardy
who once wrote 'Clouds, mist and mountains are unimportant
besides the wear on a threshold or the print of a hand, and a
beloved relative's old battered tankard is entirely superior to
the finest Greek vase.' By 'superior' he did not, of course, mean
'more beautiful', but possessing an evocative power stemming
from what he once called 'memorial associations'. So, to recall
and record his kin and what passed between him and them,
often long since, was to establish the only lien on immortality
that they, and he, could hope for. Fascinated, as his poem of
that title attests, by heredity, a sedulous genealogist, he added
to these interests something approaching total recall, a strong
'attachment to the soil of one particular spot', and an affection
as deep-rooted as it was clear-sighted. Often these qualities of
mind conspire to produce glimpses of people, 'in their habits as
they lived', drawn up from the distant past with an uncanny

55

immediacy which we have already encountered in Chapter 2 with *The Self-Unseeing* (135).

This imaginative acuity of vision which compels us to see as he does, is one of Hardy's greatest assets as a writer; by virtue of it his prose also often verges on and occasionally becomes, poetry. Yet with it goes an unusual objectivity. Hardy very rarely enlists our sympathy, still less our admiration, for himself. Yet though he contemplates his former self quite disinterestingly, his attitude is far from detached in the sense of cold or hard; warmth, tolerance, muted humour, and a love not the less profound for being inexplicit, all come together in these retrospective encounters. For, as he confesses in *The Ghost of the Past* (249/W/H/*), 'We two kept house, the Past and I,//There was in that companionship//Something of ecstasy.'

'Ecstasy' is a strong word, but there is nothing of Wordsworth's transcendental perception that 'Trailing clouds of glory do we come,' in what Hardy wrote of his own childhood. In one of the earliest glimpses of him he is seen walking *The Roman Road* (218/C/G/W/H/*) towards Weymouth. Yet, for all his well-attested enthusiasm for the Roman past of Dorchester, the ultimate significance of the scene is not some 'Visioning on the vacant air//Helmed legionaries who proudly bear//the Eagle . . . '. Rather, 'for me,' he says, 'Uprises there//A mother's form upon my ken//Guiding my infant steps . . . ' Such simple statements of simple feelings are not uncommon in Hardy; they reflect his warm approval of Leslie Stephen's formulation (already noted in Chapter 3) that the 'poet's function is to touch our hearts by showing his own'.

Childhood Among the Ferns (846/C/D/G/*) is a subtle, delicately observed vignette, of which the prose catalyst was quoted in Chapter 2. The small Hardy shelters from a downpour under the luxuriant heath-ferns which make him 'a spray-roofed house'. But the cold rain unobtrusively becomes a telling symbol of the wider, alien world beyond his ken, which he shrinks from facing; as opposed to the 'sweet breath' of the ferns drying in the kindly sun (always in Hardy's verse, a benevolent force), here an image of family love and security. Hardy used the incident for a key passage in *Jude the Obscure* (Chapter 1). He was not at all averse to recycling his materials if occasion offered.

In *He Revisits His First School* (462/*) we find his laconic, self-deprecating humour surfacing in a poem which makes a fruitful comparison with W. B. Yeats's magnificently oracular *Among Schoolchildren*. Typically, he pictures himself then as a nestling bird 'Pink, tiny, crisp-curled//My pinions yet furled// From the winds of the world.' But any hint of sentimentality is at once dispelled by his portrayal of himself *now*. 'Wanzing weak//From life's roar and reek.' Innocence confronts experience, and Hardy feels it would have been better to have gone 'as a ghost' whom passers-by might see 'by green moonlight' ' . . . just as he was//When in Walkingame he//Conned the grand Rule of Three//With the bent of a bee.' It is a playful, slightly macabre imagination that we encounter here. He concludes, drily, that if he was wrong to return, 'With an aspect of hollow-eyed care' . . . 'But yet let me say//I may right it – some day.' The ending is delightfully wry and throwaway in a poem which must have offered many temptations to pull out the emotional stops.

A similar dry-eyed vision is brought to bear on *The House of Hospitalities* (156/C/D/W/H/*). Revisiting his birthplace Hardy surveys the adjoining derelict site, scene of parties where he and his young friends had once so uproariously 'broached the Christmas barrel//Pushed up the charred log-ends'. Of these jovial occasions no trace survives; now 'the worm has bored the viol//That used to lead the tune' and – a supremely suggestive image – 'Where we sang the mole now labours,//And spiders knit.' A different kind of domesticity indeed; but there is nothing menacing in nature's resumption of what man has only borrowed. Hardy may regret but he does not resent the frailty of man's hold on his environment. Indeed, if he returns at midnight,

> When the moon sheets wall and tree,
> I see forms of old time talking
> Who smile on me.

That sense of the past as alive, as informing the present, indeed interacting with it, is a salient feature of Hardy's poetry, as it was of his prose.

His parallel conviction, that our ancestors are a part of our being, is most overtly shown in *Heredity* (363/C/D/W/*) where he asserts, somewhat grimly, but with that compressed, direct vigour of expression that he is a master of 'I am the family face//Flesh perishes, I live on.' For him this is the one '. . . eternal thing in man//That heeds no call to die.'

Hardy's well-founded premonition that he was the last in a long line prompted him to pay tribute to his ancestors, generally in the fine sonnet *A Wet Night* (229/G/W/*) and, in *One We Knew* (227/ALL/*) to his grandmother, 45 years after her death. It was from her that he had absorbed much of his local lore, having shared a bedroom with her as a small boy. The poem catches the child's wide-eyed wonder together with her own relish for her tales. It is decidedly not a celebration of 'the good old days' with its dark echo of 'a small child's shrieking// At the cart-tail under the lash', but it moves with a jaunty, infectious vigour, savouring of the country dances with which it opens, while the penultimate verse modulates from tale to teller, depicting the old lady

> With cap-framed face and long gaze into the embers –
>   We seated around her knees –
> She would dwell on such dead themes, not as one who remembers,
>   But as one who sees.

How alike is that 'long gaze' to the 'deep look' which Hardy's friends the Granville Barkers noticed as he, by then in his eighties too, gazed into the fire at Max Gate: an example of heredity in action, so to speak.

There are several good poems about Hardy's immediate family. His father's somewhat elusive personality is only touched on in *One Who Lived and Died Where He Was Born* (621/W/*) but it makes use of a structural device quite common in Hardy, representing his father's life as cyclic, and thus implying that all life is part of a recurring pattern; a pattern of conflict, in this instance between Time as creator and Time as destroyer. Samuel Hynes has argued that this pattern, which he terms 'antinomianism' is the lynchpin of Hardy's poetry, but no other critic has been ready to go so far. And indeed in this poem, where his father descends and ascends the same stairs in November (the month of both his birth and his death) 'wealth-wantless' on both occasions and thus 'wise' enough to view life as 'a vain pantomime', the predictability of the pattern blunts the point of Hardy's message somewhat. It is an occasional failing in him that he signals his punches too blatantly.

To My Father's Violin (381/C/W/*) is much more impressive. The instrument (which Hardy always kept in his study) mutely symbolises his father's own silence and remoteness after death, in the 'Mournful Meads' (an effective translation by Hardy of Virgil's phrase for the twilit underworld of classical myth). By inventing this half-world of 'Nether Gloom' Hardy deftly avoids any serious consideration of life after death. Yet what is inevitably a sad, and might have been a morose, poem is transformed from a dirge by Hardy's remarkable vivacity and dexterity in the complex stanza form. This mirrors both the father's musical skill and his son's pride in it. Changes of pace match changes of mood; now 'the homely harmony//Of the quire', now the 'merry tunes' of the dance. Such rapid, sinuous lines as

> Elusive as a jack-o-lanthorn's gleam
> And the psalm of duty shelved for trill of pleasure,

serve as verbal counterpart for the nimble fingering in a cadenza.

There are three fine poems about Jemima. One is fully analysed later, while *Bereft* (157/C/D/W/*) in a ballad-like form, with a refrain, touchingly deploys Jemima's artless recollections, at once painful and happy, of everyday life, of summer and winter mornings and the evenings 'When the supper-crock's steaming' to convey her grief. *After the Last Breath* (223/C/D/W/*), written just after his mother's death in 1910, treats of her bereaved childrens' feelings with piercing insight and painful honesty. Its flat, curt phrases, its dwelling on the now useless paraphernalia of the sick-room, suggest the tired resignation of the family as they 'note the numb relief withheld before'. But then Hardy drops into the inertia two beautiful, lapidary lines,

> Our well-beloved is prisoner in the cell
> Of Time no more.

It is a superb epitaph, and I regret that Hardy thought fit to add a, somewhat repetitive, final stanza.

Hardy's sister Mary is the subject of four poems. The best are *Molly Gone* (444/D/W/*) and the fine *Logs on the Hearth* (433/C/D/W/*) which is later analysed. It is probably Mary to whom Hardy also refers in the epigrammatic *The Comet at Yell'ham* (120) an undervalued poem, brief enough to be quoted in full:

> I
> It bends far over Yell'ham Plain,
> And we, from Yell'ham Height,
> Stand and regard its fiery train,
> So soon to swim from sight.
>
> II
> It will return long years hence, when
> As now its strange swift shine
> Will fall on Yell'ham; but not then
> On that sweet form of thine.

Hardy recalled that he saw the comet in 1858 or 1859. I think that it was probably drafted at or near the time. If so, it shows Hardy as already evincing a predilection for the plain style, using the four-line alternately-rhymed stanza so popular for hymns that it was termed *common metre*. Hardy gives the comet a striking presence succinctly; 'fiery train' and 'strange swift shine' are all we get by way of epithet to suggest the remote beauty of the phenomenon and contrast it with Mary's 'sweet form'. Yet though it contains something of that fear which science's postulation of a limitless, indifferent universe excited in Victorian minds, it also suggests that, however awesome the spectacle, only man can feel awe; that the small scrap of humanity which is his sister is more significant than a universe of comets – to Hardy.

We now come to those poems – they are not numerous – in which Hardy writes directly about himself. The last lyric in *Wessex Poems, I Look Into My Glass* (52/ALL/H/*) is one of them.

I look into my glass,
And view my wasting skin,
And say, 'Would God it came to pass
My heart had shrunk as thin!'

For then, I, undistrest
By hearts grown cold to me,
Could lonely wait my endless rest
With equanimity.

But Time, to make me grieve,
Part steals, lets part abide;
And shakes this fragile frame at eve
With throbbings of noontide.

If this has a familiar ring it is partly because the verse form
(four-line stanzas rhyming ABAB, with three beats (feet) in
lines 1, 2 and 4, increasing to four in line 3) is exceptionally
widespread in hymns and songs. But I believe the catalyst is
George Herbert's famous *The Elixir*, which is still sung today, as
in Hardy's time, in Anglican churches all over the world under
the title of its first line, *Teach Me My God and King*. I quote the
relevant verse below,

A Man that looks on glasse
On it may stay his eye;
Or if he pleaseth through it passe
And then the Heav'n espie.

The reason Hardy does, in effect, 'stay his eye' on his own
reflection is that, for him, there was no 'Heav'n' beyond to
'espie'. But if their thought necessarily differs, the two poems
share the same lucidity, the same directness and the same
vigour of expression. Hardy's final verse is masterly in its
controlled yet passionate utterance; his private wound is made
universal. The last two lines are also notable for the way in
which the language of 'shakes this fragile frame' and 'throbbings of noontide' simultaneously conveys both physical and
emotional states.

Finally *I Look Into My Glass* illustrates what Hardy said (in a
deleted passage from the *Life*) about the 'only safe way of

winning a hearty [critical] reception . . . that of shadowing the philosophy and manner of some eminent [recent] poet.' This 'royal road' he rejected, choosing to go back beyond 'Wordsworth or Browning', and, as here, often drawing on earlier and less fashionable poets – John Donne is another example – for guidance, rarely though he actually imitates them.

What Hardy said of his concern being with 'impressions' rather than 'convictions' is borne out by his infectiously exuberant celebration of life's pleasures, *Great Things* (414/C/G/W/H/ *). Written in an appropriately lilting measure – virtually that of the famous song 'Charlie is my Darling' – it tells of the joys of 'cider' when 'spinning down to Weymouth Town//By Ridgeway thirstily' (Hardy was a keen cyclist), of the dance (a pursuit he kept up into his seventies) and, in a sensuous and romantic vignette, love,

> When having drawn across the lawn
> In darkness silently,
> A figure flits like one a-wing
> Out from the nearest tree.

This plea to 'seize the moment' cannot be reconciled with the concept of Hardy as a stoical pessimist: his capacity for enjoying life was not dissipated by his awareness that life is not universally enjoyable. His duality is well brought out in *A Merry Making in Question* (398/W/H/*) in which the jovial dancers and fiddlers of the first stanza give way to the gruesome chorus of 'headstones' and 'gurgoyles' of the second, a form of macabre inversion Hardy could rarely resist. What we call 'black comedy' is not as modern as we suppose.

Lastly, there are four poems which might be categorised as farewells. The two best are fully analysed later; those with which Hardy designedly concluded his *Winter Words* are interesting because the first shows him ignoring his own precepts by hauling in his 'convictions' at the expense of the poem's integrity. For though *We Are Getting to the End* (918/C/D/W) begins quite impressively with 'We are getting near the end of visioning//The impossible within this universe', the sonnet's conclusion sags noticeably. By the end of the Great War 'nations' no longer 'lay waste//Their neighbour's heritage *by* *foot and horse'* except, one suspects, when poets need a rhyme for 'demonic force'. But when he invites us to accept war as a condition into which we are 'tickled mad' even Hardy cannot dispel the sense of bathos that intrudes. He has for once allowed us to see him mounting the soapbox to deliver a sermon. This error is not repeated in the far more effective *He Resolves To Say No More* (919/C/D/W/*) of which the last stanza will fittingly conclude this section, even if we view this late self-denying ordinance with some scepticism.

> And if my vision range beyond
> The blinkered sight of souls in bond,
> – By truth made free –
> I'll let all be,
> And show to no man what I see.

Analyses (Preliminary note on method)

Each sub-section will conclude, like this one, with the close scrutiny of a few poems, selected from the grouping just considered in more general terms to represent Hardy's best work within the category. There is no single agreed method of conducting such analyses, so it may help if I indicate the one I intend to employ. Nevertheless, with a poet as diverse and profuse as Hardy it would be pointless to try to shepherd his entire poetic creation over a single gangplank into the ark of evaluation. Accordingly the relative weight given to the three aspects of analysis set out below will necessarily vary from poem to poem.

Any analysis must try to answer three basic questions which fall into a natural sequence: (1) *What* does the poem say? (2) *How* does the poem say it? and (3) What does the poem *impart* to (as opposed to tell) the reader? Naturally this simple formula needs some amplification if it is to be useful.

(1)   Unless we understand what a poem is *about*, what it has for *subject* (even at the elementary level of putting it into our own words), we risk missing its point. Hardy is rarely obscure; he did not, he once said, think his readers should 'have to rack their brains to solve conundrums'. But he did complain of their

frequent failure to grasp what he implied rather than stated. '[My] poems of a satirical, dry, caustic or farcical tone [are] regarded . . . with the deepest seriousness.' So not only his *themes*, but the *tone* and the *mood* of a poem must be probed and assessed by the critical reader.

(2)   This is a much wider question. It ranges over Hardy's *style*, his *techniques* of versification and his *diction*. He was a tireless experimenter with verse-forms (employing more than any other English poet) and an idiosyncratic, sometimes eccentric, exponent of the immense resources of the English language. Also, like most poets, the manner in which he employed particular *images* and *symbols* was often peculiar to him. In many poems Hardy's emendations throw a strong light on his working methods, and in his quest for what he called 'poetic texture rather than poetic veneer', ('depth rather than surface decoration' we might say), Hardy's meticulous craftsmanship is often a salient factor.

(3)   A poem's impact on the reader is normally to be gauged in terms of what is implicit rather than stated; and because thought and feeling may be *imparted* in so many ways a brief example may be helpful at this juncture. The narrative poem *A Conversation at Dawn* (305) is, justly, ignored by all compilers of Hardy selections. In its seven tedious pages a wife 'tells all' to the discomfiture of her staid, smug new husband. What frail interest the narrative exerts is dispersed by the often risible dialogue, of which the husband's query 'Then what has kept, O reticent one,//Those lids [i.e. *eyelids*] unlatched?' is a fair example. But the last four lines *impart* much more than the previous 192 have *told* us.

> She answered not, lying listlessly
> With her dark dry eyes on the coppery sea,
>   That now and then
> Flung its lazy flounce at the neighbouring quay.

The first ten words give us the woman's spiritual imprisonment, her despairing impassivity and her indifference to her angry spouse. Then the beauty of dawn and the freedom of the natural world is contrasted with the stuffy prison of the hotel bedroom – and what a brilliant and menacing epithet *coppery* is here. Then the *sea*, so often in Hardy an image connoting both freedom and danger is subtly associated with the woman's nature in *lazy flounce* with its hint of the whirl of a petticoat. Verse technique figures in the strong rhythmic and alliterative emphases of lines 1 and 2 where *lying listlessly* and *dark dry eyes* are both sharply suggestive of inner torment. Next, the deliberate heavy pause at the crest of line 3, the swift *decrescendo* of *flung* and *flouce* and the quiet, unstressed ending all seem powerfully to enact the movement of an incoming wave while 'lazy' hints at the unbridled but now quiescent power of the sea. Though in her inner nature the woman may aspire to be as untameable, perhaps as amoral, as the sea at which she gazes hopelessly, she is trapped by convention and the sea seems to mock her impotence. If that seems a great deal to elicit from four lines we need to remember that the hallmark of poetry is that *every* word matters. It is this concentration which enables it, in the words of Shelley, one of Hardy's early heroes, to 'purge from our inner sight the film of familiarity that obscures from us the wonder of our being.'

A Church Romance (211/ALL/H/*)

His mother Jemima probably told Hardy of her first encounter with his father (in Stinsford Church) which he recreates in this poem. Its easy flow masks the fact that it is a sonnet, written in a variant of the technically demanding Petrarchan form with a rhyme-schme ABBA/ABBA/CDDCEE. Hardy was an extremely accomplished exponent of this highly traditional form and those who decry his craftsmanship would find reading the forty-odd sonnets scattered through *The Complete Poems* a salutary experience.

The mood is serious, though not without a glint of irony; the tone detached, as Hardy recreates a moment in time. He begins with that swift 'onset' which is essential to the form, plunging us instantly into the scene with a single, rapid sentence, slowing only where the words *sinking sad tower window light* impel the reader to pause. The next four lines (quatrain), again a single sentence, first hint at his mother's character with *pride's despite*; then the highly concentrated phrase *strenuous viol's inspirer* stresses simultaneously the intensity of the playing and the way in which Hardy's father, albeit virtually invisible except as a silhouette, could, through music, convey *his* intensity of feeling.

The last six lines (sestet) are, by contrast with the octet's swiftly sketched narrative, quietly reflective; effecting, after the conventional strong pause, a change in the direction of the poem's thought. This so-called *turn* is a familiar feature of the sonnet form. Now, with wry honesty and quiet affection, Hardy reflects upon the significance of that 'claim', declared by the musician through the music that was, perhaps more than his wife, a lifelong passion. There is a tartness reminiscent of Jemima in the phrase *when Age had scared Romance*, and even the word *bond* is double-edged: Hardy will not pretend that his parents' marriage was 'roses, roses, all the way'. Yet this very unsentimentality sharpens the impact of his mother's retrospective vision; there is a good deal of Hardy himself in that phrase *some old attitude . . . or glance*. It is the kind of impression to which his mind was continually open, and many of his poems *break upon the mind* in just this way, like a random shaft of sunlight falling on a ruin, momentarily allowing us to see it as it was in its heyday. How well, too, the penultimate line sums up Hardy's father when young, though there is a sly humour in placing the *minstrel* on the balcony, the lady on the ground. And as for the last line, the old, no longer fashionable hymn-tunes are there to remind us, indirectly, of the flux of time, the end of romance and music. For, when Hardy wrote, his father and mother were dead and the gallery, with its quire, long gone. But Hardy has invested a commonplace with such significance that he enables it to 'break upon' our minds too. And we should remember that it is only *Romance* that *Age has scared*, not love.

Afternoon Service at Mellstock (356/ALL/*) *Circa 1850*

This brief lyric is also set in Stinsford Church, some fifteen years later than *A Church Romance*, when Hardy was ten, and there with other children, since his mother would have given short shrift to any 'swaying like the trees' on the part of her son. The theme is a recurring one in Hardy's verse; the unbridgeable and hence intensely poignant gulf between past and present. As Sir John Squire acutely observed, in one of the few critiques of his poetry that we know Hardy liked, 'the contemplation of transience and the regret of things gone is the mainspring of half our deepest emotion and the source of half our poetry.'

Yet here it is the pin-bright clarity of Hardy's picture that we notice first, together with his laconic skill in establishing atmosphere succinctly. Phrases like *drowsy calm, panelled pew,* and the entire second verse suggest the tedium of those Victorian Sundays when several hours were spent in church. Moreover, in the old 'high and dry' Anglican tradition the Tate and Brady versions of the psalms tended to be done to death, and, as the children are singing 'one-voiced' (i.e. in unison as opposed to harmony) they do not need to think about the music either. This is ostensibly the world of a bored Sunday-school child with the fidgets (only their heads were visible above the *panelled pew*), further intensified by the weather ouside – Stinsford church windows had plain glass in those days – which is touched in by *rooks, elms* (in which the rooks nested) and *clouds upon the breeze*. Plainly it is spring or early summer, and how much they long to be out of doors is shown in the neat contrast between *watching* (the *elms*) and *glancing* (at their books). The verse-form is appropriately simple; indeed, but for an extra two syllables in the third line, its four-line stanzas are in the old so-called 'common metre' which was often employed by Tate and Brady (see, for example, 'O God Our Help in Ages Past'). The tone is conversational, the language devoid of complexity: all in all we have here an excellent example of how well Hardy could deploy the plain style when he chose.

Yet it would be a mistake to see this as a naive poem. Here is no easy nostalgia for a lost innocence; any such impression is sharply countered by line 9. This, with its heavy stress on *mindless* might seem the preamble to a sour, even a cynical conclusion. Yet, though rational man cannot go back to being *mindless*, the telling word *outpourings* implies an ebullience and openness to life which *subtle thought* cannot confer on us. Hardy could not shut his ears to what science was proclaiming, but such knowledge was, he knew, no highroad to happiness.

She Hears the Storm (228/C/D/W/H/*)

There was a time in former years –
    While my roof-tree was his –
When I should have been distressed by fears
    At such a night as this!

I should have murmured anxiously,
    'The pricking rain strikes cold;
His road is bare of hedge or tree,
    And he is getting old.'

But now the fitful chimney-roar,
    The drone of Thorncombe trees,
The Froom in flood upon the moor,
    The mud of Mellstock Leaze,

The candle slanting sooty-wick'ed,
    The thuds upon the thatch,
The eaves-drops on the window flicked,
    The clacking garden-hatch,

And what they mean to wayfarers,
    I scarcely heed or mind;
He has won that storm tight roof of hers
    Which Earth grants all her kind.

If Hardy had not placed this poem next to *One We Knew* (227) then we could be quite sure that the 'speaker' is his widowed mother, but he may not have wished to be too precise. Bereavement is a universal sorrow and he discarded the MS sub-title, 'The Widow's Thought', presumably because he thought it superfluous. The crucial problem for Hardy in adopting his mother's 'voice' is one of catching the appropriate tone. In the exacting task of making her say nothing that might seem, in a countrywoman, mannered or literary, he succeeds to perfection. His diction is so spare and robust, his syntax so straightforward that it might indeed be Jemima Hardy speaking. The poem is formed as a simple thought sequence, devoid – up to the penultimate line – of a single metaphor or even a simile to disturb the even flow of small sense-impressions which make its fabric. Because she is alone at night in the Bockhampton cottage these are predominantly aural, and thereby convey more tellingly, not just the acuteness of her hearing, but also her loneliness and desolation. The actual sounds are brilliantly evoked by Hardy's meticulous choice of words: *fitful chimney-roar*, *drone*, *slanting sooty-wick'd* (a candle burning like this sputters audibly), *thuds*, *eaves-drops* (perhaps an echo of coleridge's *Frost at Midnight*); all these display that loving exactitude which is no small part of his poetic art. There is a psychological insight, too, in the way in which Jemima, after her first shocked realisation of loss, allows her mind to distract itself with these once-significant details, as an anodyne for grief, only to return inescapably to the bleak fact that they are no longer meaningful for her. This also accounts for her merely fleeting reference to her husband in line 2, where the single dialectal word *roof-tree* is a pre-echo of the conclusion. The verse form is homespun too; no hymn-stanza is more familiar than that of *While shepherds watched their flocks by night* (which is Tate and Brady again!).

Hardy does not deviate from his all but plebeian diction throughout; there is nothing conventionally 'poetic' about a *storm-tight roof* (what could be a more natural concept for a builder's widow?). Yet this wonderfully apt image opens out the whole poem into a sombre yet plangent conclusion. The last two lines are both stoical and consolatory; they remind us of the Prayerbook's minatory 'Earth to earth' at the committal, and simultaneously – this is a very Wordsworthian poem – of *Lucy*, 'Rolled round in earth's diurnal course,//With rocks, and stones, and trees.' Such acceptance of the inevitable, with grief but without rancour, was part of Hardy's temperament. Country people and architects are much exposed to the harsher realities of decay and death, and he was both. But it would be hard to miss the profound compassion, unvoiced but omnipresent, which is Hardy's hallmark. NB The last two lines in the MS ran, 'He has reached the roof well known as hers//That Earth provides her kind.' I do not need to spell out how much Hardy's revisions have here improved on his first thoughts.

Logs on the Hearth (433/C/D/W/*)
A Memory of a Sister

The fire advances along the log
    Of the tree we felled,
Which bloomed and bore striped apples by the peck
    Till its last hour of bearing knelled.

The fork that first my hand would reach
    And then my foot
In climbings upward inch by inch, lies now
    Sawn, sapless, darkening with soot.

Where the bark chars is where, one year,
    It was pruned, and bled –
Then overgrew the wound. But now, at last,
    Its growings all have stagnated.

    My fellow-climber rises dim
    From her chilly grave –
Just as she was, her foot near mine on the bending limb,
    Laughing, her young brown hand awave.

December 1915

This poem, sub-titled 'A Memory of a Sister,' was written only a
month after Mary's death on 24 November 1915. In it Hardy
gazes, casually at first, at an apple-log burning on his hearth. As
his eye follows the flames' progress his memory throws up new
facets of the past, until, with a shock of recognition, he 'sees' his
fellow-climber so clearly in his mind's eye that momentarily she
becomes a revenant. And that is all the poem tells us; happiness
and grief are both left to implication. Hardy was not much
given to wearing his heart on his sleeve.

To begin with the tone is gentle, almost casual, suggesting no
more than drowsy half-attention. The alternating long and short
lines, the frequent pauses, impose a slow, meditative movement on the reader, intensified by the way in which each line's
syntax is run on into the next. Though something of Hardy's
empathy with all living things is observable in his use of words
like *bled* and *wound* of the tree, it is not sentimentalised. Its

function here is to remind us, as it reminded Hardy, of the human lives that once impinged on it. But it is also a potent image of the cyclic nature of all life, on the fact that, as King Lear says, 'Men must endure//Their going hence even as their coming hither,//Ripeness is all.'

Hardy's language is markedly plain and direct throughout, the verse form too is simple, though the strong alliteration in, for example, lines 3–4 and line 8 give resonance to his phrasing. Structurally, the notable feature is the inversion of the image pattern in the last stanza. Whereas the first three all begin with images of growth and life, darkened by a last line which returns us to the present and the burning log, the last gives us Mary's 'ghost' returning from her *chilly grave* into life. And perhaps no single word could have been more poignant in this context than *laughing*. For a moment, love and memory have defeated Time.

It is interesting that, even after it had seen print (in *Moments of Vision*) Hardy modified this poem to make it yet more reticent in mood. He deleted a refrain, 'That time O!', which came between lines 2 and 3 of each verse. Evidently he decided that there was no need to heighten the emotional emphasis like this; equally evidently, his instinct was sound. For there is already sufficient feeling concentrated in the last two lines to make us catch our breath as at a lost presence. He did not need to do more than provide us with the echo of his sister's laughter, the glimpse of *her young brown hand awave*. It is, after all, enough; we can all provide our own face and name.

Lying Awake (844/C/D/W/*)

You, Morningtide Star, now are steady-eyed, over the east,
    I know it as if I saw you;
You, Beeches, engrave on the sky your thin twigs, even the least;
    Had I paper and pencil I'd draw you.

You, Meadow, are white with your counterpane cover of dew,
    I see it as if I were there;
You, Churchyard, are lightening faint from the shade of the yew,
    The names creeping out everywhere.

First published in 1927 and probably written not much earlier, this is really a meditation on old age. In its subject, its brevity and its emphasis on the visible world it is somewhat reminiscent of the Chinese poetry which Hardy had enjoyed in Arthur Waley's translations during the 1920s. Lying awake in the small hours Hardy knows from long familiarity just what the faint dawn light is revealing outside Max Gate; he has no need to draw the curtains. By his use of lazy-paced lines, hesitating at the double-rhymes (*draw you, saw you*) he imposes on the reader a sense of that musing, dreamy state between sleep and full consciousness, but the exactitude of *steady-eyed, engrave* and *thin twigs* reinforces his assertion, *I see it as if I were there*, a phrase which very precisely identifies an important aspect of Hardy's poetic genius.

Short and strongly patterned as it is, with its direct, intimate *You* four times repeated, nevertheless the second verse is more than a variation on the first. For the *meadow* with its surprising, yet apt *counterpane cover of dew* (white, intricately patterned, counterpanes were common then) is, by this image, subtly linked both with the churchyard beyond it and with Hardy's own bedroom. Under that *counterpane* sleep his 'friends beyond'; his own name must soon join those now *creeping out everywhere*. Even the phrase *shade of the yew*, is an echo of Gray's famous 'Beneath that yew tree's shade' from his *Elegy in a Country Churchyard*, which Hardy knew more or less by heart.

What we have then is really a leave-taking, a final survey of a loved, familiar landscape. Perhaps we need to summon up imaginative sympathy to see these verses as a coming to terms with old age, frailty and the approach of death. But we can hardly miss the cool, dignified poise of a poem which, while it tells us nothing remarkable, yet imparts so cogently an impression of the octogenarian poet lying there 'In calm of mind, all passion spent.'

Afterwards (511/ALL/H/*)

Because Hardy's emendations here are so crucial I print all the important ones below, listing line numbers and giving the final text in italics too, where necessary.

Line 1 MS reads 'when night has closed its shutters on my dismantled day'.

Line 3 MS reads 'people' (for *neighbours*).

Line 7 MS reads 'nibbled' (for *wind-warped*).

Line 17 MS reads 'passing bell' (for *bell of quittance*).

Line 18 MS reads 'makes a break in its utterings' (for *cuts a pause, outrollings*)

Hardy's epitaph on himself, it was written in his seventy-seventh year. But it is not the author and public figure on the aftermath of whose death he speculates; these are far from the expectations of a vain or ambitious man hungry for posthumous fame. Indeed the poem is nearer the verbal equivalent of a shrug; death itself is dismissed offhandedly. Moreover, even though *He was a man who used to notice such things* is, in all conscience, a profoundly modest assessment, Hardy could not be certain even of so much. He leaves the posthumous judgement to those country/*neighbours* (a deliberate choice, as the MS line 3 shows us) for whom Hardy was a local lad who had done well out of writing books. He hopes they may recall his keenness of eye, his care for small creatures as they might a shepherd's or a ploughman's.

This approach requires him to efface himself from the poem in so far as overt emotion is concerned. He creates a detached mood also by his employment of an exceptionally slow-paced, almost ambling, line, which invests the whole poem with a musing, speculative tone, sprinkled as it is with *If, may*, and *will*? He 'asserts nothing'; in one of his own phrases this is a 'last look round' familiar, loved terrain, which perhaps no one, before or since, has known better.

Such a survey was bound to include much natural imagery, and he never bettered his impressions of the *May month* in the first verse, where *delicate-filmed* and *new-spun* display his genius for the compound epithet, subsequently seen in *wind-warped* and *full-starred* (if perhaps a trifle less effective in *dew-fall hawk*, where *hawk* does not, to my mind, primarily suggest a moth.) Nevertheless, meticulously as he depicts the minutiae of the scene, this is very much more than 'nature poetry'. After the first verse the prevailing atmosphere becomes that of dusk or night. All is blurred and hushed; to use his own words, *nocturnal* and *tremulous*, no doubt because he wishes to impart a sense of the mysterious, fleeting nature of life itself. The language he uses to enhance this mood is at times miraculous. To apostrophise night as *mothy and warm*, to compare a moth's almost imperceptible arrival to an *eye-lid's soundless blink*, is to add a dimension to our own imperfect perception of the physical world. It is in this way that a man who was shy and tentative in his personal relationships allows us an oblique insight into the mind of a poet who was, in Coventry Patmore's phrase, one 'singularly moved//To love the lovely that is not beloved.'

Hardy's emendations bear out what I have said. In the first, and therefore very important, line, Hardy initially failed to create quite the right sinuous flow – the metre is a very delicate and subtle one. But though the revision is smoother to the ear, he may also have felt *Night* (as an 'elegant variation' on death) was a near-cliché. Attempting to invigorate it by the metaphors of *closed its shutters* and *dismantled* he found himself arousing undertones of shops and machinery. To substitute *the Present* (for *Night*) was neat and a gain in precision (the Present *releases* us, Night *receives* us) but the revised line as a whole is masterly. For a *postern* was a small, subsidiary exit for unimportant guests, *latched* implies a casual dismissal, and *tremulous stay*, with its undertones of insecurity, impermanence, physical frailty and fear, imparts exactly that universal feeling which the Bible sums up in the famous verse, 'I am a stranger here and a sojourner, as all my fathers were.' 'Nibbled' (i.e. by sheep) was good, but *wind-warped* (hinting at an identification of the *thorn* with Hardy) is better, while his invention of *bell of quittance* adds the suggestion of debts cancelled to the ancient custom of the *passing bell*. Finally, *cuts a break* avoids the implicit contradiction in *makes a blank* (can you *make* something non-existent?), and where *utterings* would humanise it, *outrollings* perfectly captures the sound of the *bell's boom*.

The abiding impression is one of quiet truthfulness, a particuarly rare achievement in a poem as directly personal as this in its subject. As C. Day Lewis wisely said, this genre is especially perilous to poets because, in it 'false humility, egotism or emotional insincerity cannot be hidden.'

BIOGRAPHICAL POEMS

Like all novelists, Hardy was intrigued by the vagaries of human character, carrying this inquisitive, sometimes indeed nosy, habit of mind into his verse, predominantly via his narrative poems. But there is a small group of poems which treat either of personal friends or admired figures from the past. Certainly he could pay a graceful compliment when occasion offered. *In the Evening* (802) pays tribute to Frederick Treves, the famous surgeon who came from Dorset, *Concerning Agnes* (862/D) is about one of his literary protégées, and the song-like *Evelyn G[ifford] of Christminster* (578) mourns a cousin of whom he was fond. A much deeper layer of feeling is revealed in *Before Marching and After* (502/W/H/*) which recalls how Frank George, Hardy's cousin and heir-elect stayed at Max Gate on the eve of his embarkation for the ill-fated Gallipoli expedition, where he was killed in action. In this underrated poem Hardy will have nothing to do with patriotism, nor does he mention his cousin's recorded bravery. His concern is with the curious, albeit very well-attested, detachment soldiers experience before battle. Frank George stays up late, unaffected by the beauty of the starlit summer night, unmoved by 'love, friendship, home joy', hearing, yet not responding to his sleepless mother's 'restless sighing'. He muses instead on war as a 'game with Death' that he is well aware 'Death stood to win'. Hardy's grim truthfulness echoes the fatalism of the trenches: the frail hope that Frank George's name 'will not fade on the morrow', is really all Hardy can offer when the news of his death arrives. War and Death both notoriously tempt poets to gild the lily; poems presenting the unvarnished truth about both are rarities.

I cannot spare the space here to consider *Wessex Heights* (261/C/D/W/H/*) in detail. It commemorates a group of Hardy's friends but so obliquely that it needs much annotation, indeed too much. The ghosts who rise up from the past to disturb Hardy produce a more self-indulgent scenario than is usual with him and, though weirdly compelling in parts, I do not rate this a complete success. F. Giordano makes a good case for it in the *Thomas Hardy Yearbook* (V), however.

Past writers prompt some excellent commemorative verse. There is a charming fancy about *Shelley's Skylark* (66/G/W/H/*), appositely Shelleyan in manner. John Keats, whom Hardy revered, has three poems of which the best *At a House in Hampstead* (530/*), sub-titled 'Sometime the dwelling of John Keats', begins

> O Poet, come you haunting here
> Where streets have stolen up all around,
> And never a nightingale pours one
> Full-throated sound?

(The other poems are numbered 71 and 556 in CP.) *George Merdith* (243/C/W/H/*) who knew and helped Hardy in his early career, and who had had to suffer much abuse (like Hardy) for his outspokenness, has the ringing conclusion: 'His words wing on – as live words will.' The poet Swinburne, whom he knew and who was similarly castigated by the press, is remembered in *A Singer Asleep* (265/C/W/H/*). But, setting aside the two which are to be analysed in detail, the pick of this group are those about two writers, Gibbon and Shakespeare, and Hardy's most intimate friend, Horace Moule. In fact there are two poems about Moule. One, *Before My Friend Arrived* (804/*) recalls, many years afterwards, Hardy's vigil on the evening before Moule's body arrived by train. A terse, reticent, perhaps deliberately repressed poem, it is moving but not in the same class as the anguished, passionate utterance of *Standing by the Mantelpiece* (874/C/W/*). Here Hardy recreates a scene in Moule's Cambridge rooms during 1873. Moule is the speaker throughout and he begins by citing an ancient folk-tradition, 'This candle-wax is shaping like a shroud'. Then, by pressing his finger in the wax, he both foretells and chooses an early death for himself. He is ready to relinquish life because it is now 'Tonight'.

> To me twice night, that should have been
> The radiance of the midmost tick of noon,
> And close around me wintertime is seen
> That might have shone the veriest day of June!

Moule's utter despair, his tormented nihilism are painfully enacted. It is the Vicar of Fordington's brilliant and promising son who cries out

> But since all's lost and nothing really lies
> Above but shade and shadier shade below,

Whoever he had loved and pinned his hopes upon has, he implies, rejected him.

> I say no more: the rest must wait till we
> Are face to face again, yonside the tomb.

Despite the obscurity occasioned by our not knowing to whom Moule is talking, this is an extremely impressive, moving and deeply felt poem. To me it has so strong a ring of authenticity that I find it hard to believe that Hardy himself was not Moule's silent auditor, even though that supposition raises thorny questions about the nature of their relationship (which are examined in Millgate's biography, q.v. Chapter 7).

However, what matters as poetry is the terrible insight we receive into Moule's tragically divided nature, which we should nowadays classify as schizoid. Here are his warmth, his charm, his quick intelligence and romantic enthusiasm on the one hand, lurching precipitately into utter desolation and self-destructiveness on the other. Hardy spares us nothing; the lines quoted above also display a frenetic fluency in 'shade and shadier shade below' which is irrationally contradicted by 'yonside the tomb'. Writing the poem must have been a painful therapy for Hardy; he held it back from publication until *Winter Words*, by which time Moule's immediate family were dead.

Gibbon, author of *The Decline and Fall of the Roman Empire*, whose sceptical brilliance, sardonic wit and dedication to historical truth won Hardy's admiration, is the subject of a fine poem which Hardy actually wrote at *Lausanne, in Gibbon's Old Garden* (72/C/D/W/*). Hardy envisages Gibbon's 'spirit' returning (on the 110th anniversay of his completion of the *magnum opus* which coincided with Hardy's visit) to enquire 'How fares the truth . . . //Do pens but slily further her advance?' Here 'slily' refers to Gibbon's famous irony, a weapon also dear to Hardy. The reply, indicting the nineteenth century, is couched as a final query from Gibbon, but it is in fact a brilliant compression of a longer sentence by John Milton – another great defender of free speech – from his *Doctrine and Discipline of Divorce*. Hardy thus, across a spectrum of three centuries, provides us with a perspective from which to view the then recent outcry over his *Jude the Obscure* (1895). The history of our century has not dulled the edge of his concluding lines, 'Truth like a bastard comes into the world//Never without ill-fame to him who gives her birth.'

Hardy, as *Lausanne* and several other poems demonstrate, had a penchant for the so-called 'occasional' poem; one prompted by some topical event or anniversary. He might indeed, have made a good Poet Laureate though he was never canvassed for the job. *To Shakespeare* After Three Hundred Years (370/C/W/*) was commissioned for a book of 'tercentenary tributes' which proved, as one might have expected, the kiss of death for his fellow-contributors. But not for Hardy whose effort is one of the best among numerous attempts made in four centuries to give substance to that elusive genius. Hardy begins by stating the capital difficulty clearly with 'Bright baffling soul, least capturable of themes', but slips into the high-faluting in the second stanza where – even in context – the phrase 'that cow Oblivion' is hardly one of his most apposite. But once he brings on a cast of Shakespeare's fellow-Stratfordians to gossip about his death in banal exchanges: 'A worthy man and well-to-do', 'I'faith, few knew him much here,' with the squire's wife snootily summing up 'Ah, one of the tradesman's sons, I now recall', he imbues the poem with life. And the ending, with its still homely yet vivid metaphor of Shakespeare as a 'strange bright bird' which arrives mysteriously 'to mingle with the barn-door brood awhile', is both ingenious and perceptive. So, Hardy says, Shakespeare 'flew . . . into men's poesy', briefly 'Lodged there a radiant guest and sped forever thence'. The occasional uncertainty of diction is a weakness, but the reflection that Hardy was also slily suggesting what would happen in Dorchester after *his* death adds a spice to our reading.

Analyses

The next two poems are both about men whom Hardy knew well, admired and who, albeit as widely divergent in background, belief and character as could be, were collectively the most potent influences on Hardy as a writer.

The Schreckhorn, (With thoughts of Leslie Stephen)
(264/C/D/W/H)
(June 1897)

Aloof, as if a thing of mood and whim;
Now that its spare and desolate figure gleams
Upon my nearing vision, less it seems
A looming Alp-height than a guise of him
Who scaled its horn with ventured life and limb,
Drawn on by vague imaginings, maybe,
Of semblance to his personality
In its quaint glooms, keen lights, and rugged trim.

At his last change, when Life's dull coils unwind,
Will he, in old love, hitherward escape,
And the eternal essence of his mind
Enter this silent adamantine shape,
And his low voicing haunt its slipping snows
When dawn that calls the climber dyes them rose?

Stephen, who gave Hardy his breakthrough as a novelist in
1874, was a famous climber who made the first ascent of the
mountain he called 'the grimmest fiend of the Oberland'. Hardy
tells us that, when on holiday in Switzerland during 1897 and
looking at the Schreckhorn, 'I suddenly had a vivid sense of
[Stephen] as if his personality informed the mountain – gaunt
and difficult, like himself.'

This sonnet, one of the best of all climbers' poems, is written
in a mixed form. Its octet rhymes ABBA/ABBA (as in the
Petrarchan mode), its sestet DFDF/GG (as in the Shakespearian). The octet suggests Stephen was himself drawn to the
mountain by *vague imaginings* of its *semblance to his personality,*
an affinity clearly discernible to Hardy who is prompted by it to
speculate, tentatively, in the sestet, on whether such an identification is conceivable after death.

Tone is crucial here. Stephen, like Hardy, had lost his faith to
Darwinian   science,   relinquishing   Holy   Orders   and   a
Cambridge Fellowship, and writing in 1865, 'I now believe in
nothing . . . but I do not the less believe in morality.' This is
Hardy's position too; for both men found some hope in

evolutionary 'meliorism' as Hardy called it, a belief that man was capable of continuous improvement without supernatural sanctions. Hardy, therefore, can only offer, as a rather tenuous extension of this notion, the theory that at his *last change* (an evolutionary concept) some *eternal essence* will remain, somehow interfused with the mountain, to speak of Stephen's nature to us. But it is Hardy's mastery of technique and especially his resourcefulness in the use of language which gives his somewhat Wordsworthian 'argument' whatever force it has and the poem is more a memorial than a consolation.

Hardy's subtle interweaving of the man's personality with that of the mountain is first asserted by the delay in identifying Stephen until line 4, and the astute selection of epithets (*Aloof*, *mood and whim* and *spare and desolate*) which apply with equal aptness to either or both. Structurally, as in Milton's sonnets (which Stephen admired), the octet is all one sentence, so lucidly articulated that, though restrained and dignified in language, it is never rhetorical. Hardy verges just closely enough on the colloquial with *life and limb*, *maybe* and *rugged trim* to avoid any risk of a chilling formality.

The sestet is again Miltonic in its complex syntactic structure. But though it abates nothing of the octet's coolness and lucidity, a greater warmth of feeling supervenes. From *Life's dull coils* we move to *old love*; *eternal essence* is tellingly opposed to *silent adamantine shape* – life against lifelessness – and, almost as if Hardy had become impatient with his rather arid thesis, he ends with a beautiful and unashamedly romantic image. For the couplet, with its strong alliteration and musical assonances in *his/haunt*, *low/slipping snows*, *dawn/dyes* and *calls/climber*, has a warmth and a magniloquence which speaks for Hardy's grief. No wonder Stephen's daughter, Virginia Woolf, wrote to Hardy, 'That poem . . . remains in my mind as incomparably the truest and most imaginative portrait of him in existence.'

The Last Signal (412/ALL/*)

Something has been said of Hardy's relationship with Barnes in Chapter 2. In the *Life* he records the incident which prompted this poem. As he took his familiar walk over the fields towards Barnes's church, his eye caught the momentary flash of the sun on his friend's brass coffin-plate, half-a-mile or so away. Barnes was a devout Christian; Hardy would never have thought of intruding his own religious difficulties into a memorial to him. Rather his warm affection and sincere admiration for Barnes as both man and poet prompted him to pay an apparently simple tribute, by way of a homely anecdote akin to those Barnes so often deployed in his *Poems in the Dorset Dialect*. In what is the last encounter of friends and neighbours, sorrow and mourning are not to be made explicit any more than they are in Barnes's beautiful elegy *The Wife a-Lost*.

But Barnes's art is anything but naive; his homely themes are often couched in verse-forms of great sophistication. Hardy had edited a selection from Barnes and in deliberate homage to him he employs two and possibly three of the techniques Barnes had himself borrowed from poetry in the languages he had studied. Thus the internal rhyming (for example, *road/abode* in verse 1) is, in Welsh, called *union* and the elaborate consonantal pattern in, for example, line 3, where it runs LLSNSLLNS is a device termed *cynghanedd* and employed by Gerard Manley Hopkins also. But what is probably Hardy's most direct and valuable lesson was derived from Barnes's genius for the compound epithet of which he coined hundreds (for example, *thatch-brow'd* windows, *sky-backed* clouds). Here we have only *yew-boughed* and *grave-way*. On the other hand a salient feature of Anglo-Saxon verse, which Barnes admired and from which he believed his Dorset dialect was lineally descended, was its alliteration. This is very marked throughout, nowhere more so than in verse 4 where we have *To* /take/trudged/time, his/he/he/ his/hand, gate, grave-way, athwart/thus, and well/way/wave. It is also notable how seldom Hardy here employs Latinate words, which Barnes thought dispensable, using, for example, *foresay*, for *preface*. I can only find eight in this poem, none with viable equivalents.

Yet what is perhaps most impressive is the fact that all this artful and sophisticated compliment is achieved without any obvious straining for effect. The poem reads as easily as it was meant to do, a sad yet far from gloomy footnote to a long, fulfilled life. We are left feeling that Barnes has bequeathed something of himself to this wintry landscape, a remembered warmth of personality like the *brief blaze* of the sun, *signalled . . . As with a wave of his hand*.

NARRATIVE POEMS

A high proportion of Hardy's total verse output was of the kind he called 'dramatic and personative'; if bulk rather than number of poems is taken for a criterion probably more than half. Some run to several pages, some exhibit both plot and development, others are merely anecdotes. In one or two instances, where I judge the prime function of the story is as a vehicle for satire – for example, *Ah, Are you Digging on My Grave?* (269/G/ *) – narratives are considered in Chapter 6.

The sheer volume of Hardy's narrative verse coupled with its wide variations in quality suggest a few introductory generalisations. First is the fact that – as in his fiction – Hardy is virtually always better on his home ground than away, so to speak. When setting and dramatis personae both have their roots in Wessex there is always something to relish. The Mellstock Quire, as we shall see, amble into several narratives, always to welcome effect. But lurid titles like *The Duel* (379), or *The Mock Wife* (728) (which actually gives us a first line 'trailer', 'It's a dark drama this') tend to live up to their unpromising beginnings. It is as if, among the upper or middle classes, Hardy often found their conventionality so stultifying that he could not even infuse a disagreeable vivacity into their lives. Second, Hardy is far more often successful when his primary purpose is to some degree humorous; his penchant for straight-faced melodrama is not easy to share. Finally, as he once confided to his publishers, he found writing narrative verse 'easy to do' and this facility led him into the versification of some inherently prosaic episodes better left as prose. Nor, for all his jackdaw's eye for colourful scraps from the fabric of life, could he always subsume his idiosyncratic style and opinions into that impressive anonymity of manner which gives to traditional verse much of its gnomic power.

Thus, even given a promising subject, he will sometimes fail to charge it with reality. *The Peasant's Confession* (25/C) has a Napoleonic plot. The dying narrator confesses to his priest that his overmastering desire to preserve his farm from the ravages of war led him to misdirect Marshal Grouchy's relief column *en route* to Waterloo, thereby bringing about Napoleon's defeat. This might have made an excellent short story, like Hardy's

A Tradition of 1804; it *could* have made an excellent ballad in the manner of Browning's similar footnote to history, *Hervé Riel*. Alas, Hardy clogs it up with so much superfluous detail that maps and textbooks would be necessary to unravel it fully. There are 45 names of Napoleon's marshals in *five* verses; one, apart from *with*, has nothing else! Worse still, the diction oscillates uneasily between the incisive 'heard the gloomy gun//Growl through the long-sunned day' and the stilted, 'Albeit therein – as lated tongues bespake'. The ignorant peasant displays a truly encyclopaedic grasp of military history and tactics. In short, Hardy quite fails to persuade us to 'suspend our disbelief'. Although this was an early effort, the much later *At Wynyard's Gap* (718/W) is not a great improvement. True, Hardy opens promisingly: a chance encounter seems likely to lead to an adulterous, 'damn-the-consequences' affair. Yet what real interest can we take in people whose conversation (and the whole poem is cast in dialogue) bumbles along like this, its movement yet further impeded by 'stage directions',

> SHE
> Put up? Do you think so!
> HE
>   I incline to such,
> My *dear* (do you mind?)
> SHE
> Yes—Well (*more softly*), I don't much.

On the whole the I think it best to concede that the greater part of Hardy's narrative verse falls far short of his best, while no useful purpose would be served by making an Aunt Sally of his worst. Even the lively, and faintly bawdy dialect tale, *The Bride-Night Fire* (48/C/D/W/*) is, on its own ground of farcical comedy, easily outshone by the hilarious three prose pages of *Absentmindedness in a Parish Choir* (in *Life's Little Ironies*).

All this is not to say that the best of Hardy's narratives fall short of excellence in their kind. Indeed, even among those prompted – in Walter de la Mare's mordant phrase – 'by the feeblest of actuality's sparks' it is rare to find not one phrase or stanza to break upon the mind and invade the memory. But the whole is more than the part, and so, from the 150-odd which are scattered through the pages of *The Complete Poems*, I shall limit myself to a few narratives only.

The Alarm (26) shows, in total contrast with *The Peasant's Confession*, just what Hardy could do with a slice of local, indeed family, history. It tells with a wealth of – in this instance fascinating – detail, how Hardy's grandfather set off to help repel Napoleon's supposed landing, as a trooper in the Yeomanry complete with 'knapsack, firelock, spatters,// . . . Pouch, magazine and flintbox that at every quickstep clatters'. It is a vivacious and sometimes slily ironic tale, written in a galloping metre to be read aloud. Much of its infectious *élan* derives from what Hardy himself called 'parochialism'. No one knew better what went on in 'local hearts and heads'.

This applies with yet more force to the little group of poems featuring the *Mellstock Quire* (the heroes of Hardy's original title for *Under the Greenwood Tree*). They appear, with their instruments, in *The Dead Quire* (213/W/H), *The Paphian Ball* (796/C/W/*), *The Country Wedding* (612/W/*) *The Choirmaster's Burial* (489/ALL/*) and *The Rash Bride* (212/W/*), while *The Dance at the Phoenix* (28/D/W/*) is of very similar character. All have a markedly indigenous flavour, earthily reminiscent of the 'tall tales' exchanged by habitués of the 'Maltster's' in *Far from the Madding Crowd*.

The Paphian Ball turns a classical myth into a folk-tale in which the Quire is bribed by Satanic gold to play for his rout of damned souls, but 'Drowsy at length, in lieu of the dance// 'While Shepherds watched . . . ' they bowed by chance;' whereupon 'in a moment' the illusory ballroom vanished with 'all its crew' and their fee of 'heaped-up guineas'. Yet the villagers have heard the Quire all night playing carols which 'Never so thrilled the darkness through'. *The Country Wedding* is a melancholy piece, relating one of what Hardy called *Life's Little Ironies* and *The Rash Bride* a grim little tragedy of love and money.

The Dance at the Phoenix, despite its sad conclusion is a rumbustious and amusing 'cautionary tale' of a Casterbridge woman who formerly 'knew the regiment all,' (in both senses, Hardy implies). Now long reformed, the return of the 'King's Own Cavalry' to town tempts her to a valedictory night of wild dancing at which she still 'sped as shod by wings'. Exhausted, she dies in bed by her unwitting husband's side and, Hardy drily concludes, 'The King's said not a word.' *The Choirmaster's Burial*, most lyrical of the group, is about Hardy's grandfather and has been beautifully set to music by Benjamin Britten. His friends return, as ghosts, to play at his grave.

Among the best of Hardy's longer narratives is another Christmas 'ghost' story, *The Dead Quire* (first printed in *The Graphic's* Christmas number, but extensively revised for *Time's Laughingstocks*.) When it begins the Quire all 'lay by the gaunt yew tree' and there are no more 'Christmas harmonies'. On the contrary, their 'sons and grandsons' now drunkenly celebrate the season at 'a dormered inn', where, when 'the clock belled midnight' they blasphemously flout the time-honoured tradition of the toast to Christ's birth with a bawdy salutation of 'John Barleycorn', and their 'women' (i.e. *not* their wives). But, at the moment's silence which ensues,

> 'While shepherds watch'd their flocks by night' –
> Thus swells the long familiar sound
> In many a quaint symphonic flight –
> To *Glory shone around*.

Now 'abashed', frightened, and 'stilly staring at the ground' they listen and then set off to 'follow the notes afar'. Here, in nine quietly expressive stanzas – sharply differentiated from the roistering mood of the inn scenes – the ghostly 'aerial music' moves away and they follow, spell-bound.

> 'Then did the Quick pursue the Dead
> By crystal Froom that crinkled there;
> And still the viewless Quire ahead
> Voiced the old holy air.

It is done so persuasively that we can almost swallow the conclusion that of 'each sobered son . . . not one//Sat in a tavern more.'

The Lost Pyx (140/G) is another Christmas legend about the mysterious 'pillar Cross-in-Hand' which figures in *Tess*. It might be described as a lively parlour-recitation. There are a number of tart, short pieces perhaps best categorised as anecdotes. *The Children and Sir Nameless* (584/C/W), *The Carrier* (669/H) and the dry *Squire Hooper* (868/W/*) are good examples as is the genial *Farmer Dunman's Funeral* (744/*) which he arranged '. . . so as to see//Poor folk there. 'Tis their one day//To spare for following me.' His thoughtful labelling of ten rum bottles as 'drink for my funeral' also ensures them a 'jolly afternoon'!

The avowed 'ballads' are not as good as might have been hoped; the best, *A Trampwoman's Tragedy* (153/ALL/H/*), is analysed later. Only *The Harvest Supper* (746/*) stands out from the remainder as an effective re-working of the ancient ballad *The Unquiet Grave*, echoes of which sound in several of Hardy's poems. Its theme is that of excessive grief occasioning the return of the dead, and Hardy's poem, using the same ballad-stanza, could well be sung to the old, haunting tune.

Hardy's ventures out of Wessex are seldom very rewarding though the London vignette, *An East End Curate* (679/C/D/W/H) exhibits a bleak precision not untouched by admiration while *The Chapel Organist* (593/C/W), a dramatic monologue very much in the manner of Browning, displays a cutting insight into small-town hypocrisy. Finally, there is a group of short poems which, though Hardy entitled them *A Set of Country Songs* are best treated with the narratives. *The Market Girl* (197/C/*) and *The Orphaned Old Maid* (203), though slight, are both successful; *The Homecoming* (210) I think is better still. It recounts the efforts of a rough, but good-hearted, farmer from 'haunted Toller Down' to reconcile his newly-wed and now reluctant young bride to her lonely lot. It is by turns both funny and touching while Hardy deftly hits off the speech of the anxious, none too articulate bridegroom,

> 'Now don't ye rub your eyes so red; we're home and have
>   no cares;
> Here's a skimmer-cake for supper, peckled onions, and
>   some pears;
> I've got a little keg o'summat strong, too, under stairs.'

By contrast with this the eerie refrain of the wind pulses through the entire poem, 'The wind of winter mooed and mouthed their chimney like a horn//And round the house and past the house 'twas leafless and lorn.' Unquestionably the pick of the bunch is the *Dark-eyed Gentleman* (201) which goes happily to the old tune of 'Here's to the maiden of bashful fifteen'. The heroine tells her own tale. She has 'pitched her day's leazings in Crimmercrock Lane' (leazings = gleanings), so as to 'tie up my garter and jog on again' when the 'gentle-man' of the title remarks, pointedly,

> 'What do I see
> O pretty knee!'
> And he came and he tied up my garter for me.

Hardy is here drawing on not just folk-song but also the thousand-year-old Provençal tradition of the *chanson d'aventure* in which a wayfaring knight makes a proposition to a chance-met maiden, who may either accept or reject it, sometimes to humorous, sometimes to tragic effect. There is nothing tragic about this narrator's acceptance, though sex is implied rather than stated, another folk-song convention. Hardy gets his laughs by the deliberately flat, monosyllabic refrain, leaving us to fill in the spaces, as it were. The dry humour is pervasive; vocabulary and phrasing are perfectly in key with the narrator, with the merest hint of dialect. Even the jaunty, infectious rhythm implicitly contradicts her conventionally sententious, 'Ah, 'tis easy to lose what we nevermore find' in verse 2. But there is a brilliant sting in the tail, characteristically Hardeian and not at all traditional. For whereas Victorian middle-class received morality held that unchastity led inexorably to pover-ty, misery and an early grave, the undaunted narrator openly delights in her 'fine lissom lad' and ends with a Parthian shot for Mrs Grundy:

> No sorrow brings he
> And thankful I be
> That his daddy once tied up my garter for me.

On its own terms this is a complete success; one can only regret that Hardy did not use the formula more often!

Analyses

A Trampwoman's Tragedy (153/ALL/H/*)

Hardy said this was 'on the whole his most successful poem', but, since he was not given to using language loosely, we need not suppose he meant it was his best. Thought unsuitable for a 'family periodical' in England, and first printed in America, the plot, founded on fact, needs no remark, the more so in view of Hardy's plentiful comments (in the *Life*, a letter to Gosse and his note to the poem).

It is not hard to see why he thought it 'successful'. Viewed simply as a story it grips and holds the reader's interest firmly. It has enough variety of background to avoid monotony, with sufficient psychological insight to raise it above mere melodrama. Truth to tell it is not really ballad-like in form; the elaborate eight line stanza-pattern, rhyming AAA/B/CCC/B, in no way resembles the simple four-line stanzas of the traditional ballads. Hardy's form produces a markedly cumulative effect in lines 6–8 of each verse, screwing up the pressure to the terse, often clinching, eighth line with its slower rhythm and six solemn beats. I have some reservations about the repetition of the first line, which, if the poem is read *aloud*, seems to me to act as a drag on the forward thrust of the narrative.

If the wanderings of the gipsy band at one point too closely suggest a 'Guide to Good Wessex Taverns', the fatigue and temper-fraying tedium of their journey – a necessary prelude to the dramatic crisis – is well suggested by such glimpses as *shoulders sticking to our packs* and *stung by every moorland midge*. Hardy does, however, keep within the terse ballad convention by giving only hints about the character of the protagonists. The narrator keeps to an epithet for *Jeering John*, her lover is only *my fancy man* and she does not directly accuse herself, except for ignoring her lover's *dark distress*. From this taciturnity the poem gains in conviction. The narrator's actions reveal her nature; she may be wanton in manner but she has no real intention of cuckolding her lover.

The 'tragedy' lies, not in her crude baiting of her lover (we are not in drawing-room society here) but in her misjudgement of the depth of his passion. This is the Greek *hamartia* or crucial error while, since her motive in teasing him was plainly to intensify his love, we also have the Greek *peripateia* in the sense of an action's producing the opposite result to what was intended. Hardy's title is more apt than it may seem. As in the better ballads, the climax is very well and very suddenly initiated from an intense atmosphere of brooding violence where inarticulacy means that thought explodes into action. The lover's curt question eliciting only a nod, though we can easily envisage the mocking smile that would accompany it, is a brilliant piece of compression: speech would be superfluous.

There is a single twist of visual horror in the *slant ray* that *gilded John's blood and glazing eye* and then a brooding hopelessness supervenes, which the ghost's return only lightens momentarily. For a primitive way of life Hardy has contrived a dour, austere manner. But I do not believe it was a manner that came altogether naturally to a poet of such penetration into the darker recesses of the human heart, nor do I believe this to be one of his best poems, effective as it is within its limits.

The Curate's Kindness (159/C/D/W/*)
A Workhouse Irony

I

I thought they'd be strangers aroun'me,
  But she's to be there!
Let me jump out o'waggon and go back and drown me
  At Pummery or Ten-Hatches Weir.

II

I thought: 'Well, I've come to the Union –
  The workhouse at last –
After honest hard work all the week, and Communion
  O'Zundays, these fifty years past.

III

"Tis hard; but,' I thought, 'never mind it:
  There's gain in the end:
And when I get used to the place I shall find it
  A home, and may find there a friend.

IV

'Life there will be better than t'other,
  For peace is assured.
The men in one wing and their wives in another
  Is strictly the rule of the Board.'

V

Just then one young Pa'son arriving
  Steps up out of breath
To the side o'the waggon wherein we were driving
  To Union; and calls out and saith:

VI

'Old folks, that harsh order is altered,
  Be not sick of heart!
The Guardians they poohed and they pished and they
    paltered
  When urged not to keep you apart.

VII

'"It is wrong," I maintained, "to divide them,
  Near forty years wed."
"Very well, sir. We promise, then, they shall abide them
  In one wing together," they said.'

VIII

Then I sank – knew 'twas quite a foredone thing
  That misery should be
To the end! . . . To get freed of her there was the one thing
  Had made the change welcome to me.

IX

To go there was ending but badly;
  'Twas shame and 'twas pain;
'But anyhow,' thought I, 'thereby I shall gladly
  Get free of this forty years' chain.'

X

I thought they'd be strangers aroun'me,
  But she's to be there!
Let me jump out o'waggon and go back and drown me
  At Pummery or Ten-Hatches Weir.

This was sub-titled 'A Workhouse Irony' because Hardy had painfully learned that many readers could not recognise irony even when it bit them. He plunges us headlong into the situation via the aged narrator–victim: *I thought they'd be strangers around me,//But she's to be there!*. The succinct immediacy available to the dramatic monologue is at once manifest, as is the bitter emphasis on *she*; indeed Hardy has encapsulated his plot in a single stanza. In the next our sympathies are enlisted by the old man's profound humiliation at having come *to the workhouse at last*. Hardy plants his first pungent little dart of satire when he has the old man say, quite innocently (though Hardy's purpose is far from innocent) that this is made worse by coming *After honest hard work all the week and Communion// 'O Zundays, these fifty years past*. Still, the prospect of *a friend* is some compensation and, better still, the principal consolation is now revealed, with splendid straight-faced aplomb on Hardy's part, in verse 4. One can almost hear the old man's expectant sigh as he recites the *rule of the Board*. At this point the idealistic and evidently persuasive young *Pa'son* (surely a Tractarian fresh from Oxford) rushes up to announce his triumph. It is with a peculiarly savage irony that Hardy makes him say, *Be not sick of heart*, when this is the one thing that could make the narrator's gloom yet deeper. His solitary palliative is lost, his loyalty to the Church rewarded by the Church's giving him the last thing he desired (though how could he say so?). And, as a final turn of the screw, we realise that the glum repetition of his suicidal opening wish comes from someone with neither the will nor the power to achieve it.

This is in many ways an admirable poem, typical of Hardy in both its theme and its temper. The effortlessly authentic rendering of the old man's voice, the witty use of stress to bring out key phrases (it reads marvellously well aloud), the compression whereby not a word is superfluous: all are clearly to be seen. But perhaps less immediately apparent is the depth, not only of Hardy's irony, by turns funny and cruel, but also of his compassion. He suggests that life is, inherently, ironic; a far from divine comedy. For here unavoidable cruelty to one derives from a genuine, an entirely commendable impulse of kindness to many. The rule *is* inhumane: the other old couples *will* be happier together. However much our hearts go out to the narrator would we really want to reverse the Guardians' decision? The *situation* might have appealed to other poets. One may envisage the conclusion to *A Poor Law Romance* by some minor follower of Tennyson, say,

> . . . .and thus the good old pair,
> United by the Curate's urgent plea,
> Blest him and one another. So they dwelt
> For many a year in mellowing happiness
> To cease at last upon the self-same day.

But that was not Hardy's way; he never let go of the fact, truism or not, that one man's meat is another man's poison.

Julie-Jane (205/C/W/*)

> Sing; how 'a would sing!
> How 'a would raise the tune
> When we rode in the waggon from harvesting
> By the light o' the moon!
>
> Dance; how 'a would dance!
> If fiddlestring did but sound
> She would hold out her coats, give a slanting glance,
> And go round and round.
>
> Laugh; how 'a would laugh!
> Her peony lips would part
> As if none such a place for a lover to quaff
> At the deeps of a heart.
>
> Julie, O girl of joy,
> Soon, soon that lover he came.
> Ah, yes; and gave thee a baby-boy,
> But never his name . . .
>
> – Tolling for her, as you guess;
> And the baby too . . . 'Tis well.
> You knew her in maidhood likewise? – Yes,
> That's her burial bell.

'I suppose,' with a laugh, she said,
'I should blush that I'm not a wife;
But how can it matter, so soon to be dead,
What one does in life!'

When we sat making the mourning
By her death-bed side, said she,
'Dears, how can you keep from your lovers, adorning
In honour of me!'

Bubbling and brightsome eyed!
But now – O never again.
She chose her bearers before she died
From her fancy-men.

NOTE. – It is, or was, a common custom in Wessex, and
probably other country places, to prepare the mourning
beside the death-bed, the dying person sometimes
assisting, who also selects his or her bearers on such
occasions.

     'Coats' (line 7), old name for petticoats.

'Country life', said Edward Thomas when this poem first
appeared, '[Hardy] handles with a combination of power and
exactness beyond that of any poet who could be compared to
him, and for country women I should give the palm to his Julie
Jane.' Hardy's chosen form is that of a conversation – virtually a
monologue – immediately prior to a funeral; the speaker one of
the dead girl's friends. Hardy's theme here is one that often
exercised him: are we to judge people solely by their degree of
compliance with society's rules (often no more than conventions) or by some more liberal yardstick? His great novel *Tess*
was made out of this dilemma. In it his heroine 'felt herself
condemned . . . though nothing in Nature condemned her'.
Here, the case is altered with a vengeance; Julie Jane does not
give a hoot for convention. She is the ancestress of Dylan
Thomas's Polly Garter, with her cry of 'Oh isn't life a terrible
thing, thank God!'

The narrator hesitates – convincingly – between the sancti-
monious *'Tis well'* (albeit this remark also displays an un-

derstanding of the likely fate of an illegitimate orphan) and her true feeling – which the tone of the whole poem makes manifest – that her friend's life, however disturbing to the orthodox, was one that enhanced the lives of others. She yields by no means immediately to the promptings of her heart: *lover* is pretty sharply qualified by *But never his name*. Yet it emerges that Julie Jane's short life was pitched at a higher intensity than that of more earthbound mortals, a fact splendidly brought out in the first three verses. In each, the stressed opening word *Sing, Dance* or *Laugh* is followed by a marked pause, almost as if the speaker were momentarily lost for words adequate to her emotion. Then comes the homely dialect phrase to intensify the mood of admiration and lastly – moving from general to particular – an instance of Julie Jane 'in action', so to speak. The strong, echoing rhymes and the insistent alliteration reinforce the gay rhythms, like hand-claps in a jig.

Now stanzas 4 and 5 change to a more muted and conversational mood, broken up into brief exchanges and reflections. Hardy witholds the origin of the dialogue until verse 5 in which death is dealt with almost offhandedly. But then, with a brilliant stroke of juxtaposition, he allows the sound of Julie Jane's *laugh* in effect to cut across the sound of her *burial bell*. Next we hear her speak, and what she says is all of a piece with what we have already learnt of her nature as her friends perceive it. Thus her *slanting glance* of verse 2 is picked up by her faintly mocking query of verse 7. It is remarkable how full a picture of this *girl of joy* Hardy has compressed into a few lines.

Finally, with sure instinct, Hardy returns in the last stanza to the tone and pattern of the first three, but that his final verse has all the concentrated impact of an epitaph, cut in stone. He never wrote more telling epithets than *Bubbling and brightsome eyed*, nor can I ever read the second line without tears coming into my eyes as I wonder how he makes those time-worn words *never again* (with which he also ends his masterpiece *At Castle Boterel* (292/ALL/H/*)) seem so fresh minted. But even that does not prepare us for the conclusion, truthful, sardonic, defiant and sad all at once. For what other poet of Hardy's day would have used his last word? And what other word would have quite the same effect? Note, *fancy-man* is glossed in Eric Partridge's *Dictionary of Slang* as 'lover of a loose woman' and a distinctly 'low' word in nineteenth-century usage. The implication here is that Julie Jane had, at least, six lovers!

> *One Ralph Blossom Soliloquises* (238/C/*)
> ('It being deposed that vij women who were mayds
> before he knew them have been brought upon the
> towne [rates?] by the fornications of one Ralph
> Blossom, Mr. Maior inquired why he should not
> contribute xiv pence weekly toward their maynte-
> nance. But it being shewn that the sayd R. B. was
> dying of a purple feaver, no order was made.' *Bud-
> mouth Borough Minutes*: 16 —)

When I am in hell or some such place,
A-groaning over my sorry case,
What will those seven women say to me
Who, when I coaxed them, answered 'Aye' to me?

'I did not understand your sign!'
Will be the words of Caroline;
While Jane will cry, 'If I'd had proof of you,
I should have learnt to hold aloof of you!'

'I won't reproach: it was to be!'
Will dryly murmur Cicely;
And Rose: 'I feel no hostility,
For I must own I lent facility.'

Lizzy says: 'Sharp was my regret,
And sometimes it is now! But yet
I joy that, though it brought notoriousness,
I knew Love once and all its gloriousness!'

Says Patience: 'Why are we apart?
Small harm did you, my poor Sweet Heart!
A manchild born, now tall and beautiful,
Was worth the ache of days undutiful.'

And Anne cries: 'O the time was fair,
So wherefore should you burn down there?
There is a deed under the sun, my Love,
And that was ours. What's done is done, my Love.

These trumpets here in Heaven are dumb to me
With you away. Dear, come, O come to me!'

Budmouth should be Weymouth, but the original entry (which
Hardy must, at some time, have noted down) has never been
located, though it is manifestly authentic. However, this fragment of somewhat disreputable fact from Tudor times enables
Hardy not only to open one of his windows into time for us, but
also to cock an uninhibited snook at Mrs Grundy and 'respecta-
bility'. The snippet would have appealed strongly both to
Hardy's antiquarian predilections and to his penchant for the
macabre. Nevertheless, the actual situation was his invention,
deriving a hint perhaps from the well-known folk-song *Dives
and Lazarus* in which Dives speaks from Hell. Most critics have
seen it as a *jeu d'esprit* and it is, of course, meant to be amusing.
But, characteristically, Hardy's humour is alloyed with a more
serious concern that emerges as the poem progresses.

The opening, however, establishes *Ralph Blossom* – the name
is a poem in itself – as an insouciant rogue (reminiscent of
Hardy's *Tony Kytes; the Arch-Deceiver* in *Life's Little Ironies*).
The mock-repentant tone of *some such place* and *sorry case*,
suggests, as does the whole poem, that the Vicar and he would
not agree as to what 'last things' suit his case. Structurally
speaking, Hardy's immediate removal of his protagonist to the
sidelines is a stroke of genius; the crisp, succinct and dramatic
remarks that follow not only enlist our sympathy, if hardly our
approval, for him, they also sardonically establish the fact that
all his 'victims' – as convention would have labelled
them – were, to say the least, willing: certainly none feels any
real resentment. But does Hardy imply we should say 'Lucky
man?'. It is not so simple. Hardy discriminates succinctly and
with great skill between the *seven women*, employing feminine
rhymes at first to comic effect, as in Rosa's *hostility/facility*
couplet. Apart from the taciturn Cicely's *dryly* there are no
'stage directions', yet the reader needs no guidance as to the
tone of voice to use for each speaker, beginning with the coy
would-be 'innocence' of Caroline, through wry acceptance to
maternal affection.

This progression is crucial to the poem's meaning
because – though this is subtly handled – Hardy is not content

to amuse us by planting a few well-aimed darts in the hide of complacency. In addition we get something like the Seven Ages of Love, steadily intensifying into the fiery but essentially egocentric and implicitly erotic outburst of *Lizzy*, modulating into the child-centred attitude of *Patience*, whose *my poor Sweet Heart* suggests that she thinks of Ralph too as a child. But then *Anne* get six lines, the feminine rhymes are dropped but for the last couplet, and love, until now never quite disinterested, flames out in a conclusion worthy of Donne. Her simple, yet serious assertion that the world, indeed Heaven itself, may well be lost for love, gives an incandescent quality to the ending which, with its repeated *come, O come* has a lovely falling close in contrast with the heavenly *trumpets'* insistence. We realise that Hardy has here devised a miniature allegory of everyone's quest for love, with perhaps the implication that one is lucky to find it once in a lifetime, nor can we possibly accept that Ralph Blossom was a monster of depravity. The stereotype, looked at from another angle, is revealed as absurd; the richness and unpredictability of life are celebrated.

5

Poems about Seasons, Places and Things

POEMS ABOUT SEASONS AND PLACES

As a novelist Hardy is justly famed for his descriptive passages, of which the panoramic vision of Egdon Heath that opens *The Return of the Native* is only the most celebrated. From the outset of his career his evocations of landscape, weather and the seasons were recognised as poetic in their precision and intensity; even the savagely dismissive reviewer of *Desperate Remedies*, his first published novel, praised his 'remarkable sensitiveness to scenic and atmospheric effects'. As he confessed in his 1912 Preface to the same novel, he had in fact 'dissolved . . . scattered reflections and sentiments [from his poems] into prose'. Now and then, so strong was the lyric impulse within him, his prose will even deviate into or verge upon metrical form. In *Far from the Madding Crowd* (Chapter XXVIII) for example, we find,

> Above the dark margin of the earth appeared
> Foreshores and promontories of coppery cloud,
> Bounding a green and pellucid expanse
> In the western sky;

There are a further seven regular iambic lines to follow, in which the weather of the heroine Bathsheba's mind is mirrored by the skyscape, beautiful and ominous. In view of all this, and the fact that he would readily admit to 'place-enthusiasms' it is perhaps surprising to discover that descriptive poetry has only a small part to play in Hardy's output; indeed there are no more than thirty poems that can fairly be called descriptive in terms of their primary intention. There are, however, good reasons for this relative abstinence. First is the fact that, as Hardy said (in a remark already quoted), 'Nature is played out as a beauty.' He was not, that is to say, disposed to compete with such word-painters of the rural scene as his friend William Barnes with his pictures of 'Sweet Bemister that bist abound//By green an' woody hills all round.' Second, bearing in mind that the incidence of such poems becomes very much higher from *Satires of Circumstance* (1914) onwards – in which virtually all the poems had been written well after he had finished with fiction – it is fair to assume that this particular aspect of his creative imagination had been almost wholly subsumed in his prose.

Lastly, his actual handling of description was original. In one exceptionally striking and innovative poem, *After a Romantic Day* (599/D/W/*), he gives us valuable insights into both his practice and his theory. In it he is travelling at night by train – and Hardy was the first poet of the railways – after the 'romantic day' of the title. He asserts that for 'the visions of his mind'

> The bald, steep cutting, rigid, rough,
>   And moonlit, was enough
>   For poetry of place: . . .

Yet, despite this disclaimer, the first stanza ends with these lines, both exact and evocative,

> Though the frail light shed by a slim young moon
> Fell like a friendly tune.

This balances the second stanza's contention that there is a 'blank lack of any charm'. And here 'charm' is a highly significant word. For Hardy the absence of conventional, picture postcard 'beauties of nature' was no loss. He believed it was time for a reappraisal of received notions as to what should be regarded as 'beautiful'; arguing in the *Life* that 'Nature's defects', so called, may in the hands of the artist be made 'the basis of a hitherto unperceived beauty, . . . seen to be latent in them by the spiritual eye'. In expressing his admiration for Turner's painting and especially his 'much decried, mad, late' works, he adds that 'The "simply natural" is interesting no longer.'

All this means that we should not look for large-scale descriptive set pieces, especially in his earlier volumes, while, even in the later ones it is rare for *what* he depicts to be of equal importance with the idea or situation suggested by it. The stupendous sunset in *The Woodlanders* (Chapter XXVIII) or the Arctic winter landscape at Flintcomb-Ash in *Tess* (Chapter XLIII) have no counterparts in the poetry, which is, perhaps, regrettable. But, even in his earliest poems there are what might be called brilliant descriptive asides. The scene is set in *Her Dilemma* (12/C/D) dated 1867, with all an architect's informed precision,

> The two were silent in a sunless church,
> Whose mildewed walls, uneven paving-stones,
> And wasted carvings passed antique research;
> And nothing broke the clock's dull monotones.

This strong sense of locality is reinforced by the man's 'Leaning against a wormy poppy-head,//So wan and worn that he could hardly stand.' We see how much Hardy's acute sense of place sharpens the poem's impact; the decay and gloom of the setting emphasise the wasting illness of a man 'soon to die'; The 'wormy poppy-head' (a pew-end carving) with its grim undertones of death and drugs, also makes us aware of the brevity of human life set beside its age-long, slow crumbling.

But, memorable as this visual realisation is, it remains incidental to the poem's 'dilemma'. Here, asked by the dying man if she loves him, the woman, writes Hardy, ' . . . lied, her heart persuaded throughly//'Twas worth her soul to be a moment kind'. This blend of irony and compassion against a background entirely appropriate to the sombre theme, is characteristic of Hardy's method in many other poems. A line or two, maybe a stanza or two, depicts – one might says etches – a scene with great intensity, only to prove a catalyst rather than a subject in itself. Hardy's admirable little group of poems about the Boer War (*War Poems* CP 54–64), some of which will be discussed in Chapter 6, contains several glimpses of what Hardy could do in a small compass by way of giving a poem appropriate visual atmosphere. The chilling desolation of a London fog has rarely been better shown, for example, than in the first verse of *A Wife in London* (61/W/*), dated December 1899,

> She sits in the tawny vapour
> That the Thames-side lanes have uprolled,
> Behind whose webby fold on fold
> Like a waning taper
> The street-lamp glimmers cold.

This is the prelude to the arrival of the telegram announcing her husband's death in action; next day a letter arrives 'Page-full of his hoped return, ' . . . 'And of new love that they would learn', but written – it is Hardy's only comment – by 'His hand, whom the worm now knows'. Irony and weather are equally grim and desolate. The visible scene imparts the mental condition.

The first two verses of *The Souls of the Slain* (62/D/H/*) are even better, and similar discriminating perceptions occur in *Rome, Building a New Street in the Ancient Quarter* (69/C/W); for instance, opening with 'These umbered cliffs and gnarls of masonry'. Even so phrases like 'I enter a daisy-and-buttercup land' from *Growth in May* (583/*) or 'The broad, bald moon edged up where the sea was wide,//Mild, mellow-faced . . . ' from *On the Esplanade* (682/C/D/W/*) though they do, in these instances, begin poems with a markedly descriptive element, may just as often crop up in places where Hardy has entirely different ends in view. Such a suggestive title as *In Front of the Landscape* (246/C/D/W/H/*), although its second stanza contains this brilliant glimpse of the Dorset landscape,

> . . . And the coomb and the upland
> Coppice-crowned,
> Ancient chalk-pit, milestone, rills in the grass-flat
> Stroked by the light,

only offers them as a momentary break in the otherwise all-pervading mist. This, as Hardy fumbles through it, functions, like the railway cutting in *After a Romantic Day* (599), as a

mental backcloth to Hardy's equally misty and confusing recollections of the past. Even such a peremptory title as *The Place on
Map* (263/C/D/W) turns out to be less a portrayal of the
' . . . jutting height//Coloured purple with a margin of blue
sea', than of the mixed emotions 'the wonder and the wormwood' with which Hardy now views the map as it 'revives her
words, the spot, the time'. There is not much doubt that this
poem refers to Hardy's Cornish romance with his first wife
Emma. And, of course, the poems of 1912–13 offer frequent,
vivid glimpses of the ruggedly beautiful scenery and the fickle
weather which formed the background, and sometimes the
foreground of the Hardys' experiences together. But even such
effortlessly evocative vignettes as 'Bos with its flounce flinging
mist', the 'haunted heights//The Atlantic smites//And the blind
gales sweep' are really incidental to Hardy's purpose. However,
Where They Lived (392/D/W/*), one of the less well known of the
poems set in Cornwall, is perhaps an exception to Hardy's
general avoidance of straight descriptive verse. It begins with
an extended image of autumnal decay:

> Dishevelled leaves creep down
> Upon that bank today
> Some green, some yellow and some pale brown;
> The wet bents bob and sway;
> The once warm slippery turf is sodden
> Where we laughingly sat or lay.

The second verse further intensifies Hardy's sense, on his
return, of 'the nakedness of the place' (the once-beautiful
garden of a house the young lovers had stayed in with friends
now lost). His dejected mood could hardly be more sharply
conjured up than it is by his dismal, rain-sodden surroundings.
But I feel he underlines the significance in a rather too heavy-
handed manner when he concludes 'And instead of a voice that
called, "Come in, Dears,"//Time calls, "Pass below!"'. For surely
his 'blind drifts of vapour' that now obscure the 'hills of blue'
make their impact unaided; Hardy's unhappiness declares itself
through the medium of the scene and the weather; the last
line's rather jerky transition to another level of metaphor adds
little, maybe even detracts from, the poem's impact.

A very similar pattern – one we have already met, of course – is employed in a better poem, *At Middle-Field Gate in February* (421/C/D/W/*). This is, I think, the first to which the term 'descriptive' can unequivocally be applied, and it deserves to be quoted in full.

> The bars are thick with drops that show
>   As they gather themselves from the fog
> Like silver buttons ranged in a row,
> And as evenly spaced as if measured, although
>   They fall at the feeblest jog.
>
> They load the leafless hedge hard by,
>   And the blades of last year's grass,
> While the fallow ploughland turned up nigh
> In raw rolls, clammy and clogging lie –
>   Too clogging for feet to pass.
>
> How dry it was on a far-back day
>   When the straws hung the hedge and around,
> When amid the sheaves in amorous play
> In curtained bonnets and light array
>   Bloomed a bevy now underground!
> *Bockhampton Lane*

I am not aware of any poet who has better caught the windless, dank silence; the all-pervading gloom of a sunless winter's day than Hardy in his first two verses. If a gleam of beauty is suggested in the 'silver buttons' it is at once dispersed by the ploughland's mud in 'raw rolls, clammy and clogging', a description which anyone who has ever tried to run across fallow land will at once accept as definitive! Yet this is all by way of prelude and in contrast to the snapshot of high summer and harvest, which with its few but telling details leads in to Hardy's one-line retrospect of 'a bevy now underground.' That is the only authorial comment; the close, lovingly detailed delineation of the place and the weather is enough to summon up the emotional response. Hardy's thought, one might say, is wintry: past summers may be recalled, but the human part of what made that 'far-back day' so intense an experience is now irrecoverably lost. Set against our awareness that even the 'leafless hedge' will be thick with blossom again in Spring his use of the word 'bloomed' for those who once shared in 'amorous play' is particularly telling. The poem might have made an epigraph for the great tragic novel *Tess of the D'Urbervilles* whose heroine might well have been one of that 'bevy now underground'. What might be thought a simple, albeit sharp-eyed description can, if our ears are sharp enough to catch Hardy's murmured suggestions, impart a strong sense of the fragility and brevity of human life and love.

Three poems rather tenuously linked with the Hardys' early married life at Sturminster Newton (Nos. 424–6 in CP) have extended descriptive sections which lead into succinct reflections on their relationship. The best is *On Sturminster Footbridge* (426/D/W/*) which Hardy sub-titled *Onomatopoeic*; justifiably in view of its brilliant rendering of water sounds. Phrases like 'the wind skims irritably', 'the current clucks smartly', and swallows 'arrow off and drop like stones' come near to persuading the reader that he is *listening* to the river Stour. But in this and the other two poems the 'turn' at the end is perhaps a little *too* sudden; the formula, even in Hardy's hands, does not always come off.

No such reservation need be made of *The Five Students* (439/D/W/*), a fine if commonly undervalued poem. Again Hardy employs a pattern where his evocations of season and weather prompt reflections on mutability. His formula, considered simply as a formula, is that used in a cruder form by such 'cumulative' folk-songs as 'Ten Green Bottles' or 'Ten Little Nigger Boys': Death picks off the five students one after another, leaving only Hardy to reflect upon the frailty of his own hold on life. Thus baldly put, the theme suggests nothing of the emotional charge delivered by the five stanzas of seasonal change and the subtly varied diminuendo of the refrain. For each stanza – concentrated as a Bewick tailpiece – offers us a masterly miniature landscape. The first is Spring:

> The sparrow dips in his wheel-rut bath,
> 　The sun grows passionate-eyed,
> And boils the dew to smoke by the paddock-path;
> 　As strenuously we stride, –
> Five of us; dark He, fair He, dark She, fair She, I,
> 　All beating by.

The poem, more than most, needs to be read aloud; this brings out Hardy's skilful contrast of the tiny sparrow with the sun itself, the sheer vigour of his phrasing, *'boils* the dew to *smoke'* and 'passionate-eyed' for example. More importantly – the 'life' and the springing movement (to which his strong alliteration in *s* contributes) are seen to contrast with the slow, musing refrain. The 'strenuous stride' of the first four lines is deliberately checked by the sombre iteration of the fifth which only looks odd on the page, as it were, but read (at a decelerating pace) communicates exactly both the precision and the sadness of Hardy's retrospect. Yet, as a whole, the verse is most Spring-like, instinct with the optimism, the 'high-uplifted hearts' (to borrow another phrase of Hardy's) of his youthful five 'students'. For what it is worth, the five, other than Hardy, were most probably Horace Moule (*dark he*), Tryphena Sparks (*dark she*), Hooper Tolbort (*fair he* and a brilliant fellow student of Hardy's Dorchester days) and Emma (*fair she*). The chronology does not quite fit, nor can all five have really walked together. What matters is that Hardy loved them all in different ways. This is their joint memorial.

There is not space to quote the whole poem though the intervening verses are equally felicitous. But by the last all has suffered a grim transformation:

> Icicles tag the church-aisle leads,
>   The flag-rope gibbers hoarse,
>   The home-bound foot-folk wrap their snow-flaked heads,
>   Yet I still stalk the course–
> One of us . . . Dark and fair He, dark and fair She, gone:
>   The rest–anon.

It is a death-cold landscape now, yet in how few details Hardy has captured it. The crucial effect is in the choice and disposition of phrases like 'icicles tag', 'gibbers hoarse' and 'snow-flaked heads', allied to the now heavy, dragging rhythm; compare, for example, 'I still stalk the course' with 'As strenuously we stride,' and notice how the poem falters at 'One of us . . . ', then resumes the list with the final hammer-blow of *gone* and finally tails away in emptiness and despair. This is a highly orchestrated poem; its gradations are infinitely skilful.

Yet it exemplifies Hardy's determination to offer 'impressions not convictions'. To be sure, it could never have been written by anyone who was not affected by an overwhelming sense of the tragic significance of Time, of the ever-present symbolism of the seasons' immemorial cycle. But he does not spell out for us what gives the poem its ineffable sadness; the fact that all these episodes of the turning year will recur unseen by those once on their 'urgent way'. Only the survivor remembers them, only his words give them any kind of continuance, and soon – it is a whispered postscript – 'The rest-anon'. And what must add a little more to our respect for Hardy's creative integrity is the fact that he originally wrote two stanzas envisaging the four 'Who trod that track with me' in 'yon Pale Land' (i.e. a possible afterlife) and debating whether they 'strode . . . for naught at all', or *per contra*, 'saw aureola'd far//Heaven's central star?' It need hardly be said how much that extraneous discussion would have marred the integrity of both Hardy's theme and imagery which *show* us everything by *telling* us almost nothing.

The poem which immediately follows in *Moments of Vision*, *The Wind's Prophecy* (440/C/D/W/*) combines, in each stanza, an initial four lines of quite brilliant visual imagery with a subsequent four of imagined dialogue between Hardy and the soothsaying wind. I am afraid that the 'art of sinking' has seldom been better demonstrated than in the transition from this suberb picture of sky and seascape, which Tennyson might have envied,

> The all-prevailing clouds exclude
> The one quick timorous transient star;
> The waves outside where breakers are
> Huzza like a mad multitude.

to this exchange

> 'Where the sun ups it, mist-imbued,'
> I cry, 'there reigns the star for me!'
> The wind outshrieks from points and peaks:
> 'Here, westward, where it downs, mean ye!'

It is all very well to ensure, like Alice's Humpty-Dumpty, that words 'know who is master', but to take them by the scruff and yank them about like this to fit a predetermined pattern is indefensible. It is an odd kedgeree of Victorian sentimentality and his own intense realisation of the thing seen that Hardy has here, he tells us, *'Rewritten from an old copy'*. Nevertheless, it contains an unrivalled evocation of the wild North Atlantic coast of Cornwall, which is, curiously enough, entirely self-contained and could, to its great advantage, be detached from the turgid prophesyings of the wind. Interestingly enough, nearly all Hardy's MS revisions relate to the descriptive passages.

Not until his penultimate volume, *Human Shows* (1922), did Hardy print a whole series of poems which can be called purely descriptive in that the places he depicts constitute, in themselves, the true core of the poems. Collectively, this unusually homogenous group is of very high quality indeed, and since they were probably all written at about the same time, I shall, for convenience, discuss them in the order of their original appearance.

Last Week in October (673/C/G/W/*) devotes ten lines to a meticulous recording of leaf-fall, only the single word 'undressing' used metaphorically of the trees, hinting at a human parallel. *The Later Autumn* (675/C/G/*) makes an instructive contrast with Keats's celebrated *Ode to Autumn*. Hardy is not concerned with the 'Season of mists and mellow fruitfulness', however, but with the impending onset of Winter. The first verse, with its rapid, somewhat irregular rhythm, suggests the equally swift disappearance of all signs of growth and life, the opening line perhaps gently mocking earlier poets' predilection for personifying Autumn, with its frank picture of courting couples for whom the absence of foliage and the cold are a disincentive.

> Gone are the lovers, under the bush
> > Stretched at their ease;
> > Gone the bees,
> Tangling themselves in your hair as they rush
> > On the line of your track,

> Leg-laden, back
> With a dip to their hive
> In a prepossessed dive.

This vigorous opening gives way in stanzas 2 and 3 to silence and a damp, misty stillness, atmospherically conveyed in the second stanza,

> Toadsmeat is mangy, frosted, and sere;
> Apples in grass
> Crunch as we pass,
> And rot ere the men who make cyder appear.
> Couch-fires abound
> On fallows around,
> And shades far extend
> Like lives soon to end.

The detail is all-important here; small indications like 'Toadsmeat [i.e. a fungus] is mangy, frosted and sere' are part of the countryman's time-clock. Hardy is, indeed, far more precise than Keats, though not, of course, more impressive on that account. Rather the reverse, in fact: if we take 'impressive' in its sense of 'making an immediate impact' then much of Hardy's best poetry will often seem – I will not say unimpressive – but unobtrusive. The varieties of experience he puts to use are often not striking, nor is his handling of them commonly dramatic. Yet *The Later Autumn* is one among many of Hardy's less well-known poems that takes root in the reader's mind.

Hardy's interest in history and his 'place-enthusiasms' coalesce in *A Spellbound Palace* (688/D/W), a poem of which the opening is exceptionally suggestive, even for him, of the look and feel of Hampton Court, its subject. It begins,

> On this kindly yellow day of mild low-travelling winter sun
> The stirless depths of the yews
> Are vague with misty blues.

How well that catches the brooding stillness of a place as thick with historical associations as any in England, and how telling is the later image of the 'enfeebled fountain' which 'lays an insistent numbness on the place, like a cold hand's touch'. That chilling premonition heralds the apparition – purely in Hardy's mind – of 'the Shade of a straddling King, plumed, sworded, with sensual face' accompanied by Wolsey who built the palace. But the shades only drift momentarily into our view. Hardy returns us to the 'mindless fountain' and its tinkling. Even the most powerful of men once dead can no more influence events than the most trivial artefect he leaves behind him. This poem is one of Hardy's bolder experiments in form. Though he retains rhyme he employs a six-line pattern for verses one and two, then increasing to seven lines for the third and decreasing to four lines (two rhyming couplets) for the fourth, while varying both rhyme-schemes and line-lengths also from stanza to stanza. The overall effect is impressive and curiously modern, showing Hardy as a bridge-builder between the nineteenth and twentieth centuries.

Poems 698 to 708 in the *Complete Poems* comprise, with one exception, an unusually homogenous group, but because four are to be fully analysed later I shall only say that all are rewarding, especially *A Light Snowfall After Frost* (702/D/W/*) which is the perfect verbal complement to Turner's great winter landscape *A Frosty Morning*, while *Ice on the Highway* (704/C/G/ *) offers a glimpse of Hardy's fun, here quite devoid of satirical intent. Finally, *Winter Night in Woodland* (703/C/G/W/*), which Hardy noted referred to *Old Time*, is a vigorous survey, alive with local knowledge, not so much of Bockhampton Wood itself as of the life that fills it; a fox, poachers, smugglers and the Mellstock Quire 'on their long yearly rounds'.

A little later comes *Last Look Round St. Martin's Fair* (730/C/W/ *). This is a cinematic panorama of the fairground at the end of a hot summer's day. The lurid quality of the scene is stressed, 'The sun is like an open furnace door', the rising moon 'like a brass dial gone green' and the gipsy stall-holder 'redder in the flare-lamp than the sun'. The coarse, brash but lively, atmosphere is summoned up by many shrewdly chosen details. In total contrast is *The Sheepboy* (764/D/*) which depicts Egdon Heath (the location of *The Return of the Native*) in two moods, first basking in sunshine with 'myriads' of bees, and then, on the same day, suddenly shrouded in mist, rising 'out of the sea in swirls//Flexuous and solid, clammy vapour-curls', a silent, threatening presence.

Hardy's last volume, *Winter Words* (1928), has very few descriptive pieces. The two best, *An Unkindly May* (825/C/D/W/ *) and *Suspense* (879/C/*), both display the unwelcome face of the English climate; its capacity for disagreeableness has seldom been better attested than in these lines from the first poem, with its deft sequence 'blurting', 'dirty', 'rusty':

> The sour spring wind is blurting boisterous-wise,
> And bears on it dirty clouds across the skies;
> Plantation timbers creak like rusty cranes.

Hardy's disdain for those who would romanticise the country and its people is shown in the impervious figure of the 'shepherd' who stands at a gate 'Unnoting all things save the counting his flock'. Lastly, I quote the first verse only of *Suspense*,

> A clamminess hangs over all like a clout,
> The fields are a water-colour washed out,
> The sky at its rim leaves a chink of light,
> Like the lid of a pot that will not close tight.

That is entirely characteristic of Hardy. Not at all engaging or 'pretty', it gives an instantly recognisable image of a lowering, sullen day which exactly matches and symbolises the glum despair of the lovers whose lowering fate the poem tells of in its last two verses.

Analyses

(Note: *Weathers* (512/ALL/*) was considered in some detail in Chapter 3. Otherwise it, too, would have been analysed here, of course.)

Snow in the Suburbs (ALL/H/*)

The title, integral to the poem in that it allows Hardy to employ *it* in the first line, refers to a winter in the years 1878–81 when the Hardys were living in Upper Tooting (a name Hardy struck out of the original title, probably because of its faintly ludicrous connotations). This is a well-known and much-anthologised piece; no doubt because it succeeds so admirably in its primary – though not sole – purpose, to depict a snow-bound scene with all the exactitude that verbal artistry can command. The structure is basically simple. Hardy uses rhymed couplets, though he varies his lines greatly in length, and reduces what are really five verses to four by amalgamating the first two, thereby unifying his initial picture of the snow itself. The first four short lines neatly convey the density and the muffling effect of the snow, while the triple-rhymes – *big with it* and *twig with it* institute a light-hearted tone. In the next four lines the irregular, swirling movement, the weightless quality of the snowflakes are enacted by a meticulous disposition of language, in which Hardy's revisions play an important part. He replaced the MS 'float' with *grope* in line 5 thereby reinforcing the *lost* appearance of the flakes. In lines 6 and 7 he substituted, respectively, *meandering* for MS 'coming' and *glued* for MS 'joined', both stronger, more expressive verbs; while in line 8 *there is no waft* takes the place of 'there's not a whiff', the MS phrase introducing an inappropriate association with scent as against sight. Alliteration keeps the lines fluid, despite their length variations; Hardy deploys it profusely, in *w*, and *f* especially. The last line with its clinching phrase *fleecy fall* sums up Hardy's vision of a still, white, lifeless landscape.

Now a sparrow, that symbol of Cockney impudence, disturbs the calm; playing a comic part and bringing life to the scene. Hardy speeds up the pace with a succession of clipped, rapid lines, speeding up to a hectic finale. He repeats his jokey rhyming with *overturns* and *inurns*, implying that the little bird is indestructible, and once again his detailed revisions in wording reward attention. His change from the run-of-the-mill 'falls on a lower twig' to the more exact *lights on a nether twig* suggests the sparrow's flitting arrival, the much more suggestive *volley* displaces 'cascade' which, besides suggesting water, has no implication of noise, while *lodged lumps* seem more precarious than 'waiting' ones. These may perhaps appear rather finicking details to catalogue, but it is a mistake to imagine that poetry can be produced inspirationally and effortlessly, and this poem exemplifies Hardy's attitude to his craft particularly well. He knew exactly what effect he wanted to achieve and nothing was too much trouble for him in his search for the precise words which would achieve it.

Up to now the poem has had something of the quality of a photograph, one taken from the window of a warm room by an uninvolved spectator. The actual technique is wonderfully assured but just a touch inhuman perhaps. But the last four simple, almost monosyllabic lines, with their picture of the starving cat (the only *black* spot in an otherwise wholly white poem) make a moving and effective coda. The snow is undeniably lovely, the sparrow's antics entertaining, but what about those, human or animal, that have to be out in it? They see it quite differently, as Hardy's characteristically unemphatic conclusion reminds us with its matter-of-fact compassion. No doubt the cat took up residence at 'The Larches, Upper Tooting!'

Life and Death at Sunrise (Near Dogbury Gate, 1867)
(698/C/W/*)

The hills uncap their tops
Of woodland, pasture, copse,
And look on the layers of mist,
At their foot that still persist:
They are like awakened sleepers on one elbow lifted,
Who gaze around to learn if things during night have shifted.

A waggon creaks up from the fog
With a laboured leisurely jog;
Then a horseman from off the hill-tip
Comes clapping down into the dip;
While woodlarks, finches, sparrows, try to entune at one time,
And cocks and hens and cows and bulls take up the chime.

With a shouldered basket and flagon
A man meets the one with the waggon,
And both the men halt of long use.
'Well,' the waggoner says, 'what's the news?'
' – 'Tis a boy this time. You've just met the doctor trotting back.
She's doing very well. And we think we shall call him "Jack".

'And what have you got covered there?'
He nods to the waggon and mare.
'Oh, a coffin for old John Thinn:
  We are just going to put him in.'
' – So he's gone at last. He always had a good constitution.'
' – He was ninety-odd. He could call up the French
  Revolution.'

It should be pointed out that Dogbury 'Gate' is actually a road
junction at the crest of a rise – a 'pass' one might almost call
it – in the hilly terrain some ten miles north of Dorchester.
When Hardy witnessed this early morning encounter in 1867 he
either stored it in his capacious memory or perhaps made a
note; the poem itself, though undated, can hardly be early,
since the deleted MS title was *A Long-Ago Sunrise at Dogbury
Gate*. The revised title neatly summarises the theme of the
poem, without nudging the reader too sharply. The meat of
Hardy's achievement here is his superb setting of the scene,
without which we should have an odd coincidence but little
more.

He opens quietly, at the moment of sunrise, subtly identifying the hills with man by means of *uncap, look on, their foot* and
the extended simile which concludes the first verse, so that the
effect of the hills as he depicts them is that of some great
semi-abstract sculpture by Henry Moore. But there is a hint of
bucolic humour too, seen in the image itself and in the
lifted//shifted rhyme.

Since Hardy is plainly a spectator on the ridge, his rendering
of the mist-bound valley must be aural. The noise level
increases – as, of course, it does at dawn in the countryside – and we can see Hardy orchestrating his effects here
through his revisions. He altered his MS's uninspired 'slowest,
possible jog' to the drowsy, rhythmic *laboured, leisurely jog* we
have now. The present lines 9–10 take the place of his MS 'And
a trotting horse then nighs//Slacks, passes over the rise', to
effect a much more telling contrast. The discordant hullabaloo,
as the dawn light reaches the animal world in the valley, is
again good humoured as well as authentic.

All this scrupulous fidelity to observation, however, is there
to underpin the laconic dialogue that ensues. Hardy, who was,

of course, a past master at this kind of exchange, perfectly catches its off-hand amicability. The moment in time he shows us is, certainly, significant to the father; and of mild interest to the waggoner, but, to Hardy as to us, it is the juxtaposition of their errands (the significance of which quite escapes them, of course) that gives the encounter its representative symbolic status. In this background has a vital part to play, albeit not an explicit one: thus the sunlit hills stand for new life, as does the dawn itself; the sun was always a 'warm god' to Hardy. It disperses the mist – an image of silence and death – in the valley from which the waggon comes. The swift horse stands for youthful vigour, as does the young father's eager, rapid speech. The slow, creaking wagon suggests old age, as does the waggoner's more studied talk. The dry, unemphatic dialogue points up, without labouring, the theme of the poem, clinched by the neat play on the names *Jack* and *John*. Here Hardy, understandably, 'Put his thumb on the scale', because the MS shows the old man's name originally to have been *Andrew Thinn*, though there is no reason to suppose that either name is anything but fictitious. For once, we actually *see* an idea take root and flower. The overall impression is of a hopeful augury; there is nothing very tragic about a death at ninety and there is a comfortable sense of an achieved life in the homely Dorset phrase *We are just going to put him in*, so redolent of husbandry, while the waggoner's final tribute, with its far echoes of blood and havoc long past, makes a satisfying conclusion. Hardy has no need to say that life, like day and night, is cyclic, that death is as necessary as birth; the time, the place, the simple words of two countrymen, have done it all for him, leaving nothing to add.

Nobody Comes (715/ALL/H/*)

This brief lyric is one of the last of Hardy's poems to carry a date. The setting is plainly his home, Max Gate, and he, aged 84, is standing by its roadside gate, watching the last of sunset fade over nearby Dorchester. If we needed evidence that the coming of old age brought no weakening either of the impulse, or the ability, to write poetry, here it is. The poem makes an interesting contrast with the *Dogbury Gate* encounter, nearly sixty years earlier. Hardy depicts the twilight scene, so different in its implications from dawn, with the same acute precision of observed detail. Here too, however, the cumulative effect of his descriptive phrasing has a deeper significance. His choice of words in *labour, fainting light, crawling night, darkening land*, with the ghostly imagery of the last two lines, all have a dual function, a more than visual significance. Hardy would have scorned any overt reference to his age, but his whole approach to this familiar scene suggests a sense of a weakening hold on life. As the landscape fades, so the tide of life seems to ebb.

The noisy, lurid advent of the car (Hardy had nothing against cars in themselves, often travelling in them) disturbs the silence and darkness, as the telegraph wire's sound had done. Both are symbols of an alien, indifferent world, a world in a hurry and self-absorbed. Indeed, Hardy's phrase *whangs along in a world of its own* is a very early presentiment indeed of the now well-attested insulating effect that cars exert on their occupants' thoughts and feelings towards the outside world. Its speed, too, is well caught in the verse's first two lines: notice how, read aloud, the sequence *lamps full-glare//That flash upon a tree*: enforces a brisk pace on the reader. Similarly the flat disclaimer of line three returns us to the observing eye. The end, as suits a poem empty of humanity, is muted. The line *Leaving a blacker air* obviously denotes the momentary loss of vision that follows the passing of the car's lights, but *blacker air* has far deeper connotations besides, of all those figurative associations of darkness, of gloom, despair, even death. In this, and in the grim, dour statements of the last two lines Hardy accepts, what he once admitted he sometimes felt in company uncongenial to him, a sense that he has become almost a ghost, stranded out of his time as the world he knew recedes into shadow and a new, confident, 'mechanical' one leaves him behind. At Dogbury Gate the young Hardy could identify easily with the scene and its human dimension; here his sense of estrangement is all but complete, his loneliness achingly evident; in both the title and its echoing last line.

POEMS ABOUT THINGS, ANIMALS, BIRDS, PLANTS, ETC.

Hardy did not often write about inanimate things and when he did choose them as subjects it is not surprising that it was of their associations rather than the objects in themselves that he wrote. *Green Slates* (678/W/*) and *The New Boots* (891) for example, do not say much about rock and leather, while *The Little Old Table* (609/C/*) a delightful short lyric, only 'speaks', by its creakings, 'Of one who gave you to me', something future owners 'will never know.' Similarly, Hardy's architectural expertise is not brought into play as often as one might expect. This is a pity because the part it takes in *Heiress and Architect* (49/D), which Hardy dedicated to his former employer, A. W. Blomfield, is not inconsiderable. So, too, in *A Cathedral Façade at Midnight* (667/C/D/*) his splendid evocation of the 'moonlight creeping' over the West Front of Salisbury, so that

> . . . each austere form
> Was blanched its whole length brightly
> Of prophet, king, queen, cardinal in state,
> That dead men's tools had striven to simulate;
> And the stiff images stood irradiate.

easily outweighs, to my mind, the somewhat forced, ratiocinative conclusion to the effect that 'Reason's movement' must make 'meaningless//The coded creeds of old-time godliness'. I suspect, from the need to personify 'Reason' and the lack-lustre jingle of the last line, that Hardy's heart was not in his argument. His confessed life-long 'churchiness', his trained eye for both the magnificent craftsmanship and the grandeur of the medieval architect's concept were too much for him and his 'impression' wins hands down over the 'conviction' in this instance.

On a more mundane level *Old Furniture* (428/ALL/*) is analysed in detail but *A Gentleman's Second-Hand Suit* (869/W/*) – and who but Hady would ever have written a poem about such a thing until he gave a lead to younger poets? – deserves attention. The suit 'hanging in the sun//By the pawn shop door' and cut 'rather in bygone style' prompts Hardy to speculate on the 'print of powder' on the sleeve. The poem, written in a somewhat waltz-like rhythm, carries us back to the days when 'within its clasp//Fair partners hung'. It is a fittingly light and airy poem: Hardy loved to dance himself, and the note on which it comes to a graceful conclusion, is, though sad perhaps, not at all gloomy. It has perhaps a touch of the subdued melancholy often detectable in Viennese waltzes,

Some of them may forget him quite
  Who smudged his sleeve,
Some think of a wild and whirling night
  With him, and grieve.

I must beg forgiveness of animal-lovers, not to say of Hardy's shade, if I have seemed so far to be indiscriminately lumping together the animate and inanimate worlds. At all events, it is a tribute to Hardy's exceptionally wide-ranging interests and sympathies that a significant number of the poems should be about dogs, cats, horses, trees, flowers and even in one instance, insects. *An August Midnight* (113/ALL/*), the poem in question, is interesting in more ways than one. Writing at his desk by a 'shaded lamp' with the window open, Hardy is interrupted by 'A longlegs, a moth, and a dumbledore', 'while mid my page there idly stands//A sleepy fly, that rubs its hands . . .' Most of us would be irritated to the point of swatting them; to Hardy they are 'My guests' even though they 'smear' his 'new-penned' line,//Or bang at the lamp and fall supine.' He concludes 'God's humblest they!' I muse. Yet why//They know earth-secrets that know not I.' As a convinced Darwinian Hardy contended that animals were 'our kind, having the same ancestry' and this belief, together with what H. W. Nevinson acutely termed his 'extreme sensitiveness to other people's pain' made him a strong supporter of the Royal Society for the Prevention of Cruelty to Animals, a cause he shared with both his wives and his sister Mary. Indeed, he wrote an Ode, *Compassion* (805/C), for the Society's centenary in 1924 which, if not very memorable, nevertheless has a fine, ringing conclusion. Two other poems deal directly with cruelty to animals, one *Horses Abroad* (757/G) describes remounts for the Great War being shipped out to become 'war-waste', 'wrenched awry// From the scheme Nature planned for them, – wondering why'. The other, and more effective, is *Bags of Meat* (787/C/*) which makes savage play with the attitudes of auctioneers and customers at a cattle-auction where the beasts are treated as if already so many joints on a butcher's block. Of a 'timid, quivering steer', for example, the auctioneer remarks 'He'd be worth the money to kill//And give away Christmas for good-will' – an acidulated cut, typical of several. Hardy was not a vegetarian or a total sentimentalist; it is the callous indifference, the assumption that animals have no feelings, that offends him.

Hardy was much attached to his own pets, even if 'Wessex', his over-indulged dog, was often attached, in quite another sense, to the Hardys' human guests. But his two poems about Wessex, *A Popular Personage at Home* (776/C/*) and *Dead Wessex, the Dog to the Household* (907/G/*) though not without their moments, nowhere approach *Last words to a Dumb Friend* (619/C/G/W/*) an elegy for Snowdove, his favourite cat, killed on the nearby railway line and buried in the pets' cemetery at Max Gate. This poem, though I should not be disposed to rate it quite as highly as some critics, is certainly a masterpiece in its kind. For Hardy it is unusually traditional in form, written throughout in simple rhymed couplets of the kind that can, carelessly handled, easily degenerate into doggerel. Hardy never puts a foot wrong, and only once, forgivably, does he verge on sentimentality, when he speaks of the cat's 'little look.' His picture of the 'Purrer of the spotless hue,//Plumy tail and wistful gaze' in the first stanza, is displaced by a desire to 'Selfishly escape distress//By contrived forgetfulness'. But the more he attempts to do so, the more small details like 'the claw-worn pine-tree bark' spring out to remind him of 'this speechless thing'. The fourth and fifth stanzas move from reminiscential to elegiac mood. The diction, up to this point affectionate and intimate, now becomes serious and dignified as Hardy explores the idea that, to the cat, he and Emma were godlike; their pet a 'Timid pensioner of us Powers//His existence ruled by ours.' Now, his death makes him ' . . . part above man's will,//Of the Imperturbable.' The cat has returned to the mysterious otherness from which it came; its 'insignificance' reminds Hardy, and us, of his own. The last six lines, themselves a moving epitaph, make a restrained but dignified and moving conclusion:

> Housemate, I can think you still
> Bounding to the window-sill,
> Over which I vaguely see
> Your small mound beneath the tree,
> Showing in the autumn shade
> That you moulder where you played.

For birds, with their beautiful plumage, their song (both exploited so ruthlessly by man) and their apparent freedom of the elements – often illusory – Hardy felt a particular affinity. There is a moment in *The Return of the Native* where the dying Mrs Yeobright, lying exhausted on the heath, looks up from where the ants 'toiled, a never-ending and heavy-laden throng', to see a heron come 'dripping wet from some pool . . . and as he flew the edges and lining of his wings, his thighs and his breast were so caught by bright sunbeams that he appeared as if formed of burnished silver. Up in the zenith where he was seemed a free and happy place'. The symbolism is obvious enough but there is another, darker side to Hardy's bird-imagery. An especially poignant moment in *Tess* occurs when his heroine, herself so wounded in spirit as to be near despair, finds the will to put scores of maimed pheasants – shot and left to die – out of their misery, saying, 'Poor darlings – to suppose myself the most miserable being on earth in the sight of such misery as yours!' It is no surprise to find that there are at least a dozen poems about birds, while *The Darkling Thrush* (119/ALL/ H/*) certainly one of Hardy's greatest and fully analysed at the end of this section, has a bird for its protagonist, a winter landscape for its setting.

Nearly all these poems display an interest in lyrical form; it may be because Hardy thought that appropriate to Nature's musicians. Their other common feature is Hardy's empathy; his sense of what may here be called with perfect aptness, a bird's-eye view of the world. The transience and frailty of these tiny creatures, their dependence on the vagaries of the weather and – occasionally – human kindness, is repeatedly stressed. As Hardy saw it, this was equally true of mankind; seen *sub specie aeternitatis* our existence, too, is brief and tenuous in the extreme. Thus, his *The Bullfinches* (86) chorus

> Come then, brethren let us sing,
> From the dawn to evening! –
> For we know not that we go not
> When the day's pale pinions fold
> Where those be that sang of old.

It is a neat and effective touch so to symbolise night and death with the roosting of birds, while their enviable freedom from the burden of consciousness is also touched in. A small group of bird poems (114–117 and 119 in CP) contains, besides *The Darkling Thrush* already mentioned, two of particular interest. *The Caged Thrush Freed and Home Again* (114/W), a *villanelle* in which the alternating and opposed refrains are 'Men know but little more than we' and 'How happy days are made to be', plays graceful but also disenchanted variations on the liberated thrush's discovery that his captors ' . . . cannot change the Frost's decree' any more than the birds can do so. The frost is an important image in Hardy's work and F. B. Pinion has devoted a whole essay to it (see Chapter 8). In contrast, *Birds at Winter Nightfall* (125/D/W/*) is a *triolet* that particularly well displays Hardy's remarkable skill in making, within a highly artificial form, a succinct lyrical statement which, rather like the Japanese haiku, is both visually and mentally satisfying; and much harder to do than it looks!

Perhaps the best is *The Blinded Bird* (375/G/W/H/*) which refers to the then not uncommon practice of blinding a bird with a red-hot needle so that it would then sing almost incessantly. This fiendish device revolted Hardy but the crux of his poem is not the anger he feels but controls. It is rather the way in which the bird's plight mirrors that of many men and women for whom life, metaphorically and perhaps literally too, resembles the bird's.

> Eternal dark thy lot,
> Groping thy whole life long,
> After that stab of fire;
> Enjailed in pitiless wire;
> Resenting not such wrong!

In the concluding stanza Hardy paraphrases a famous passage from the Bible, St Paul's summary of the Christian virtues (in Corinthians 13: 4–7), to make of the blinded but still singing bird a two-edged symbol, on the one hand of man's appalling inhumanity to man and to all other living things, on the other of what heights of patience, long suffering and hope it is possible for him to rise to. This is only partly a poem about cruelty to animals; more crucially it is about the need for those virtues which St Paul entreats us to observe in dealing with our fellow men to be extended over that wider family of living things which Darwin taught were also our ancestors in a sense. Yet the bird, and it is a savagely ironic point, seems to embody a far higher moral attitude than mankind, which blinded him not even for food but for entertainment. It is an uncomfortable poem still. We may not blind birds any longer but what would a returned Hardy have had to say about battery farming I wonder?

The Caged Goldfinch (436/C/W) is an example of Hardy's skill in using an observation simply to ask a question; within its eight lines it is perfectly achieved. Much the same could be said of *Proud Songsters* (816/C/D/W/*) in which 'thrushes . . . finches . . . and nightingales', 'Pipe as they can when April wears,//As if all Time were theirs', yet 'a year ago'

> No finches were, nor nightingales
> Nor thrushes,
> But only particles of grain,
> And earth, and air, and rain.

Hardy has no need to say that, aside from the differing time-scale, it is much the same with us, and perhaps we should learn from the birds the lesson he enjoins on us in another poem *Let Me Enjoy* (193/D/W/H/*)

> Let me enjoy the earth no less
> Because the all-enacting might
> That fashioned forth its loveliness
> Had other aims than my delight . .

Those lines, with their Wordsworthian gravity and resonance, would make a fitting epigraph for this chapter.

There remain, however, a handful of poems about plants; flowers and trees figuring also in Hardy's view of Nature as 'the Great Mother' (a phrase he uses in *Far from the Madding Crowd*). Of these *To Flowers From Italy in Winter* (92), a poem which has all Walter Savage Landor's poised elegance of form and language, is one of Hardy's most successful ventures into the 'pure lyric' and could easily be mistaken for, say, Tennyson's work. To quote one verse only is to do the poem no sort of justice, but will at least display the cool grace and musicality which Hardy is often said to have lacked in his creative make-up.

> Frail luckless exiles hither brought!
> Your dust will not regain
> Old sunny haunts of Classic thought
> When you shall waste and wane;

In the whole poem there is not one eccentric word, nor one unusual stress or syntactical variation. Hardy wonders in this poem whether 'all organic things//Be sentient . . . as some men say.' Two good poems explore this sense of the mysteriousness of nature from different angles. *The Last Chrysanthemum* (118/C/D/G) questions why the flower is 'Waking but now' when 'Nothing remains for it but shivering//In tempests turbulent.' He accepts that this is to suppose the flower has 'sense to work its mind'; but concludes that this 'is but one mask of many worn//By the Great Face behind.' Science then, does not hold all the answers, and in *The Year's Awakening* (275/C/D/W*) he addresses himself to the same question from the other end, so to speak. A striking series of astrological images lead into the baffling capacity of bird and flower alike to sense, with no tangible evidence, the onset of Spring. Neither poem offers any sort of answer and it has always seemed to me that these poems – and there are good many more like them – provide a telling answer to critics who use Hardy's supposedly life-denying philosophy as a stick with which to beat his poetic achievement. For they exemplify compactly what Keats, in a famous passage in his *Letters*, posited as an essential quality for the poet – one which he said,

> . . . Shakespeare possessed so enormously – I mean *Negative Capability*, that is, when a man is capable of being in uncertainties, mysteries, doubts, without an irritable reaching after fact and reason.

There is little doubt that Hardy knew the passage; he was deeply versed in Keats. What he so often said himself about his verse expressing 'impressions, not convictions' amounts to another way of saying what Keats said. It is further exemplified in the late *Throwing a Tree* (837/C/G/W/*). This is a superbly graphic and detailed account of two lumberjacks felling some huge New Forest tree. Its long-lined, laborious rhythms well enact the physical laboriousness of the task and the massive size and strength of the tree as it stubbornly resists their efforts. The last verse runs,

Then, lastly, the living mast sways, further sways: with a shout
Job and Ike rush aside. Reached the end of its long staying
   powers
The tree crashes downwards: it shakes all its neighbours
   throughout
And two hundred years' steady growth has been ended in less
   than two hours.

The only authorial comment, and that is a simple statement of fact, comes in the very last line; nor does Hardy tell us whether the tree was rotten or not. A good poem does not have to have a 'message': authenticity of experience *can* be enough and on that score Hardy can seldom if ever be faulted.

Analyses

Old Furniture (428/ALL/*)

The furniture is that of Hardy's birthplace and the poem expresses his persuasion that, as he said in his admirable lecture, *Memories of Church Restoration*, 'The protection of an ancient edifice . . . is the preservation of memories, history, fellowship, fraternities. Life, after all, is more than art . . . ' Here, alternately rhymed five-line stanzas make delicate use of feminine rhymes which, with the diminuendo effect of the brief final line, make a perfect vehicle for the gentle, hesitant, one might say lingering, quality of Hardy's thought. After the introductory stanza Hardy gives five glimpses of what he 'sees', all but the last significantly treating of *hands*. He subtly suggests the everyday small pleasures we derive, as we know he did, from each *shiny familiar thing* by phrases like *in play* (stanza 2) neatly poising between enjoyment and routine operation, *dallying*, and *dancing* (stanza 5). Stanza 3 contains, within its sharply observed simile, a telling metaphor of ancestry. Hardy's 'family face' is called to mind (see *Heredity*/363), it too growing '*frailer// As it recedes*'. Stanza 4 is particularly brilliant in expression. The complementary images of *dull dial* and *foggy finger* convey the hazy, spectral quality of Hardy's vision, the concern for *minutes* of one for whom time no longer has meaning is gently ironic, and the clinching symbol of the *moth*, for Hardy always an emblem of beauty and frailty combined, is especially poignant, suggesting that human life, on the time-scale of the poem, is hardly more than a summer's night for the moth.

A similar loving exactitude is displayed in stanza 5; surely the rapid, intricate dexterity of the fiddler's art could not be better suggested. (Hardy's MS had a further verse, after 5, elaborating on the *viol*, and for once I regret his decision to delete it; possibly because he thought it stressed one artefact and one person too strongly, though, to me, it does not seem inferior as verse.)

In the poem as a whole the insubstantial, wavering quality of Hardy's imagery imparts to us his regret for the fragility of our hold on memory; the solitary human *face* is only momentarily lit up, and then by a *flinty spark*, with *flinty* suggesting coldness and hardness and the melancholy progression curtly ended by ' . . . *goes out stark*', utterly, absolutely, that is. The final stanza is, superficially, an apology for what the world might condemn as aimless maunderings. But its ironic undertones make clear what Hardy really thought of such *up and doing* utilitarianism. He was, we might say, a conservationist, distrusting 'progress' and valuing continuity as giving meaning to our lives.

A Sheep Fair (700/ALL/H/*)

There were half a million sheep in Dorset in the mid-nineteenth century, so that the seasonal fairs at Poundbury Hill (*Pummery* is the local pronunciation) in Dorchester went on regardless of inimical weather. The theme – if a poem so bent on descriptive realism can be said to have one – is an age-old topos (or stock subject). The Roman poet Ovid summed it up in the phrase *Tempus edax rerum*, 'Time the devourer of all things.' Hardy's method here is to construct, very precisely, a poem of the 'Past and the Present'; his *Postscript* shifting the poet's and the reader's viewpoint from *then* to *now*. If that seems a very simple device we should remember that it underlies some of our very greatest poetry; Shakespeare's Sonnets, for example, often deploy it.

However simple the subject, the treatment is sophisticated and elaborate. The ten-line stanzas Hardy devised rhyme A/B/A/B//CCC//D/B, with the penultimate rhyme repeated in the ninth lines of verses 2 and 3, helping to unify the poem as a whole. In each verse the opening quatrain offers a succinct general statement, which is exemplified by the next quatrain with its calculatedly repetitive rhymes. The elongated ninth line shows the movement down, and the last, virtually repeating the second, acts as refrain. The overall effect, contrived with consummate artistry, is one of deliberate monotony. The rain, the resultant discomfort for animals and men alike, the auctioneer's automatic gestures: all seem to go on for ever, to be 'timeless' in no happy sense at all.

This is certainly no advertisement for holidays in Wessex. Hardy makes masterly use of predominantly tactile imagery, built up by such words as *sodden, wrings out, wipes, bedrenched, smeared, sponge, jammed tight*, and *reek* to achieve a both literally and metaphorically saturating effect on the envisaged scene. There is perhaps the faintest glimmer of humour in *the buyers' hat-brims*, as they *fill like pails*, but his many small touches of exact observation enable us to experience vicariously the intense discomfort, exacerbated by boredom, that attends upon rural life at times. Only someone born to such a world would have spotted the sheeps' horns *soft as finger-nails* and only Hardy would have thought it worth putting in a poem perhaps.

The Postscript suggests that this is a feat of memory, no doubt prompted by a much later visit to Poundbury. There is a slight change of tone in verse 2 where *woolly wear* and *meek, mewed head* imply some sympathy for the hapless sheep. But the repeated *Ands* (echoing those in verse 1) and the cumulative effect of the reiterated rhymes, together with the sardonic juxtoposition of the auctioneer's *Going, going* with his own death, primarily suggest that life repeats its patterns, while the poem, with its clear-eyed authenticity, as well as imparting to us what it feels like to be a sheep or shepherd in the rain all day, suggests that 'In life', to borrow a phrase of Dr Samuel Johnson's, 'there is always more to be endured than enjoyed'.

The Darkling Thrush (119/ALL/H/*)

This justly celebrated poem first appeared under the far more peremptory title *By the Century's Deathbed* in *The Graphic* magazine for 29 December 1900. There is MS evidence to suggest that Hardy was unsure whether to regard 1899 or 1900 as the 'last' year of the century, but that is of little significance; the *occasion* he wishes to commemorate is plain enough, as is his valedictory purpose.

The word *darkling* in his revised title (the original one clarifies line 10) has a distinguished ancestry, appearing in famous poems by Milton, Keats and Matthew Arnold. An adjective (*not* a noun), it means literally 'in the dark' and probably here – as in Keats's *Ode to the Nightingale* where the poet applies it to himself – metaphorically too. Poems by Robert Burns, William Cowper, and John Keble have all been suggested as analogues for Hardy's lyric. Each of his predecessors used a winter songster as a symbol of hope: Burns's is indeed a thrush, and Keble's a robin, but Cowper's ornithologically more improbable *To the Nightingale* (heard on New Year's Day, 1792) may have provided Hardy with a verse model, since Hardy's eight-line stanzas are only formally distinct from Cowper's four-line verses of which I quote one,

> O sings't thou rather under force
> Of some divine command,
> Commission'd to presage a course
> Of happier days at hand.

Though this is interesting as showing Hardy's assimilation of tradition, it is peripheral to his purpose. The originality of his poem was to lie in its implicit themes and its treatment, not in its form. Indeed his stanzas, like Cowper's, are simply the old four-lined ballad stanza, alternately rhymed, used in innumerable folk-songs and hymns and often, as we have seen, by Hardy, but masked in this instance by being 'doubled-up'.

Hardy opens with a landscape, exhibiting his usual precision, but his images, though visually authentic, also give off a subdued menace, and he substitutes *Frost* (line 2) for his MS *shades*, personifying a natural phenomenon which, for him, always had a doom-laden, malevolent quality. Last summer's ruin, shown in *winter's dregs* and *tangled bine-stems*, intensifies the feeling of desolation, as does the *weakening eye* of the sun, Hardy's beneficent 'deity'. Romance is figuratively destroyed by his image of *strings of broken lyres* (the lyre was a favourite symbol in Romantic poetry). The compound epithet *spectre-gray* and the ambiguous *haunted* intensify the eerie quality of the scene. The cumulative effect is of a terrible overall bleakness and barrenness, in which Hardy's vision is in dreary accord with the landscape he surveys.

A dead land is now neatly turned into an image of a dead century. Each simile is quite unforced, yet each is more withering than the last. The freezing of the *'ancient pulse of germ and birth'* is an echo of King Lear's curse 'All germens spill at once', and Hardy falls away into a flat assertion – utterly dispirited and dispiriting – of his own inner despair. Perhaps the most remarkable thing about verse 3 is its perfect balance; the way in which it refuses all temptation to overstate the contrast with what has gone before. True, Hardy does give a wonderfully vibrant warmth to the thrush's *evensong* (like *carollings'*, a subdued Christian reference). *Full-hearted,   joy   illimited* – suggesting both 'unlimited' and 'illimitable' – and *fling his soul* all suggest that the song is some kind of universal augury of hope. But – and this is the touchstone of Hardy's genius – the thrush itself (and the point is hammered home) is *aged, frail, small* and *gaunt* (which replaced the less telling *thin* in the MS). The *twigs* remain *bleak*, the *gloom growing*. He declines to pull out any of the available romantic stops: this is not a 'wise thrush' like Browning's, nor, like Shelley's *Skylark*, a 'blithe spirit//Bird thou ever wert.' It is time-battered, and what a brilliant phrase *blast-beruffled plume* is in that we think of *plume* in terms of beauty and colour; it is weary. Like the poet himself it seems to have no good reason to sing. Largely because we can accept the truthfulness of Hardy's telling, we can also accept his musings on the significance of his tale. So, in the last verse, he refers us back to the foreboding scene and only draws the most tentative conclusion: *I could think, there trembled through,'* he says.

It is the way in which Hardy is driven, against all the evidence of his senses, to accept the possibility, however faint,

of *some blessed Hope*, the perfect equipoise between reason and
emotion in the poem, the contrast between the deathless beauty
of the music and the deathstruck setting for it, with, perhaps
above all else, the hesitance, the shyness almost of Hardy's
'impression', that makes this a great poem. And whether we
accept the *Hope* or not, the image of the thrush remains in the
mind, gallant and unconquerable, an image of Man himself,
'slighted but enduring'. Its quality makes this poem an
appropriate coda to this chapter; its theme provides a link with
the next for, like all the very best of Hardy's poems, it ultimately
defies categorisation.

6

Poems about Ideas

In the Postscript he wrote for the 1912 edition of *Jude the Obscure* Hardy roundly asserted that 'Britons hate ideas'. In this, his most controversial, most reviled novel, he had certainly given his readers a good few 'ideas' to hate: sexual incompatibility, the 'new woman', child suicide, Oxbridge arrogance, and religious hysteria among them. In this sense then he cannot be said to have 'hated ideas' himself; indeed, so far from being an ivory-tower-dwelling recluse, he held strong opinions on many social issues, was a staunch Liberal in politics, and repeatedly took the part, as he drily put it in his fine essay *The Dorsetshire Labourer*, of 'those unimportant scores of millions of outsiders in civilised society . . . who [are] neither University men nor Churchmen.' In an interview with William Archer he asked, 'What are my books but one long plea against 'man's inhumanity to man' – to woman – and to the lower animals?' adding that he hoped, '[All] mankind may be, and one day will be, viewed as members of one corporeal frame.'

This did not prevent many essays and articles with titles like *Hardy; Prince of Pessimists* being published by those who claimed to detect in his work, and especially his poetry, a nihilistic, life-denying 'philosophy', a ruthless application of scientific materialism to every aspect of human life. As late as 1920 Hardy was declaring himself 'an irrationalist rather than a rationalist, on account of his inconsistencies . . . his views mere impressions that frequently change.' He was perfectly sincere in his contentions but we need to take them with a pinch of salt. How, for example, can one view the caustic late epigram, *Christmas 1924* (904/C/D/W/*), as a tentative query?

> 'Peace upon earth!' was said. We sing it
> And pay a million priest to bring it.
> After two thousand years of mass
> We've got as far as poison gas.

The answer is that one cannot, of course; it is a strongly held 'impression' mordantly expressed, intentionally provocative. But there is, or so Hardy thought, all the difference in the world between entertaining and indeed expressing views on any particular *aspect* of the human predicament, on what in *A Sign Seeker* (30/C/D/*) he termed, 'All the vast various moils that mean a world alive', and articulating them into a structured, self-consistent philosophy of life. As W. H. Auden memorably put it, in his poetry Hardy displays a 'hawk's-eye view' of the world, but that is not at all the same thing as holding a unified world-view, such as Hardy thought the older Wordsworth and Browning had both subscribed to, thereby weakening their poetry.

When all is said and done, there is nothing very paradoxical or contradictory in Hardy's position, which amounted to a certainty that, while neither poets or anybody else could change Nature, everybody was capable of changing, and ought to endeavour to change, *human* nature. For, as he said, 'Whatever may be the inherent good or evil of life, it is certain that men make it much worse than it need be.' He was convinced that life was painful; all the more then that the chief aim of man should be to ensure that 'pain shall be kept down to a minimum by loving-kindness', as he declared in the *Apology* to *Late Lyrics and Earlier*.

This enables us to distinguish, in his verse, between those poems which exhibit a corrective, sometimes an overtly reformative, purpose; concerned to answer the question ' *How* is betterment to be achieved?' and those which explore and speculate on the much larger question *Why*?

> . . . we are here as on a darkling plain
> Swept with confused alarms of struggle and flight,
> Where ignorant armies clash by night.

as Matthew Arnold put it in his famous poem, *Dover Beach*, which Hardy admired and echoed unmistakably in the closing lines of his *A Plaint to Man* (266/C/D/*). The first category I have ventured to call 'didactic', which the dictionary defines as 'meant to instruct or teach', and this includes his satirical poems and poems about War, God and Nature. For the second, and more important, those poems of a predominantly speculative, explorative description, following his own practice, I have termed reveries. The first category can be sub-divided conveniently, according to the subjects Hardy chooses to treat.

SATIRICAL POEMS

Satire, by ridiculing the person, the idea or the institution selected as a target, aims to strip off the layers of humbug and thereby conduce to reform. The Victorians were uneasy with verse satire, and myopic reviewers discouraged Hardy from employing his undoubted gift for the form. Indeed, he grumbled that this poetry was often misunderstood by 'men accustomed to Dickensian [but] not to Swiftian humour' and the reference to the author of the greatest satire in English, *A Modest Proposal*, makes it clear that the weapon of mockery and what we now call 'black comedy' was one Hardy relished. Two of his satires are of a coruscating brilliance equal to Swift's best verse; none of the others can quite sustain this level, though many plant barbed little darts in the sizeable target of Victorian social convention and institutionalised hypocrisy. *The Milkmaid* (126/C/*) is an entertaining jibe at the townsman's proclivity for sentimentalising the country, a pastoral with the lid off, so to speak. *Architectural Masks* (130/D) exposes the folly of judging by externals, in this instance houses. *The Conformers* (181/W) examines with tart urbanity the conflict between illusion and reality as exemplified in courtship and marriage. It has a beautifully straight-faced, sardonic conclusion. The deaths of the pair whose 'night-screened, divine//Stolen trysts' were once a byword for romance, are mourned with 'in them we lose/A worthy pair, who helped advance//Sound parish views.' The dull thud of the last three words sounds like earth on the coffin. *The Pink Frock* (409/*) is only marred by the fact that its first verse, a malevolent miniature portrait, does not really need supplementing, good as the two succeeding verses are,

> 'O my pretty pink frock,
> I sha'n't be able to wear it!

> Why is he dying just now?
> I can hardly bear it.'

Considered as an epigram it has all the pungency of the best eighteenth-century work in the genre.

I find it harder to enthuse about the group of fourteen collectively entitled *Satires of Circumstance* (337–351 and variously represented in ALL/*). These originally appeared early in the volume that took its title – most inappropriately – from them, but were subsequently, no doubt because of their marked incongruity with the *Poems of 1912–13*, shifted to the end. To my mind they lack, on the one hand the controlled hilarity of *The Ruined Maid* (128/C/D/W/*), on the other the devastating irony of *Ah, Are You Digging On My Grave?* (269/G/ *). Though often ingenious, their limited range of subject and their repetitive structural pattern, after one or two examples, cause the reader's attention to flag. *II. In Church* (332/D/*) is one of the best; it is also entirely typical. We catch the tail end of a sermon so tear-jerkingly emotive that 'each listener chokes'. But then a 'Bible class' pupil who 'adores' the preacher as one 'without gloss or guile' has her hero's clay feet revealed to her when he celebrates by re-enacting ' . . . at the vestry glass' (an acidulated touch), 'Each pulpit gesture in deft dumb-show// That had moved the congregation so.' The hit is palpable enough: the same kind of volte-face repeated becomes tedious. The corrosive *VI. In the Cemetery* (342/ALL/*) and the more subtle exploration of the shabby-genteel *VIII. In the Study* (344/C/D/W/*) are the best of the others, apart from *XII. At the Drapers* (348/D/W/*). This is a dialogue, carried off with superb, macabre panache. The dying, tubercular husband informs his fashion-conscious wife, with an ice-cold detachment that hones the irony to a razor-edge, of the chance that has led to his seeing her selecting her mourning outfit in advance of his demise. He says, urbanely,

> You were viewing some lovely things. *"Soon required*
> *For a widow: of latest fashion,"*
> And I knew 'twould upset you to meet the man
> Who had to be cold and ashen
> And laid in a box . . .

Though *Whispered at the Church Opening* (888/*) offers a glint of
dry humour in this vein, Hardy scarcely touched satire again
after this broadside. *The Christening* (214/*), however, merits
fuller treatment; is indeed one of Hardy's most pungent pieces
of social comment. The target seems at first to be that aspect of
Victorian social hypocrisy which displayed such alacrity in
casting the first stone, exemplified in the angy furore which
greeted Hardy's sub-title for *Tess, A Pure Woman*, because she
had had an illegitimate child, and therefore was, by definition,
'impure'. Hardy begins with a calculated stroke of disinformation, an innocent-seeming glimpse of a lovely child beautifully
dressed, a 'paragon'. 'At so superb a thing//The congregation
smile'. Indeed, the first three verses are like a Victorian genre
painting; that wave of sentimental warmth babies always
generate is felt by the entire congregation, and the reader too.
Then the mother appears 'in deep disgrace' with 'furtive
feverish air' and – the very phrasing oozes smug disapproval – 'ah, they are shocked anon'. Her assertion that the
baby is 'a gem of the race//The decent fain would smother'
seem hysterical. Surely the most unbending pillar of rectitude
would not wish that? But Hardy has not finished: having made
his initial point, that Nature does not reserve her bounty for the
'virtuous', he goes on to stand another convention on its head.
For when the mother is asked for the whereabouts of the father
who has left her in the lurch, she drops a bombshell into the
laps of her inquisitors, and strikes at that lynchpin of respecta-
bility, the institution of matrimony itself, announcing blithely
that he is not only 'in the woods afar' (and so perhaps a gipsy,
which is bad enough) but also that he and she have no
intention of 'slovening//As vulgar man and wife' though he
will be always ready,

> 'To clasp me in lovelike weather,
> Wish fixing when,
> He says: To be together
> At will, just now and then,
> Makes him the best of men;

The universal gasp of horror at her advocacy of free love can
readily be imagined; though it should not be supposed that

Hardy is unreservedly commending it. He rather poses a hard question. Granted that 'Wish fixing when' is an ideal, Shelleyan notion, doomed to disillusion (and, one may note, the man's idea anyway), is not marriage an emotional cocoon? Doesn't its legalistic aspect make it often what the mother, admittedly quoting her absent lover, says it is, 'Sweet love's sepulchring'? It is a theme Hardy elaborated in *Jude the Obscure*, of course, but not so pungently and perhaps not so even-handedly as here.

Analyses

The Ruined Maid (128/C/D/W/*)

'O 'Melia, my dear, this does everything crown!
Who could have supposed I should meet you in Town?
And whence such fair garments, such prosperi-ty?' –
'O didn't you know I'd been ruined?' said she.

– 'You left us in tatters, without shoes or socks,
Tired of digging potatoes, and spudding up docks;
And now you've gay bracelets and bright feathers three! –
'Yes: that's how we dress when we're ruined,' said she.

– 'At home in the barton you said "thee" and "thou",
And "thik oon", and "theäs oon", and "t'other"; but now
Your talking quite fits 'ee for high compa-ny!' –
'Some polish is gained with one's ruin,' said she.

– 'Your hands were like paws then, your face blue and bleak
But now I'm bewitched by your delicate cheek,
And your little gloves fit as on any la-dy!' –
'We never do work when we're ruined,' said she.

– 'You used to call home-life a hag-ridden dream,
And you'd sigh, and you'd sock; but at present you seem
To know not of megrims or melancholy!' –
'True. One's pretty lively when ruined,' said she.

– 'I wish I had feathers, a fine sweeping gown,
And a delicate face, and could strut about Town!' –
'My dear – a raw country girl, such as you be,
Cannot quite expect that. You ain't ruined,' said she.

Westbourne Park Villas, 1866

When he wrote this Hardy was a Londoner. Dated 1866, it is one of his best early poems. He had himself been solicited in Piccadilly, where prostitution was a commonplace, so it was not hard for him to envisage his rustic newcomer as flabbergasted by *'Melia's* metamorphosis into a tinselly butterfly. Her ingenuousness makes a perfect foil for *'Melia's* rather superficial sophistication, which is exposed as a recently acquired veneer by her residual Dorset syntax in the last two lines.

Hardy's extraordinary deftness in handling the dialogue is immediately evident. Read aloud this is hilarious; one of the funniest things he ever wrote. Some of the humour derives from simple incongruity, the contrast between the two speakers, one so utterly green, the other so street-wise and hard-boiled. But form has an important part to play too. Hardy chooses rhymed couplets in simple quatrains but the lines are cast in a lilting, predominantly *anapaestic* metre which, though sometimes appearing in folk-song, was far more common in music-hall ballads of a comic type. 'The Daring Young Man on the Flying Trapeze' is one example, but the once-famous song with the chorus 'Sing toorah li-oorah, li-oorah, li-ay//You don't get five hams off a pig every day', which hinges on the adventures of an 'innocent' rustic in London seems a likely analogue to me. This jaunty, if crude, rhythm not only signals the poem's intentions, it also allows Hardy to emphasise the speech-rhythms. His *ingénue's* voice climbs, at the end of her breathless sentences, to a positive squeak of envious admiration on *la deeeeeee*, while her laboured iteration of *pros-per-ity* and *mel-an-chol-y* admirably convey her pop-eyed amazement, offset by the yawning, languid replies of *'Melia*, where the authentic cadences of pseudo-sophistication are caught unerringly. Hardy's, actually quite sparing, use of dialect not only further points up the contrast, it also makes starkly evident the utter misery and degradation of rural labouring at its worst. We ask ourselves, as he intended, whether, compared with *dressing in tatters* with *hands like paws* and *face blue and bleak, ruin* is really a worse fate?

So, as in all great satirical writing, underlying the humour is anger. It was Hardy's mentor Swift whose epitaph spoke of 'fierce indignation tearing at his heart' and this is a more profound poem than it seems at a first reading. For Hardy's anger has two objectives. The less significant is his wish to expose what might be called the 'merry milkmaid myth'; *'Melia*'s half-starved, dirty, ragged friend has surely, driven by her wretched life in the country, come up to town to try her prentice hand at 'the game' herself. But deeper still is his detestation for the sort of society which by tolerating acute agricultural depression and so promoting the economic situation which drove poor women to prostitution, could then stand back and condemn it as morally repugnant. Hardy exposes – for the humbug it was – the received idea, so gratifying to the righteous and respectable, that, as *The Times* ironically put it, 'All prostitutes are Magdalens *in esse* or *in posse* . . . cowering under gateways or preparing to throw themselves from Waterloo Bridge.' It is all blown up in a gust of laughter; to be *ruined* is to have reached an enviable, professional, status. A masterstroke of semantic wit, edged with compassion, there is nothing else like it in Victorian poetry. If it *was* one of the early efforts which Hardy submitted to mid-Victorian periodicals it is not hard to see why it was rejected!

Ah, Are you Digging on My Grave? (269/G/*)

'Ah, are you digging on my grave,
  My loved one? – planting rue?'
– 'No: yesterday he went to wed
One of the brightest wealth has bred.
"It cannot hurt her now," he said,
  "That I should not be true."'

'Then who is digging on my grave?
  My nearest dearest kin?'
– 'Ah, no: they sit and think, "What use!
What good will planting flowers produce?
No tendance of her mount can loose
  Her spirit from Death's gin."'

'But some one digs upon my grave?
  My enemy? – prodding sly?'
– 'Nay: when she heard you had passed the Gate
That shuts on all flesh soon or late,
She thought you no more worth her hate,
  And cares not where you lie.'

'Then, who is digging on my grave?
　Say – since I have not guessed!'
– 'O it is I, my mistress dear,
Your little dog, who still lives near,
And much I hope my movements here
　Have not disturbed your rest?'

'Ah, yes! *You* dig upon my grave . . .
　Why flashed it not on me
That one true heart was left behind!
What feeling do we ever find
To equal among human kind
　A dog's fidelity!'

'Mistress, I dug upon your grave
　To bury a bone, in case
I should be hungry near this spot
When passing on my daily trot.
I am sorry, but I quite forgot
　It was your resting-place.'

It is curious that A. E. Housman's well-known poem *Is My Team Ploughing?* (Hardy's favourite from *The Shropshire Lad* according to Housman) has been put forward as the origin of this dialogue with the dead, the only feature they share. It seems much more likely that both poets – steeped as they were in the anonymous Ballads – derived their structural pivot from one of the many variants of *The Unquiet Grave*. In this famous ballad, with its hauntingly beautiful tune, the dead girl asks her grief-stricken lover 'O who sits weeping by my grave//And will not let me sleep?' Since Hardy actually uses this ballad as the central theme of *The Harvest Supper* (746/*) and since the figure of a revenant appears in several poems besides, there is no need for so contemporary a source to be suggested, and, in any event, the twist Hardy adds with his canine interlocutor, is entirely original. I think he must also have had in mind two characteristically Victorian obsessions, with death and with sentimentalised animals, seen in so many genre paintings, in the Edinburgh memorial to Greyfriars Bobby (whose vigil by his dead master's grave went on for years) and in Wordsworth's well-known *Fidelity* where a dog 'with strength of feeling//Above all human estimate' guards his master's body in the mountains for months.

Hardy was fond, perhaps too fond, of his own pets, but it is human illusions about both human and animal nature that he is concerned to expose here by taking two Victorian 'myths' and standing them on their heads, to devastating effect.

He shrewdly delays revealing the digger's identity until he has given us three desolating verses in each of which the eager hopefulness of the dead woman is mercilessly quenched by the dog's unemotional, flat statements of fact. The dog – a particularly effective touch – expresses no *opinion* on the actions of the humans. This cruel prelude makes the fourth verse, with its hints of affection in *mistress dear* and *little dog*, and perhaps of commiseration in the last two lines, arouse the reader's as well as the dead woman's hopes. Then – it is a wickedly effective turn of the screw – in the fifth Hardy modifies the mistress' speech so as to approximate it to 'doggy talk', *one true heart* is a typical cliché, and the last three lines come close to paraphrasing Wordsworth's (whose title is indeed the concluding word), perhaps deliberately.

This prepares the ground for the terrible last verse in which the dog's matter-of-fact, almost monosyllabic explanation of the whole incident pricks the balloon of sentimental expectation that his mistress (and probably Hardy's readers, too) have inflated. Her last consolation has been shown to be an illusion like all the others; yet – a proof of Hardy's fundamental compassion – we feel, just below the surface of this blackest of black comedies, a profound, an excoriating, sadness. Comedy and tragedy, as Hardy often demonstrated in both his novels and his poems, here interact.

WAR POEMS

This is a small, clearly defined section of Hardy's verse needing only brief preliminary remarks. The Boer War, to which the series *War Poems* (86–97) refers, was regarded by Hardy as an unjust and unnecessary war, although, as he confessed, he was still stirred 'by patriotism and gallantry,' an ambiguity of response that is much more marked in the 1914–15 group *Poems* *of War and Patriotism* (493–505) inasmuch as Hardy swallowed, more or less whole, the initial outraged response to Germany's invasion of Belgium, with its attendant atrocity stories. So, while he could assure his friend Mrs Henniker, wife of a serving officer, that none of his Boer War poems 'was 'Jingo or Imperial', some at least of his 1914 verse *could* be so described. Even so, the wave of patriotic fervour in Rupert Brooke's sonnet, 'Now God be thanked who has matched us with His hour!', found only a muted echo in Hardy's heart. He had recently ended his great verse-drama of the Napoleonic Wars, *The Dynasts*, on a note of qualified optimism. Now his wife wrote, two weeks after the outbreak of hostilities, 'I think he feels the horror of it so keenly that he loses all interest in life.' His despair was to deepen as the war dragged its bloody length along for four years. Hardy hailed – though hailed is hardly the word – the armistice of 1918 in a dour little poem, *The Peace Peal* (774/*), in which a jackdaw that has happily nested in the belfry for four years of unbroken silence perceives the 'joyous' peal as a 'baleful thing'. So, says Hardy sardonically, 'mortal motives are misread' whether 'of pens or politics'.

The Boer War poems are mostly occasional; one batch was prompted by Hardy's seeing Major Henniker off to Africa at Southampton. Though the first, *Embarcation* (54/W/H), begins with a patriotic glance at Henry V whose 'army leapt afloat to win//Convincing triumphs', Hardy, like Shakespeare before him, probes more deeply into the 'tragical to-be', ending on a wan note, 'Wives, sisters, parents, wave white hands and smile//As if they knew not that they weep the while.' *The Colonel's Soliloquy* (56/W) and *The Going of the Battery* (57/G/W/ H/*) are similarly ambivalent, but *At The War Office, London* (58) and *A Christmas Ghost Story* (59/*), both written later, oppose war more overtly. In the *Christmas Ghost Story*, 'South of the line, inland from far Durban,//A mouldering soldier's puzzled phantom' enquires as to what purpose is served by our tacking 'Anno Domini' on each year. 'When tarries yet the cause for which He died?' The question and the poem set off an angry correspondence, in which Hardy vigorously joined, denying that he wished to denigrate heroism. Two poems stand out from the group as major achievements. *Drummer Hodge* (60/ ALL/H/*) is fully analysed later; and the sole reason why I have

refrained from so handling *The Souls of the Slain* (62/C/D/H/*)
which I regard as a prophetic masterpiece, looking forward to
Wilfred Owen, is its length. It takes the form of a dream-vision
in which Hardy sees the returning spirits of the Wessex dead as
a 'dim-discerned train, [Of] friendless souls.' They are met at
'the Isle by the Race' (i.e. Portland Bill) by a 'senior soul-flame'
who asks them where they are going. They reply 'We bear
homeward and hearthward//To feast on our fame!' Their
mentor disillusions them. His sweeping overview of their
families and lovers shows how deluded they were in supposing
that their gallantry has earned them an immortal garland. It is,
instead, their 'Deeds of home that live yet//Fresh as
new . . . and they are obliged to accept their 'war-mightiness'
as irrelevant,

> – 'Alas! then it seems that our Glory
> Weighs less in their thought
> Than our old homely acts,
> And the long-ago commonplace facts
> Of our lives – held by us as scarce part of our story,
> And rated as nought!

This realisation embitters some who return to 'the Race . . .

> That engulphing, ghast, sinister place –
> Where headlong they plunged, to the fathomless regions
> Of myriads forgot.

whereas 'Those whose record was lovely and true//Bore to
northward for home.' In scope, scale and handling this is a most
impressive poem to which brief extracts do scant justice. If what
Hardy has to say is not, to us, surprising, his effortless handling
of an elaborate verse-form, his tactful and restrained use of the
supernatural 'apparatus', his diction, which moves from sober
dignity to robust and sometimes dry dialogue, all combine to
invest the poem with a universality that is every bit as applic-
able to the Russian conscript returned from Afghanistan as to
his Dorset predecessors.

The First World War produced nothing as good, though
Edward Thomas, writing disparagingly of the flood of Jingoistic

ullage that appeared in 1914, said Hardy's *Song of the Soldiers* (i.e. *Men Who March Away*/493/W/H/*) was 'the only good one.' Right from the start Hardy, though he believes that the soldiers 'well see what [they] are doing' and admires their conviction that 'Victory crowns the just', is himself present in the poem as a 'Friend with a musing eye', who watches the marchers 'With doubt and dolorous sigh'. Even his perfectly justifiable anger on behalf of the Belgian refugees is, all things considered, remarkably free from the fire-and-brimstone maledictions then so widespread. By 1915 the carnage had sickened him and *The Pity of It* (498/W) records, with regret, the affinities between such Wessex dialectal words as 'Ich woll' and 'Thu bist' and German expressions. He perceives that it is not the German people, 'kin folk, kin tongued', but the 'gangs whose glory threats and slaughters are' whom we should detest; a stance that took moral courage at the time. A poem similar in tone is *Often When Warring* (503/W/*) where a soldier pauses, in the heat of battle, to give water to a wounded enemy. The soldier's nationality is purposely left ambiguous, but he is seen as 'triumphing in the act//Over the throes of artificial rage', so leaving 'War's apology wholly stultified.' Perhaps these are not among his best poems, but they do tell us why those young soldier poets who were fortunate enough to survive the Great War hastened to sit at Hardy's feet. He had divined what they had discovered empirically in the trenches, that, in Nurse Edith Cavell's immortal words 'Patriotism is not enough. I must have no hatred or bitterness towards anyone.' – a leading theme of his three finest war poems, now to be considered in detail.

Analyses

Drummer Hodge (60/ALL/H/*)

This first appeared as *The Dead Drummer* in 1899, with a note that 'One of the drummers killed was a native of a village near Casterbridge [Dorchester].' But the drummer-boy's name, *Hodge*, was subsequently and calculatedly chosen to sharpen the thrust of the poem. For *Hodge* was the music-hall comedian's generic term for the boorish, comic, country bumpkin and Hardy loathed it. He makes Angel Clare, studying farm management in *Tess*, discover that 'the pitiable dummy known as Hodge [was] obliterated after a few days . . . at close quarters no Hodge was to be seen.' Used here, of course, the name not only points up the callous indifference of the army who treat *Hodge* as mere flotsam from the battle, and thus also displays the de-humanising effects of war generally; it additionally reveals the propensity we all share for taking refuge in labels and categories, so as to avoid contact with the uncomfortable fact of our common humanity.

Hardy's opening, with its brutal immediacy, is also deliberate. He would have nothing to do with the sort of sentimental gobbledegook that Rupert Brooke was to write (before he saw battle) about 'some corner of a foreign field//That is forever England'. He is rather concerned to bring out the strangeness and emptiness of the *veldt*, and his use of the Afrikaans words *kopje* and *Karoo* suggest Hodge's alienation from his *Wessex home*. In verse 2 this sense of distance is compounded with Hodge's ignorance alike of his whereabouts and of the circumstances which have brought him there, to infuse the poem with an undercurrent of waste and futility. No note of patriotism or heroism is struck; Hardy does not need to say that this boy's death will achieve nothing.

In the third verse Hodge is, literally and metaphorically, assimilated into the land and this conveys, I think, a very subtle and subdued implication that the country boy has more in common with the Boers who farm the *dusty loam* to which his body now gives fertility than with the politicians and diamond-brokers who sent him there to die.

The form of the poem with its three six-line stanzas is as straightforward as its language is plain and direct: Hardy has set simple words to a simple tune in effect, aware that an elaborate verse form and elevated diction would not suit the occasion. Yet that restraint and honesty endow the poem with a noble dignity of tone. The use of the stars, the *strange-eyed constellations* of the Southern hemisphere, as a semi-refrain, is particularly effective. They were for Hardy, as for most of us, always symbolic of remoteness and eternity; their timeless indifference reduces Man, with his petty concerns and brief span, to his true dimension. Nevertheless, through this anonymous drummer-boy in his unmarked grave, Hardy has evoked without a trace of rhetoric or anger, an overwhelming sense of what Wilfrid Owen was later to call 'the pity of war, the pity war distilled.'

The Man he Killed (236/ALL/H/*)

It is perhaps a pity that Hardy subsequently omitted his brief 'stage directions' to this dramatic monologue; first published in the American *Harper's Weekly* in 1902. They run '*Scene*: The settle of 'The Fox', Stagfoot Lane. *The speaker* A returned soldier, and his friends, natives of the hamlet'. (i.e. Hartfoot Lane, a few miles from Puddletown and Hardy's home). A later product of the Boer War than *Drummer Hodge*, it was quite possibly prompted by something Hardy overheard.

What the speaker says is simple enough. His expression is halting, clumsy, almost inchoate; which was, of course, precisely what Hardy intended. Apart from *infantry*, *nipperkin* (meaning tot) and *curious*, there is no word over two syllables. We are listening to a very ordinary, indeed simple, man. Hardy does not employ the dialect, except in *traps* (gear, tools) and *old* as an intensifier (*old ancient* meaning very ancient); to have done so would have narrowed his frame of reference. But the language is authentically vernacular and the verse form could hardly be simpler; a variant of the *common metre* we have already encountered in *I Look Into My Glass* (52) and *Afternoon Service at Mellstock* (356). The overall effect is designedly homespun and it is Hardy's acute psychological insight – so much in evidence in his novels – which makes this poem so successful. Hardy's grasp of his speaker's mental processes is as firm as his command of his phrasing. He is not grief-stricken or guilty, to a member of the PBI (the army's sardonic abbreviation for Poor Bloody Infantry) such emotions would have been a luxury he could not afford. Nor is he a pacifist in the making, which would have been highly implausible. He is just bewildered and it is with remarkable skill that Hardy renders his slow, inarticulate groping towards an understanding of *why* he had to kill. He never really reaches it: there is a terrible poignancy about his dubious *That's clear enough* where we can see him, as it were, shaking his head. Abstractions are beyond him, but the moment he returns to a personal level identification with his *foe* (a tellingly artificial word in this context) is possible. We hear him hesitate on *although* and then there follows, in the terse, broken-up, almost inconsequential phrases of verse 4, an extraordinarily powerful exposure of the folly and futility of war. The last verse with its more measured, almost proverbial structure, clinches the poem by showing the soldier as having battled his way through to self-expression. Incidentally, like Shakespeare's rough archers in *Henry V* on the eve of Agincourt, he has shown his supposed intellectual superiors the truth, which they prefer to ignore, about war.

In Time of the 'Breaking of Nations' (500/ALL/H/*)

The very full information we have from Hardy (*Life* pp. 78–9 and 378) about the circumstances of its composition make this poem of special interest. On 18 August 1870, when the Franco-Prussian War was at its height, he and Emma were reading Tennyson in the Rectory garden at St Juliot when Hardy's eye was caught by the old horse harrowing the field in the valley below the garden. On 31 December 1915, the year when the First World War had plumbed new depths of horror with poison gas, air raids, the débâcle at Gallipoli and the carnage of Ypres and Arras, the Editor of *The Saturday Review* wrote to ask Hardy for a poem. The long-ago incident came back into his mind, 'as fresh as when interred', no doubt prompted by the advent of a New Year that promised to be even more horrific than the last. Hardy there and then drafted the poem on the Editor's letter.

The title's Biblical quotation (actually a paraphrase, the original is 'break in pieces the nations') is from Jeremiah, whose doom-laden pages have given us the word 'Jeremiad'. The whole book is redolent of war and destruction; as Hardy read it phrase after phrase must have struck home with terrible aptness. 'The sword shall devour and be sated and drink its fill of blood', 'the flower of the young men shall perish', 'the land trembles and writhes in pain' are typical extracts. But of equal or even greater importance is Jeremiah's proclamation of the 'New Covenant' between God and his Chosen People, in which much emphasis is placed upon God's establishment of a 'fixed order [of the seasons]' when 'the planters shall plant and shall enjoy the fruit' and life shall be 'like a watered garden'.

So it is out of these opposed Biblical images of betrayal, death and discord on the one hand and of pastoral life, cyclic renewal and harmony on the other that Hardy has taken the raw materials for his poem. He avoids all topical reference, he restricts his imagery to events that are timeless, pares his language down to a bone-bare simplicity and so gives the poem a lapidary quality appropriate to both its origins and its purposes.

The first verse in both movement and language enacts the leisurely pace of the work it depicts, suggesting that man and horse are so sublimely indifferent to anything but their repetitive yet necessary task that a battle in the next field would hardly distract them. The sequence *clods, slow, silent, stumbles, asleep, stalk*, enforces this repetitive, drowsy rhythm on the reader. In verse 2 the smouldering *couch-grass* perhaps hints at the fire and fury that the *Dynasties* are now engendering. But that is a necessary, not a wanton, destruction. Scarcely noticeable – *without flame* – yet part of an immemorial cycle of regeneration.

Finally, human love, another necessary element in the regenerative process, appears, with its symbolic assertion – and how effective a word is *whispering* here – that war, like the *heaps of couch-grass*, is ephemeral and finally impotent. Perhaps we can no longer share Hardy's confidence; but the weight of his minatory utterance remains unabated.

POEMS ABOUT GOD AND NATURE

I had better begin by saying that whenever one of these topics occurs, as both often do, in Hardy's verse, it is most unlikely to augur a good poem. It is not that A. E. Housman's formulation 'the troubles of our proud and angry dust' had, in Hardy's day, lost its cogency as a subject for poetry; his contemporaries, Matthew Arnold and, from a wholly different perspective, Gerard Manley Hopkins, show us what could be made of this theme. But for Hardy, the 'harmless agnostic' as he called himself, the insoluble difficulty lay in finding a suitable vehicle for the problem of 'all the ills endured//By earth's poor, patient kind.' (*By the Earth's Corpse*/89/C/*). In the same poem he displays his apparent inability to find an appropriate diction for his excursions into cosmology, breaking out into archaic poeticisms like 'I ween', 'as ere' and 'repenteth me' which somehow seem to proliferate the moment he has God in his sights. Though he very well knew of the capital difficulty all writers encounter if they try to portray God, even prefacing his poem *A Philosophical Fantasy* (884/C) with Walter Bagehot's complaint that 'Milton . . . made God argue', he himself is prone to making God *chat*, like some 'remote and ineffectual don', as follows:

> I mean, of course, well knowing
> They present conformation
> But a unit of my tentatives,
> Whereof such heaps lie blowing.

The quasi-philosophical terminology of 'tentatives' and, elsewhere, 'purposeless propension', doggerel rhyming like 'sex is//vexes', with strained coinages like 'life-shotten', make it impossible for the reader to identify with either the mood or the tone of this rambling disquisition, all too typical of others like it. When, in *A Sign Seeker* (30/*) Hardy complains 'that which I fain would wot of shuns my sense' we are tempted to murmur, disrespectfully, 'Ours too!' Nor are his attempts to adduce evidence disproving Wordsworth's contention that some 'Power', evidently Nature, 'maintains a deep and reverential care//For the unoffending creatures whom He loves' – an easy target – very much better, despite occasional stanzas of impressive dignity and weight like

> Has some Vast Imbecility
> Mighty to build and blend
> But impotent to tend,
> Framed us in jest and left us now to hazardry?

which comes from *Nature's Questioning* (43/C/D/W/*).

Hardy's continual returns to this issue and associated questions leads us on to those quite numerous other poems in which he concerns himself with Christianity in action, so to speak. Though he once said, 'I have been looking for God for fifty years, and if He exists I think I should have found him', Hardy

also admitted to being 'churchy' all his life, and whatever
reservations he had about Christ's divinity, he had none about
his pre-eminence as a moral teacher and exemplar. The Bible,
the Prayer book, much of Anglican hymnody, were all in his
blood and bones. If he could not accept the supernatural
sanctions of Christianity, its ethical and moral codes remained
for him the ultimate touchstone of Man as he might be.

His *Surview* (662/*) which concludes *Late Lyrics and Earlier*, is
plainly intended as a last testimony from a man of 82, and the
whole poem is a tissue of citations and paraphrases (though not
word-for-word quotations) from St Paul's *Epistle to the Corinthians* where the Apostle elaborates his argument that charity
(or, as Hardy preferred to translate it 'loving-kindness') is the
pre-eminent human attribute. Only a man who knew the Bible
exceptionally well could have woven so seamless a fabric from
it. The opening 'cry from the green-grained sticks of the fire'
echoes Psalm 39 and reminds us of a passage about the prophet
Elijah (from *Kings* I. xix) where he hears 'after the fire a still
small voice'. This, one of Hardy's favourite passages, also forms
the core of his *Quid Hic Agis* (371/C/W/*). In the third stanza
Hardy moves into *Corinthians* I. 13 to examine his own life and
his 'teaching' – obviously his writings – in the cold light of
what is manifestly his own conscience, concluding

> *'You taught not that which you set about,'*
>   Said my own voice talking to me;
> *That the greatest of things is Charity . . . '*
> – And the sticks burnt low and the fire went out,
>   And my voice ceased talking to me.

Very few poets, Christian or otherwise, have written with a
more genuine humility than that, and the whole poem is an
impressive testimony to the sincerity with which Hardy argued
in his *Apology* to *Late Lyrics and Earlier* that the 'chief aim' of
man should be to ensure that pain should 'be kept down to a
minimum by loving-kindness'.

Several other poems treating of Christian themes deserve
consideration. *Christmastide* (829/*), a dry, but not at all cynical
anecdote, is one, *The Wood Fire* (574/W/*), which is a poignant
treatment of the aftermath of the Crucifixion, is another, while

one of the very best, *The Impercipient* (44/ALL/*) has Hardy as a member of the congregation at Salisbury, one of his favourite cathedrals, unhappily aware that while the 'bright believing band' around him 'hear the promise of immortality that the Service offers' as like the sound of 'a glorious distant sea' to him it is no more than the wail of 'yon dark//And wind-swept pine to me!' L. E. W. Smith has admirably analysed this poem (see Further Reading List).

Despite these exceptions, however, it is hard to avoid the conclusion that, by and large, when Hardy ignored his own persuasion that neither the pulpit nor the soapbox was a proper vantage point for the poet, he did so at his peril.

Analyses

The Oxen (403/ALL/H/*)

The tradition on which Hardy based this poem was very ancient and widespread. Shakespeare refers to it in *Hamlet* and the diarist, the Reverend Francis Kilvert, actually met an old man who claimed he had 'seen the oxen kneeling . . . with the tears running down their faces'. This lyric has been repeatedly set to music, something to which its simple 'common metre' stanzas conduce, though my own preference is for the lovely modal melody of the *Coventry Carol*. Hardy's abrupt opening makes the point that no one, at the time – his boyhood presumably – needed to be told who the *they* of line 2 were. (His title neatly satisfies the reader's need to know.) His use, for the human gathering, of the biblical *flock* also suggests their simplicity and innocence, which the second verse further emphasises. The date of this poem has to be taken into account: to any soldier in the trenches who happened to read a copy of *The Times* for 24 December 1915 in which *The Oxen* first appeared, the picture of the *meek, mild creatures* in their *strawy pen* must have been almost unbearably poignant. Though Hardy's only reference to the war is the phrase *In these years!*, the second half of the poem reveals his characteristic rejection of easy sentiment. There is indeed a small but significant emendation in line 9 where *weave*, in *The Times*, reads 'believe'. The dissyllabic word impedes the run of the line where the alliterated *weave* improves it, but *weave* also means 'to create' and 'to tell', implying that Hardy is conscious that his doing so may seem odd, perhaps even naive. But, more importantly, he would not have wished to suggest that he 'believed' in it, however *fair a fancy* it might be. Instead, with that precision and scrupulosity always evident in his treatment of such themes, he sets out his own position. The last two, reflective, stanzas poise with an extraordinary delicacy between the pitfall of nostalgia on the one hand and of 'scientific' rationalism on the other. What Hardy *feels* is perfectly plain; who does not share his regret for the irrecoverably lost child's-eye vision? But the stress on *Hoping* leaves the poem open for us all to make up our own minds. Not everything we *feel* is susceptible to logical analysis. No other poem by Hardy holds in such moving equipoise his own enduring *wish* to believe; his own incapacity to make the intellectual leap in the dark that belief imposes.

REVERIES

Reverie is Old French in origin, from the same root as gives us *rêver* (i.e. to dream). Perhaps its original sense of dream-vision had, as Hardy employed it, come to mean something more like a daydream with visionary elements, but it was the sort of elusive, ambivalent term which suited Hardy, who distrusted the segregation of poems into 'kinds', and that may be why he used it to categorise the opening section of *Satires of Circumstance*, though he qualifies it there too by linking it with *Lyrics*. None the less, there are three basic ingredients in Hardy's reveries. Though they do not receive equal weight in all the poems I shall dwell on, when they all occur together in a poem it is likely to be a 'reverie'. These ingredients are an intensely personal mood, a meditative tone and a theme which is, in one way or another, visionary. On the negative side they are not assertive, still less didactic or dogmatic: they ask questions, but rarely, if ever, provide answers, giving us a very strong sense indeed of a mind given to brooding and pondering, an intellect exploring concepts without attempting to articulate a philosophy, without any of that 'irritable reaching after fact and reason,' to which John Keats objected. To call them, as I have done, *Poems about Ideas*, is perhaps close enough to Hardy's alternative categorisation of *Reflective Poems*.

In *Wessex Poems* only the engaging and much anthologised *Friends Beyond* (36/C/D/W/H/*) qualifies as a reverie. Its pungent turns of phrase, and neat encapsulation of character, its jocund verse-form, its ease of manner, are all immediately noticeable. But, collectively, Hardy's 'local hearts and heads' exemplify a theme he often returned to, that of the 'triumph of time'. They have attained in death, paradoxically, that 'very god's composure . . . ignoring all that haps beneath the moon' which, in life they never once desired. It is a simple framework, in medieval poems termed the '*Ubi sunt*' (i.e. 'Where are [they now]?') theme, but one he was to use to superb effect elsewhere.

A Commonplace Day (78/W/H/*) is a little-known and undervalued poem. Yet its very title is significant; who else would have thought such a day had any potential for poetry? Hardy depicts, with great subtlety and skill, the fabric of routine tasks that give the day its unexceptional 'flavour'. Verse 2 will show how well he evokes the dull, depressing atmosphere

> I part the fire-gnawed logs,
> Rake forth the embers, spoil the busy flames, and lay the ends
> Upon the shining dogs;
> Further and further from the nooks the twilight's stride extends
> And beamless black impends.

Every detail here of the onset of night, and of a more than merely physical darkness, intensifies the sombre mood. The long drawn-out second and fourth lines, with their slow, deliberate pace, suggest both Hardy's boredom as he distracts himself with trivia, and the way the 'weather' of his mind is affected by his surroundings. In itself this is a fairly universal experience, his 'colourless thoughts' are familiar to anyone who thinks at all. But Hardy gropes his way towards an explanation of his mental malaise. Because it is possible that, even on this 'dullest of dull-hued days', somewhere, in 'some soul . . . some impulse rose, . . . Of that enkindling ardency from whose maturer glows//The world's amendment flows', we may regret the passing of *any* day with good cause, an idea that, if developed, might give the day some 'radiance'. But Hardy cannot console himself; rather he feels his depression springs from his being attuned to the 'undervoicings' of a 'loss to man's futurity'; the 'ardency' he senses, was 'benumbed at birth' and it is that loss which 'May wake regret in me'. Hardy suffered spiritually from his perception of what he called the 'unfulfilled purpose' in man; everywhere he detected potential unrealised. In this muted, grey-toned, probing poem he gives the idea a memorable utterance.

The next poem, *At a Lunar Eclipse* (79/C/D/G/H) is a powerful, compressed meditation on shadow and substance, illusion and reality; more formal and dignified in expression than is usual with Hardy and an impressive instance of his gift for the sonnet form.

The To-Be-Forgotten (110/C/*) is the most explicit and extensive expression of an idea to which Hardy often returned; too often perhaps. As we have seen in *The Souls of the Slain* (62) he thought that what frail claim we have on 'immortality' lies in the memories of those we knew. When they die all but the towering geniuses are doomed to a 'second death' along with them. It is hardly an original idea but in this poem he gives it a sonorous, measured gravity of expression, especially in the closing verses, which he rarely bettered.

> 'But what has been will be –
> First memory, then oblivion's swallowing sea;
> Like men foregone, shall we merge into those
>   Whose story no one knows.
>
> 'For which of us could hope
> To show in life that world-awakening scope
> Granted the few whose memory none lets die,
>   But all men magnify?

The link with the 'unfulfilled intention' of *A Commonplace Day* (78) is plain, and can also be detected in the poems now to be considered, collectively entitled *In Tenebris I–III* (136–138/C/D/W/H – II only/*). These deeply felt, profoundly melancholy poems are so characteristic of Hardy that they all deserve close analysis, but limitations of space confined me to the first, though what I have to say of it may throw some light on II and

III, now to be discussed more briefly.

Hardy chose II for his own *Chosen Poems*. Its pungent irony, lively movement, and less overtly sombre tone make it seem rather less of a reverie than I and III. But all the poems deal with his sense of isolation and his reasons for this. II is concerned with his alienation from the unthinking majority of the human race, who, as Hardy sees it, prefer not 'to see things as they are' (the phrase is from Matthew Arnold's book, *Culture and Anarchy* which plainly influenced this poem considerably). The first three lines of each verse are given over to Arnold's 'Philistines'. Both Hardy's phrasing and his rhythms mock their bombastic euphoria with a jostling, bumptious vigour. Lines like ' . . . things are all as they best may be, save a few to be right ere long' and 'nothing is much the matter; there are many smiles to a tear' catch exactly that note of smug, sanguine assurance that so much annoyed both Arnold and Hardy, who shared a darker, and far more rational, view of the human predicament. To Hardy, the idea that life was an escalator labelled 'Progress' was absurd and the last line in each verse, apparently so tentative and self-deprecating, must accordingly be taken with a large pinch of intellectual salt. But though he impales his 'stout upstanders' on such beautifully sardonic lines as 'Breezily go they, breezily come; their dust smokes round their career'; which suit the 1990s quite as well as the 1890s, his summing up of his own position in verse 4 is a sad, quiet, entirely serious, confession of helplessness. The *In Tenebris* series casts light on Hardy's abandonment of prose for verse. It was written just after Hardy's traumatic experiences with *Jude the Obscure*, most desolate and most desolating of his novels, and reflects his despair at ever seeing in England that 'free play of the mind' which Arnold had postulated as essential to true progress. The final verse of II is very skilfully modulated in pace to suit its change in temper from irony to dejection,

> Let him in whose ears the low-voiced Best is killed by the
>   clash of the First,
> Who holds that if way to the Better there be, it exacts a full
>   look at the Worst,
> Who feels that delight is a delicate growth cramped by
>   crookedness, custom and fear,

Get him up and begone as one shaped awry; he disturbs the
order here.

It is no surprise that he chose the second line to stand for his
own attitude, when he felt a need to define it.

In Tenebris III is the slow movement of the series; *grave* would
be its musical tempo marking. It is retrospective in mood as
Hardy considers his life before he learned that 'the world was a
welter of futile doing'. There is a touching innocence, too, about
the anecdote in verse 2 where, as a child, he 'cast forth the snow
from the crocus-border' hoping to make 'a summer-seeming
order' But its prevailing mood is one of intense despondency
mirroring Hardy's statement in an interview at the time with
William Archer where he said, 'If it is pessimisim to think, with
Sophocles, that "not to have been born is best" then I am a
pessimist', adding that 'much of the sniggering optimism of
recent literature is cowardly and insincere.'

There is a high concentration of reveries in two volumes of
Hardy's verse, *Satires of Circumstance* and *Moments of Vision*
(1914 and 1917), several of which are analysed in detail later.
One, *Copying Architecture in An Old Minster* (369/W/*), is a
strange curate's egg of a poem, though the good parts are very
good indeed. It opens in a jocular vein,

> How smartly the quarters of the hour march by
>   That the jack-o'-clock never forgets;
> Ding-dong; and before I have traced a cusp's eye,
> Or got the true twist of the ogee over,
>   A double ding-dong ricochetts.

The irregular, indeed ametrical, first line, the 'cusp's eye'
rhyme, with such verbal tricks as 'ogee over' and 'double
ding-dong' institute a frivolous tone kept up by Hardy's
treatment of the 'ghosts' in verses 3 and 4, whose speech is
described as 'cheepings', while lines 1 and 2 of verse 5 have
already been cited (in Chapter 3) as an instance of Hardy's
parodying himself. Yet, in midstream, the mood alters, the
diction loses its jokey eccentricity, becoming notably plain and
direct, and the tone assumes that musing timbre that marks the
great reveries. Hardy rarely wrote better than the last two verses

in which his deletion of a few syllables smooths and strengthens the rhythmic flow to a remarkable degree.

> Or perhaps they speak to the yet unborn,
>   And caution them not to come
> To a world so ancient and trouble-torn,
> Of foiled intents, vain lovingkindness,
>   And ardours chilled and numb.
>
> They waste to fog as I stir and stand,
>   And move from the arched recess,
> And pick up the drawing that slipped from my hand,
> And feel for the pencil I dropped in the cranny
>   In a moment's forgetfulness.

Though there is no direct influence discernible, they remind me strongly of Philip Larkin's *An Arundel Tomb* in their gravity and restraint, in the way they allow us to enter Hardy's mind, and see with his eyes. A brief, unemphatic lyric *Drawing Details in an Old Church* (655/W/*) is a companion piece which, like *Waiting Both* (663/C/H/*) a conversation – in ten lines – with a star, could hardly have been better done within its limits. Hardy could now and then write with all the compressed poignancy of a Japanese *haiku*.

Only a little longer is *Paying Calls* (454/W/H/*) which is a truly delightful poem, very little appreciated. It is written to a common folk-song measure (set out in eight-line stanzas it perfectly fits the lovely tune *Van Diemen's Land*). It does not seem like a reverie at all, beginning as it does with a variation on the time-worn 'As I roved out' opening, and using other stock phrases. It is only in the last verse that we realise Hardy has been gently pulling his reader's leg,

> I spoke to one and other of them
>   By mound and stone and tree
> Of things we had done ere days were dim,
>   But they spoke not to me.

It is the last line that obliquely reveals where we are, in Stinsford churchyard. This is Hardy's tribute to his, and our, ancestors, 'each in his quiet cell forever laid,' as Thomas Gray put it in his *Elegy in a Country Churchyard*. It is a deliberately ambiguous poem, superficially artless at first glance, then craftily misleading, but finally breathing a quiet profundity. The way in which Hardy drops his simple monosyllables into the silence of his conclusion is beyond praise.

Finally, *Voices from Things Growing in a Country Churchyard* (580/C/D/W/*) is set again in Stinsford churchyard, which Hardy visited with the poet Walter de la Mare, having just written the poem, on 17 June 1921. The theme resembles that of *Drummer Hodge* (60) analysed earlier in this chapter, namely that after death we become a renewed part of the animate world. But that grim, scarecely consolatory notion, is here treated much more lightly, in a series of miniscule dramatic monologues which effect variety. The tombstones are real, the stories reputedly true, only the names are changed, and the plant reincarnations aptly chosen. Thus the boozy 'Thomas Voss's' legendary red nose lives on in the yew berries, while 'Eve Greensleeves', beautiful and amoral in life, becomes in death the 'innocent withwind' for which the country name is 'Virgin's Bower'. The mocking repetition of 'Sir or Madam' reminds us that we are all equal in the grave; the refrain is curiously gay, not at all macabre. It is a delightfully poised, elegant poem, a tribute to Hardy's enduring poetic skill at 82.

Hardy's postscript to the Victorian age has the self-deprecating title *An Ancient to Ancients* (660/C/D/W/*). It is something of a *tour de force*, replete with sly humour. He cast it in the form of an after-dinner speech offering the customary blend of regret, nostalgia and anecdote. In the 1920s when he wrote it, Victorian culture was much more widely derided than now, and part of the joke is the fact that the names he praises were then so many red rags to the avant-garde bull. But Hardy was only half-serious; he himself had never been a passionate advocate of Victorian 'values' and had collided head on with Mrs Grundy on many occasions. Yet what is 'new' and 'experimental' is not therefore excellent, and his genuine admiration for Tennyson is made clear in the fine verse where the absurdly low esteem in which the laureate's verse was held is likened to the decay of that archetypical Victorian artefact, a summerhouse. For the 'red-lipped and smooth-browed' young men in a hurry he has some barbed advice, and his dry conclusion 'Nay rush not, time serves; we are going,' perfectly rounds off a poised, elegant, sometime sardonic, sometimes elegiac performance.

I think of Hardy writing it as like the ancient Chinese sages in W. B. Yeats's poem, *Lapis Lazuli*, of whom he says, 'Their eyes, their glittering eyes, are gay.'

Analyses

To an Unborn Pauper Child (91/C/D/G/H/*)

I

Breathe not, hid Heart cease silently,
And though thy birth-hour beckons thee,
   Sleep the long sleep:
   The Doomsters heap
Travails and teens around us here,
And Time-wraiths turn our songsingings to fear.

II

Hark, how the peoples surge and sigh,
And laughters fail, and greetings die:
   Hopes dwindle; yea,
   Faiths waste away,
Affections and enthusiasms numb;
Thou canst not mend these things if thou dost come.

III

Had I the ear of wombèd souls
Ere their terrestrial chart unrolls,
   And thou wert free
   To cease, or be,
Then would I tell thee all I know,
And put it to thee: Wilt thou take Life so?

IV

Vain vow! No hint of mine may hence
To theeward fly: to thy locked sense.
   Explain none can
   Life's pending plan:
Thou wilt thy ignorant entry make
Though skies spout fire and blood and nations quake.

V

Fain would I, dear, find some shut plot
Of earth's wide wold for thee, where not
    One tear, one qualm,
    Should break the calm.
But I am weak as thou and bare;
No man can change the common lot to rare.

VI

Must come and bide. And such are we –
Unreasoning, sanguine, visionary –
    That I can hope
    Health, love, friends, scope
In full for thee; can dream thou'lt find
Joys seldom yet attained by humankind!

Hardy's MS adds 'She must go to the Union-house [i.e. workhouse] to have her baby', a note made at Dorchester Petty Sessions. His principal theme is stated in his own version of Sophocles' line ' . . . the good of knowing no birth at all', and reiterated in *Jude* where he calls children 'helpless creatures who . . . had never been asked if they would choose life.' But this is to over-simplify; life is always unpredictable, and anyway – once the inevitability of birth is conceded – Hardy's sympathy is further aroused by the fact that this particular child will be even more disadvantaged than most. Whatever a *pauper's* natural endowments, his or her chances of evading the cycle of deprivation were negligible. Typically, he offers a truthful, and therefore gloomy forecast, but not an entirely nihilistic one. And, faint as the glimmer of hope may be, there is much more than a glimmer, there is indeed a blaze, of compassion.

This largely derives from Hardy's diction; for the most part notably spare, often monosyllabic, and of a markedly Anglo-Saxon and Biblical flavour; *hid heart, birth-hour, to theeward, shut plot* and *wide wold* do not exhaust the list, and abstractions are few. Thus the poem has a plain, direct tone; appropriate to the child who is, nominally, the listener. Stanza I begins almost in a whisper *Breathe not, hid heart*, and its simple language and alliteration, picked up by *cease silently* and *sleep the long sleep*, impart a gentleness to the first three lines which contrasts with the more unsettled rhythms of the last three.

Stanzas II and III, which are, in effect, illustrative 'asides', use a more elaborate vocabulary as the pity implicit in Hardy's advice to reject life assimilates the child's individual destiny with that of suffering humanity. The final line of Stanza II, with its dour, insistent monosyllables drives home the inevitable quality of what it avers; its aphoristic bite is echoed in nearly all the concluding lines. Nevertheless, the harshness of stanza II is qualified by the gentle tone of III; only for its benign query *Wilt thou take life so?* to receive a bitter answer, *Vain vow*, reimposing reality with *locked sense* and *ignorant entry*, and the apocalyptic imagery, Hiroshima-like in its implications, of the last two lines.

Yet hope, and that 'loving-kindness' Hardy thought the noblest of human attributes, supervenes in stanza V with a beautiful evocation of Hardy's wishes – of all our wishes – for this and every child. With what infinite tenderness he expresses his desire, which logic cannot stifle, for the child to find some refuge like King Arthur's Avalon, where 'Nor sorrow comes, nor tears, nor tired old age', and how affecting is the one word *dear* (which similarly appears in two other great poems by him). Yet he will never allow sentiment to lapse into sentimentality. He returns upon himself in two lines as splendidly austere as any in English: *But I am weak as thou and bare;//No man can change the common lot to rare*. It might be Shakespeare or the Gospels speaking and it is followed by the quiet, resigned, musing close of stanza VI. His revision to the last line of stanza V just cited is an example of his unrelenting search for truth. His original 'No man can move the stony gods to spare' is by no means a bad line, but these 'stony gods' are superfluous and he does not really believe in them anyway; neither illusion nor poeticism must dull the edge of veracity.

Here then we recognise ourselves, *unreasoning, sanguine, visionary*, in Hardy who will neither evade nor seek to palliate the child's likely fate. But though his vision seems as dark as night itself, it is not quite devoid of hope. If man will accept the fact of his own weakness and littleness his destiny, like that of the pauper child who is one of us, may possibly be bettered by the exercise of insight tempered with compassion. The child's future is not wholly within our control, but neither is it totally beyond it. And the evidence that Hardy believed that too is his one-word emendation in the last line where he first altered *seldom* to 'never' and then, with that passion for truth as opposed to dramatic effect that is one of his greatest attributes, changed it back again to *seldom*.

In Tenebris I (136/C/D/W/*)
'Percussus sum sicut fœnum, et aruit cor meum.' – Ps. CI

> Wintertime nighs;
> But my bereavement-pain
> It cannot bring again:
>   Twice no one dies.
>
> Flower-petals flee;
> But, since it once hath been,
> No more that severing scene
>   Can harrow me.
>
> Birds faint in dread:
> I shall not lose old strength
> In the lone frost's black length:
>   Strength long since fled!
>
> Leaves freeze to dun;
> But friends can not turn cold
> This season as of old
>   For him with none.
>
> Tempests may scath;
> But love can not make smart
> Again this year his heart
>   Who no heart hath.
>
> Black is night's cope;
> But death will not appal
> One who, past doubtings all,
>   Waits in unhope.

In both theme and structure this is the simplest of the *In Tenebris* group, and its consequent unity of impression, with its brevity, make it, in some ways the most impressive. Its insistent patterning is reinforced by the alternately rhymed, hymn-like verses, with their curt, dimetric opening and closing lines, like so many drumbeats. Each offers a terse image of winter's onset, simultaneously implying the advent of a winter of heart and mind, a freezing-up of the life force. The qualifications which open each second line intensify the sense of an intellectual desolation so all-embracing that no mere external circumstance can worsen it. All those auguries of winter which normally occur in sequence seem here to be happening simultaneously, with withered flowers, dead leaves, dying birds, killing frost and storms in huggermugger, intensifying yet further the mood of despair, a mood not uncommon in the *Book of Psalms*, which provides both the general title and the individual epigraphs for each poem. In Psalm 88 Hardy may well have found the nucleus of this poem. It is the solitary psalm which is an outcry of unmitigated anguish. In it Hardy could have found, in the words of an unknown Hebrew poet of 3000 years ago, an echo of his own despondency.

In the *Authorised Version*, not only does the phrase 'in darkness' conclude the psalm, it also occurs in verses 4 and 12, always carrying, as today, a double sense of both mental and physical night. There are other resemblances of which the psalm's conclusion, 'Lover and friend hast thou put far from me and my acquaintance into darkness', is the most significant. Hardy's own climax, *Black is night's cope*, is similarly all-encompassing. Thus *unhope* (his own coinage, though he may have had the Old English 'wanhope' in mind) does not just connote hopelessness, but the reverse of hope, a negative certainty that what is to come will be worse than what has gone. This exactitude of phrase, everywhere apparent, makes it odd that the great historian G. M. Young should have selected *harrow* as a 'lifeless word'. But Young made the definitive comment on the *In Tenebris* poems when he wrote, '[In them] we hear . . . the voice of an age, of a generation carried beyond sight of its old land-marks, and gazing doubtfully down an illimitable vista, of cosmic changes endlessly proceeding, and ephemeral suffering endlessly to be renewed.'

For the Psalmist, God was there even if deaf to his entreaties; Hardy's poem about the dark night of the soul is made more terrible by his inability to believe that he had a soul.

Yet the nadir of the poem is reached in verse 3, where the birds, which, as we have seen in Chapter 5 are for Hardy a symbol of cheerful indomitability, confront his other symbol of malevolent 'uncreating' force, the *frost*, and *faint in dread*. It is indeed a *black* frost, without either the beauty or the fragility of the white hoar-frost and, by tradition, both more bitter and more enduring (hence *length*). So with excoriating sadness, Hardy seems to identify his solitariness with that of the *lone frost*, unloved by anyone or anything. It would be hard to find a more pitiless exposition of what it means to feel – absolutely and irrevocably – alone, than this poem.

The Convergence of the Twain (248/ALL/H/*)

Written only days after the loss of the 'Titanic' on 15 April 1912 and first printed in the Programme of a Covent Garden Charity Concert in aid of the disaster fund, this is another superb 'occasional' poem. The newspapers were full of the sinking for weeks, and one widespread, if perhaps apocryphal tale was that a seaman had comforted a nervous passenger by saying 'Lady, God himself couldn't sink this ship!' The Greeks had a word, hubris, for such overweening pride, offensive to the gods, and Hardy's prime concern is not to offer consolation to the victims or the survivors, some of whom he knew personally, but to offer a sombre reflection on Man's arrogance, which has lost little of its point in nearly a century. We are quite as prone as the Edwardians to flatter ourselves on being masters of the universe, quite as astounded and resentful when we are proved wrong.

Hardy takes what some might regard as tragic coincidence as tragic inevitability; the *Shape of Ice* and the *smart ship* are conceived and constructed in parallel, so to speak, their subsequently converging courses ordained by *The Immanent Will that stirs and urges everything*. This is an idea closely akin to the concept of Nemesis in Greek Tragedy, but Hardy's *Spinner of the Years* is perhaps indebted also to Milton's 'blind Fury with the abhorred shears' for something more than the rhyme. Hardy's poem – like Milton's *Lycidas* about a shipwreck – has also a great deal to do with the state of the nation, so full of *human vanity* and the *Pride of life*. So has *Lycidas*.

The overall structure is very deliberate. Five retrospective stanzas plunge the reader at once into the *vaingloriousness down* [there] and the question – everyone's question at the time – of how and why the calamity occurred, is posed, ironically, by the *moon-eyed fishes*, unearthly creatures alien to our world. The next five stanzas provide Hardy's minatory answer, the last unites both threads climactically in a terrible *consummation* (a word ordinarily used of marriage).

Hardy's language is throughout finely calculated to reflect the shifts in mood. It is not one of pity or anger; those emotions he did not wish to exacerbate. Nor is there any reference to those who perished with the ship, except by implication in verses III and IV. As in Greek Tragedy, the 'plot' is known to all: even today the very word 'titanic' is shunned as of evil omen. Everything therefore hinges on Hardy's treatment and he presents his protagonist, the ship, with its pristine splendours, its engineering *tours-de-force*, its *salamandrine [i.e. inextinguishable] fires*, and its *Jewels . . . designed//To ravish the sensuous mind'* to maximum effect against the shockingly incongruous background of the *bleared and black and blind* underwater world. Nevertheless, the diction in these five stanzas is highly emotive, initial dismay giving way to fear and repulsion. By contrast, the antagonist, the iceberg, is pictured in an appropriately icy, detached, terminology; *sinister, dissociate, shadowy,* just as Hardy changes his perspective from that of the *sea-worm* and *fishes* to the equally unearthly, but even more remote, viewpoint of the *Immanent Will*; a power like that of the Spirits who preside over *The Dynasts*, calm, objective and quite inhuman. The final verse effects a shattering collision which we can hear as well as see.

Hardy's haste to meet the deadline for the Titanic Fund programme led to a very large crop of revisions for the text in *Satires of Circumstance* two years later. Thus, surprisingly, stanza V, with its crucial *query*; the lynchpin, it seems, of the second half of the poem, was not even in the Fund Programme (hereafter simply TP). But the text we have is an even later revision, for the verse, as first published formally in *The Fortnightly Review* (June 1912) had an intermediate form, reading

Dim moon-eyed [for early *moon-eyen*) fishes near
The daintily gilded gear
Gaze querying: 'What does all this sumptuousness
     down here?'

No doubt Hardy thought 'eyen' a pointless archaism, 'daintily'
detracts from rather than adds to the grim emphasis of *gilded
gear*, while, with the loss of 'sumptuousness', Edwardian pomp
gives way to a much more Biblical weight of utterance. TP III.3
ran 'The sea-worm creeps – grotesque, unweeting, mean, content.' Not only does the revised line flow more easily but each of
the last three words sharpens both the sense and the suggestive
impact of the line. Thus, 'unweeting' besides its obscurity
contradicts 'content' (if the sea-worm can be 'content' it can
feel). 'Mean' is perhaps slightly ambiguous, not to say inap-
posite, 'slimed' provokes repulsion, 'dumb, indifferent' is both
scientifically accurate and suggests the frightening non-human
qualities of the deep-sea world. TP. IV.3 had 'flashes' where we
read *sparkles*. Finally, TP XI.1 had 'Mover' for which the change
to *Spinner* strengthens the link with Greek Tragedy in which the
Fates spun the thread of every mortal's life. Hardy also subsequently altered the jerky stutter of TP XI.2 'The which each
hears' to the simpler wording we have, while TP XI.3 had the
verb 'clouds' instead of *jars*. 'Clouds' was well enough for the
gloom which the catastrophe cast over the Western world, but
jars delivers instead the climactic *physical* shock which the
whole poem has been moving towards, besides effectively
echoing the sound of the preceding rhymes.

There are many other changes, all of interest as demonstrat-
ing the energy and persistence with which Hardy set about
improving what was already a most impressive poem. They
constitute a testimony to both his skill and the integrity with
which he adhered to his belief in poetic truth. *The Convergence
of the Twain* is completely free from humbug, sentimentality
and recrimination; its restraint, implicit compassion and admo-
nitory force make most writing on disasters appear trivial.

Beyond the Last Lamp (257/ALL/H/*)

The poem is retrospective, like so many of Hardy's reveries.
Written in 1911, the incident it records occurred in 1881, when

Hardy was living at 1 Arundel Terrace, Upper Tooting. The subrub was then still semi-rural; not all its streets were gaslit. There is precious little 'plot', two brief glimpses are recorded in three verses; two more verses ruminate on them 30 years later. What matters is the evocation of a scene and a mood, the one as melancholy as the other, and Hardy's meditations upon them: two moments in time, neither meaningful without the other.

So, among the other qualities of this poem we have to reckon with its elusiveness. It is not easy to be sure what Hardy's purposes were in it. We must glance at a less effective poem, *An Experience* (571/*), for help. There Hardy writes of an encounter wholly unremarkable 'to even the subtlest one . . . //For anything that was said, for anything that was done', which, nevertheless, he asserts, 'came as a salutation', a piercingly revelatory moment that is. The word derives from the *Salutation* of the Virgin Mary to whom the birth of Christ was announced by an Angel, but such moments, for which another term is 'epiphanies' are not, at a less exalted level, all that uncommon. Most of us experience times when life is lived more intensely than usual, with heightened awareness of the significance of the material world, and such 'epiphanies' enable poets to make poetry out of the flotsam and jetsam of experience.

The crux of the poem, what etched the scene into Hardy's memory, was the fact that returning, hours later, he found the lovers still caught, as we should say, in a 'time-warp', unable either to resolve or break away from their dilemma. Because one person's 'epiphany' may be another's commonplace, for him to summon up simultaneously both the ordinary and the extra-ordinary qualities of that distant scene was a challenge to Hardy's skill. For the actual behaviour of the *mysterious tragic pair* is, inherently, unexciting and repetitive, its trance-like monotony crucial to its significance.

Hardy's basic verse-form is very simple, itself potentially monotonous. But his octosyllabic rhymed couplets, though their steady beat suggests feet trudging wearily onwards, are interrupted by the ingenious internal refrain with its slight variations. With its reiterated *slowly* and *sadly* the plight of the *sorrowful pair* is continually stressed, while it also links past and present. The sodden, empty, miserable scene is sharply envisaged, too, with many telling phrases, lines 4–5 of stanza 1, the lamplight's *yellow glance* with its queer suggestion that the lamps are sentient, in stanza II, the unexpected *droop of day* (Hardy's emendation from his MS 'death of day') in stanza III, and the strongly alliterated *what wild woe* of stanzas III's last line are some examples of his verbal resourcefulness, his unerring touch.

In contrast, as James Gibson has shrewdly pointed out, there is 'a shadowiness about [the lovers] which seems to make them into a symbol of all unhappy couples everywhere.' Even the title (changed from the neutral MS phrase *In the Suburbs*), is, as he says, charged with significance, suggesting that the couple 'both literally and metaphorically, are going into the dark'.

We are left to infer that what Shakespeare called 'the dark backward and abysm of Time' has engulfed the lovers, the lane, their despair and indeed Hardy, as it will engulf us. That tragic sense of the fleeting, tenuous nature of our grasp on happiness is the mainspring of a poem which, paradoxically, confers a kind of immortality upon the linked loiterers by a feat of imaginative resurrection.

Midnight on the Great Western (465/ALL/*)

For Hardy the railway was a potent symbol of the way in which the Industrial Revolution was uprooting traditional life-styles, and adding to its new horizons a new loneliness of deracination. The boy's *ticket* and his *key* are both of symbolic significance, blending hope and fear. Where is he going? What (apart from his box) will the *key* unlock by way of a future? This is another of Hardy's 'epiphanies', a run-of-the-mill occurrence charged with meaning. The train, as he was the first poet to remark, offers a powerful Time-image; the boy is suspended momentarily between his past and his future; neither he nor Hardy is able either to foretell or alter it.

Technically the point to notice is the *journeying boy* refrain. Tapped out with the fingers, jõur/nēy/īng bóy, the hypnotic clack of train wheels running over rail-joints can be heard, while the internal rhymes in line 4 of each verse less emphatically carry on the metrical pulse. This rhythm suggests to us the boy's tired, bemused state, also pointed up in the *oily flame* of the lamp, his *listless form and face*, and the last two lines of stanza 2, where the unusual verb *bewrapt* clinches the impression of a life at some mysterious crossroads. Only the *key* with its *twinkled gleams* seems alive; everything else is hazy and indefinite. Accordingly the boy himself is depicted as *incurious quite* (an interesting change from the MS 'indifferent quite'; there is a significant difference between not *caring* and not *wanting* to know one's future). Such preternatural calmness puzzles Hardy who perceives that it is long odds against the boy's *plunge alone* (the implicit image is of life as a fathomless gulf) being a happy one.

But he now moves the poem into a new dimension and the language becomes, unusually for Hardy, unmistakably religious in implication. The contrast between the *sphere* of the *soul* – Heaven – and the *rude realms*, of Earth (*rude* is used in the sense of crude or imperfect) leads to the plainly mystical conception of another existence in which the feeble, friendless, one might easily say 'despised and rejected', child was (and will be?) omnipotent and omniscient, as is shown by *spacious vision* and *mark and mete* (for *mete* implies the dispensation of justice.) I am suggesting that this is Hardy's version of the Second Coming. The boy is a Christ figure, maybe *en route* to a new Calvary, he is *in* but not *of* this world, a distinction continually dwelt on in the Gospels. Nor do I recall the word *sin* elsewhere in Hardy's verse.

Yet, characteristically, these last two stanzas are couched as musing queries: it is only tentatively and obliquely that Hardy will advance his hypothesis. This reticence, with all it implies of his fear for the journeying boy's vulnerability, his sense of his oneness with humanity in *its* frailty and bewilderment, makes Hardy's solitary venture into territory he usually entered sceptically and combatively all the more impressive. In W. B. Yeats's *The Second Coming* it is a 'rough beast [that] slouches towards Bethlehem to be born': in Hardy's, much less apocalyptically but perhaps more persuasively, it is a solitary child benighted in a third-class carriage, appropriately enough, unaware of his destiny,

> Bewrapt past knowing to what he was going
> Or whence he came.

During Wind and Rain (441/ALL/*)

As Hardy's MS is reproduced as the frontispiece it may readily be compared with the text all the selections print. But this was arrived at by stages. As printed in the first edition of *Moments of Vision* (1917) the MS version of the refrains (i.e. 'Ah, no: the years O! and 'yea' *throughout* the poem) was unchanged, but altered to what we have in the second edition of 1919, when MS 'birds' was also changed to *fowl*. MS 'webbed' before *white* in the last line of stanza 2 was not deleted until the second (1923) edition of the *Collected Poems* when *carved* in the last line replaced 'chiselled'.

All critics agree with Tom Paulin that this is 'one of the greatest poems of [this] century', but a little background helps elucidate the initial question, 'What is the poem *about*, what does it say? In fact Emma's *Some Recollections*, first read by Hardy after her death in 1912, not only provides the catalyst for the poem but also, sometimes even to phrasing, the leading image of each stanza. Her ingenuous vignettes of her Plymouth girlhood mention, for example, a 'mania for keeping handsome fowl' and use the term 'elders' while she refers to the rain as a 'steady torrent [and] watery omen . . . of sorrows.' This shows that Hardy's use of the anonymous forms *he*, *she* and *they* was deliberate. He did not wish to refer the reader to the poem's origins, and though it is an elegiac poem it is remarkably impersonal. Only the last two lines of each stanza convey the intensity of his feelings, imparting, by their direct, dramatic attack upon the reader a grief the more anguished because it is seen to be unavailing. It is an ancient topos, of course, a fine folk-song, *What's the Life of a Man?*, which also concludes with the 'names' in a churchyard, ends its chorus with 'Below in the wide world [man] appears fine and gay,//Like the leaf he must wither and soon fade away', and Hardy's variation on *Ah, no: the years . . .* is scarcely less simple and traditional; divorced from their context these lines might come from a Victorian parlour ballad. So how does he contrive from this and a few scraps of Emma's artless reminiscences to strike chords so profound, so resonant?

There is no single answer, though Hardy's structural skill has a large part to play. By unobtrusive variations in stress and line-length the first five lines of each stanza are given the flavour of casual, colloquial talk; inconsequential snippets from the fabric of memory. Across this unruffled surface the refrains and their dependent moments of tormented vision cut – like the title's wind and rain – with savage immediacy, the impact of which is sharpened by a double contrast with the narrative vignettes that precede them. The first contrast is contrived by technique. Thus, the long-delayed but marvellously telling return to the opening rhyme at the end of each stanza links a serene opening with an arrest of blank dismay, thus nakedly exposing the unbridgeable gap between past and present. Then the light, rising tempo of lines 2–5 in each stanza, is checked by the sombre, long-drawn-out refrain and clinched by the stony iambic beat of the last line (of which the monosyllabic weight is increased by Hardy's revisions.)

These revisions, even more significantly, strengthen the intensity of emotion. Probably Hardy felt the earlier version of the refrain over-insistent and maybe – with its internal rhymes (no/O!) in every verse – over-'poetical' too. The tune may distract us from the words. But he also aimed to 'intensify the inner meaning'. His verb *reel* (for the neutral 'drop') both enacts the movement of the leaves and disturbingly suggests a drunken dance. The *rotten rose* is a crucial change. Whereas 'creeper' is an inert word, *rose* is thick with associations, signifying both in William Blake's famous *The Sick Rose* and in folk-song generally, sexual passion, its decay symbolising the death of love. And *ript* gives us the active malevolence of Time where 'lets go' implies only a weak resignation.

The weather and seasons have their part to play; the past is suffused with summery radiance, but the wind and rain of winter's advent and the ominous *white storm birds* impel the poem to a resolution which the violent destruction of the rose may seem to have already stated. But there are two strokes of genius in store. First comes the last stanza's touching picture of the hectic, confused, unreflecting happiness of youth, in which, surely, those carelessly disregarded *brightest things that are theirs* symbolise their health, their beauty and friendship, all to be dispersed by time. Then come the revisions in the last line. The MS version would have delighted most poets, conveying, as it does, stillness and finality. But Hardy's *raindrop*, symbol of everything soft and gentle, connoting rebirth and growth, displaces 'lichen' and, with the more active *ploughs* (incidentally a better rhyme for *house*) moves the whole line into a new dimension of what I can only call metaphysical brilliance, a Donne-like leap in meaning. For surely the last word we expect as predicate of raindrop is *ploughs*? Yet the more we consider it the more telling the juxtoposition becomes. 'Lichen' only covers but rain makes elemental. So soft in itself, it will yet, in alliance with wind, frost and time, erode the hardest stone, erase the most deeply cut names, and at length return the stone to the condition of soil that will ultimately feel the plough again. And so the cycle is inevitable: the poem, while it exhales an intense sadness, is none the less, as no stone can be, a valid defiance of time. The last line alone has the lapidary perfection of a fragment from the Greek Anthology.

Here then, as I believe, is Hardy's elegy for life itself, and its particular wisdom, while offering us no consolation, while indeed opening up a grim vista of loss and loneliness, also imparts to us an extraordinarily poignant vision of the everyday beauty and richness of life, mediated to us by glimpses of ordinary people doing commonplace things, quite unaware of their felicity. If in this it echoes the bitter-sweet song of Feste in *Twelfth Night*, with its haunting refrain, 'Hey-ho the wind and the rain,//For the rain it raineth every day' it only shows Hardy as not too modest to take a hint from Shakespeare, the great central theme of whose *Sonnets* he has here triumphantly reworked.

7

Love Poems I

. . . Love and its ecstasy
Will always have been great things'
Great things to me.
Great Things (414/C/G/W/H/*)

That this affirmation is true no one could doubt for a moment after reading through the *Complete Poems*. Nearly two hundred of them, over a fifth of Hardy's large output, may fairly be classed as love poetry. They are scattered through all eight volumes of his verse and, taken as a whole, they constitute the ultimate touchstone of his poetic genius. No one else in this century, not even W. B. Yeats, has produced so extensive, so varied and so majestic a tribute to that force in human life which Dr Samuel Johnson – surely the last man to be called sentimental – categorised as 'A passion which he who has never felt never was happy, and he who laughs at never deserves to feel; a passion which has caused the change of empires and the loss of worlds.' For anything approaching Hardy's testimony in scope and scale we must go back to Browning and beyond him to Donne, whose poetry both Browning and Hardy admired.

I have spoken here of Hardy's 'love poetry' as if no further definition were needed, and I may be accused of evading the issue if I confine myself to saying that I intend to treat of those poems that deal directly and personally (not, that is to say, through the medium of fictitious narrative) with that complex of thoughts and feelings which, happily when reciprocated, unhappily when not, embrace the experience we call 'being in love'. After all, there can scarcely be a single reader who has not formed his or her views on this, to all intents and purposes universal, experience.

Of course, this begs the larger question, 'What then is love?'. But poets, philosophers, artists, theologians and others have been worrying away at this bone of contention for two milennia and more, and as anything I could add would be both perfunctory and derivative, I shall content myself with recommending those who want to pursue the question further to Walter de la Mare's superb anthology *Love* (Faber, 1943) and to his long, acute and probing introduction.

   As to what kind or kinds of love poetry Hardy wrote, I should prefer to avoid generalising ahead of the evidence, so to speak, and to let answers emerge piecemeal as the poems come under scrutiny. But it is perhaps necessary to say that Hardy scarcely ever writes in that vein of the ecstatic here-and-now which Donne often, though by no means always employs; the theme of Eros Triumphant one might say. Rather Hardy treats, for the most part retrospectively, of love lost, frustrated or illusory: in so far as it is possible to summarise his theme it is that of Eros Defeated. But this admits of exceptions, and in any event the impact on the reader even of his most tragic love poetry is scarcely ever dispiriting or ultimately depressing. This is no doubt because the greatest of his love poems, whatever depths of present despair and misery that may betray, are never quite without some remembered gleam of 'far-back' days as 'Lit by a living love//The wilted world knew nothing of.' (*A Spot*/104/*). Indeed, the dismissive phrase 'wilted world' has a most Donne-like conviction that love can 'Make one little room an everywhere.' What John Dryden (translating the Latin of Horace, *Odes* III xxix) wrote so magniloquently,

   Not Heav'n itself upon the past has power,
   But what has been, has been, and I have had my hour.

is not only echoed (perhaps consciously – Hardy knew Horace well) in *To Meet Or Otherwise* (251/W/H)

      From briefest meeting something sure is won
      Nor God nor Demon can undo the done.

but provides a leitmotif, a continually recurring chord, sounding through all Hardy's later love poems, growing stronger and more plangent as he grew older and his poetry wiser, gentler and more clear-sighted. As he wrote – to whom we cannot be certain, but the words might just as well be addressed to his readers –

> Between us now and here . . .
> Let there be truth,
> Even if despair;
>
> (*Between Us Now*/99/C/*)

That heavy stress on truth is no accident; 'The mind,' said Dr Johnson, 'can only repose on the stability of truth', and Hardy's love poetry has much more to do with the mind than the body, suggesting nothing of Donne's or Yeats's naked sensuality, though it is far from bloodless or dispassionate. This is hardly surprising; the greater part of it was written when Hardy was over 60; most of the acknowledge triumphs when he was over 70, 73 indeed when he produced, in *Poems of 1912–13*, some of the greatest elegiac love poems in this or any other language. Nevertheless we do possess a significant number of really early love poems, which help the reader, in so far as this chapter is concerned, to trace the development of Hardy's art more clearly than is elsewhere feasible. So I have arranged the three sections that follow chronologically.

EARLY LOVE POEMS

There are just over twenty poems, mostly dated 1866 or 1867, and often subscribed WPV (i.e. Westbourne Park Villas) where Hardy lodged while working for Blomfield in London. Most of them were printed in *Wessex Poems*, a few more in *Poems of the Past and the Present*, and one or two later still. Tempting as it is to suppose that what we have here is what the young, ardent, ambitious Hardy penned in his lamplit room, far into the London night and in high hopes of publication, we need to be cautious in our assumptions. The MS of *Wessex Poems* is a 'fair copy', destined for the printers, in no sense an early draft (indeed we have only one surviving early draft of a poem). Even so the MS is often heavily revised, *Neutral Tones* (9/ALL/H/*) for example, later to be analysed, displays nine emendations, three at least of real significance. If, at this relatively late juncture, Hardy was ready to put so much effort into revision, it is a virtual certainty that there had been more drastic revision of what were, after all, juvenilia, at an earlier stage. We also know, from his 1912 note to *Desperate Remedies* that 'certain scattered reflections . . . are the same in substance with some in the *Wessex Poems* – and elsewhere' (the phrase 'swaying like the trees' from *Afternoon Service at Mellstock* (356) is a case in point), and it is manifestly improbable that Hardy simply recycled the prose back into verse again. Finally, with reference to the little group of sonnets, *She to Him, I–IV* (14–17) in *Wessex Poems*, Hardy writes of 'a much larger number that perished', though he does not say how, or how many. It may be he mislaid them, or discarded them as too jejune or too derivative from Shakespeare's sonnets. But I suspect that what we have is a heavily cut, heavily revised residuum of what Hardy wrote, to judge from the whole series of titles with *She* or *Her* in them, as a full-blown sonnet *sequence*, in which sonnets telling a story (fictitious or semi-fictitious, it is impossible to say which) are interspersed with other types of lyric verse, after the model of Sir Philip Sidney's great original, *Astrophel and Stella*. The really striking departure from the norm of Victorian poetry, however, is that they are all – as was the whole sequence if my guess is correct – written from the point of view of, and 'spoken' by, a woman, the eponymous *She* in fact. Later Hardy was to get further inside the skin of his female characters than any male English novelist before him; here he was essaying something so unusual that it is hardly surprising that those archetypal Victorians, the magazine editors, should have jibbed at publishing his verse, the more so if he sent them the whole *opus*, as he may well have done because, in a literary sense, he was very much a beginner then.

All this is by way of a preliminary caution before considering these early efforts. If 'In the spring a young man's fancy// Lightly turns to thoughts of love', what we are dealing with is a distinctly autumnal recasting of that 'fancy' and those 'thoughts'.

Nevertheless it remains true that these – the earliest examples we possess of Hardy's verse – do, however much tinkered with, betray some common features which mark them as a young man's work. Their diction often wavers uncertainly between Hardy's own knotty idiosyncrasy and that 'golden' or Elizabethan manner which he tells us he only abandoned completely 'after leaving London.' They are also, self-evidently, fictitious to the extent that their dramatis personae are invented or at least heavily disguised. Finally, their gloom is a touch mannered, their disillusion laid on rather too thickly to be entirely convincing. It is not that they are insincere, or lacking in conviction; rather one feels that their inspiration is bookish as opposed to experiential. Certainly the influence of Shakespeare's sonnets is evident in this fine conceit from *She to Him III* (16/D) where lost love is said to be

>   Numb as a vane that cankers on its point,
>   True to the wind that kissed ere canker came

but the subsequent phrase 'dexterities in witchery' is decidedly Hardeian. *She to Him II* (15) has an equally Shakespearean opening, 'When you shall see me in the toils of time,//My lauded beauties carried off from me,' but by line 10 both the idea and its expression have become unmistakably his own. 'Sportsman Time but rears his brood to kill,' has the lovers as partridges and – somewhat more appositely – Time as the gamekeeper! What could more more Hardeian than that?

To this uncertainty about manner, which even in the best of these early poems is not fully resolved, albeit Hardy's MS revisions generally tend towards a simpler diction, we have to add, I think, some reservations about the vicarious nature of the experiences presented. The mask Hardy chooses to assume, that of a wronged woman, makes demands on both technique and sophistication which he could not yet fully sustain, though much later in *Poems of 1912–13* and elsewhere, he uses the device triumphantly, in *The Haunter* (284/ALL/*) to give just one example.

Although his use of a woman's persona in many of these apprentice pieces tends to emphasise the uncertain nature of Hardy's engagement with his material, there is no very marked improvement when he writes in his own person. All in all these early poems contain too many 'keen lessons that love deceives' and assert too often that 'joy lies slain' to command our assent.

Thus in the sonnet *Revulsion* (13/C/D), besides the faintly ludicrous solemnity of the disillusioned lover's profession never again to endure 'the fateful thrilling//That devastates the love-lorn wooer's frame', there are several phrases both forced and repetitive in addition to the hackneyed poeticism of 'love-lorn wooer'. One feels Hardy would, later in his career, have seen expressions like 'the hot ado of fevered hopes' as somewhat hollow and hectic, and in this poem, like most of its contemporaries, we are left with an overall impression of straining after effect. As against the totally untheatrical anguish that he was to impart over 40 years later, what we see here is the Byronic 'pageant of a bleeding heart'. In only a few of these poems is it easy to accept that Hardy's heart is as fully involved as his pen.

Curiously enough, two exceptions to these strictures are both to some extent derivative. One, the famous *Neutral Tones* (9/ALL/H/*), is fully analysed, the other, *1967* (167/C/W), just as Edward Thomas pointed out on its first appearance, gives off a marked flavour of John Donne, the solitary poet whose *direct* influence Hardy twice acknowledges. The poem looks forward a century from its conception. It is a succinct, indeed compressed lyric of only twelve lines, mounting a vigorous, colloquial 'attack' on the reader, and couched, as Donne's poems usually were, as an address to the woman in question. He and she, Hardy accepts, will in the twentieth century's 'vivid view' be reduced to a mere 'pinch of dust or two'. But, albeit *1967* may show 'a scope above this blinkered time' he asks,

> – Yet what to me how far above?
> For I would only ask thereof
> That thy worm should be my worm, Love!

The macabre theme, the, at first sardonic, then passionately sincere tone, the simple, sensuous language, are very unlike most of the poetry that was being written in the 1860s, though *Modern Love* (1862), by his early adviser George Meredith, is an exception, probably an influential one.

Only two years later, however, when Hardy was lodging in Weymouth, he was already working his way towards his own individual utterance. It is not so much that *At Waking* (174/C/D/ W) which is dated 1869, deserves to rank among Hardy's best poems, rather that it embodies some of that hard thinking which he blends with deep feeling to produce a characteristic tension between the head and the heart. His 'vision' at dawn is of his 'Love', 'Amid cold clouds drifting//Dead-white as a corpse outlaid.' He now sees her 'in bare//Hard lines unfold' until she 'seemed but a sample//Of earth's poor average kind.' That bleak, sour phrasing underlines the 'appalling' nature of his insight, 'that the prize I drew//Is a blank to me!'. A very similar theme was handled in *The Well-Beloved* (96/*), a rather later, undated poem, where a vision, this time of the goddess of love, Venus herself, appears in medieval fashion to the poet near her former temple. She speaks to the lover, who has mistaken her for his bride-to-be, cruelly shattering his illusions,

> Brides are not what they seem.
> Thou lovest what thou dreamest her.
> I am thy very dream.

Though scarcely one of Hardy's most memorable poems, the theme, which he was later to treat extensively in his novel of the same title, is of such central importance to an appreciation of his love poetry that it must be briefly considered. Basically, it is the conflict, as Hardy sees it the inevitable conflict, in the lover's mind between illusion and reality that he is concerned with in this 'fantastic tale'. In his *Journal* (28 October 1891) Hardy wrote, 'A man sees . . . the Venus in his Beloved, but what he loves is the difference . . . what differentiates the real one from the imaginary.' To remain fixated on the visionary conception is to doom oneself (and the Beloved too, of course) to the misery that stems from disillusion, which in this poem occurs at the actual wedding

> – When I arrived and met my bride
> Her look was pinched and thin,
> As if her soul had shrunk and died,
> And left a waste within.

I have for the moment abandoned the broadly chronological approach I intend to employ in this chapter; *The Well-Beloved* is to be dated from the period 1891–2 according to Hardy. But by 1871 he had indisputably found his own voice. *The Minute before Meeting* (191) is interestingly dated – alone among his poems – 1871 and it is the only one, with the exception of the much slighter *Ditty* (18/D/H) which is inscribed to her, that Emma can have seen in print, among those Hardy wrote about her or to her. It illustrates such a marked advance in both feeling and technique that it demands notice here.

The poem derives from those long train journeys, ending in Launceston Station, which Hardy repeatedly made in the early seventies so as to snatch a day or two with Emma. The train, one might say, is slowing down to enter the station. A sonnet, its octet is not only Shakespearian in its alternately rhymed quatrains, but also in its insistent emphasis on the role of Time in Love. Its long, slow-marching lines skilfully suggest the paradox by which the train's progress, really so swift, seems to re-enact the 'grey gaunt days' dividing the lovers. Then there is a further paradox, intricate and 'witty' in a Donne-like way, playing around the word 'expectance' in lines 5–7, and suggesting that expectancy is, perhaps, preferable to realisation. The octet ends with a remarkably protracted closing line of ten monosyllables 'On my long need while these slow blank months passed' suggesting, with its decelerating movement, that the train, and the poem, have ground to a halt.

In striking contrast is the sestet's terse rapidity, echoing Hardy's unhappy awareness that the 'full-up measure of felicity' he has longed for will be denied him by his own foreknowledge of 'more dividing months', that will ensure. This is no sort of Valentine's Day compliment, but neither is it a literary exercise though it still displays traditional affiliations. One may wonder what Emma made of it perhaps, but there can be no doubt of its determination to get at, and to express, both the strength and the complexity of Hardy's feeling for her, of his refusal to be satisfied with a conventional protestation of unvarying devotion. In short, it is a mature love poem; and Hardy had come a long way in a few years. But for *Neutral Tones*, now to be analysed in detail, it might have been enough to say that it was simply better than its predecessors. But that, as will appear, would be an over-simplification.

Analyses

Neutral Tones (9/ALL/H/*)

The very first reviewer to address himself to Hardy's verse paused in his wholesale demolition of *Wessex Poems* for the *Saturday Review* in 1899 to allow this poem as an instance of Hardy's 'mature strength'; Middleton Murry in 1919 unhesitatingly termed it 'major poetry' and in 1929 F. R. Leavis included it in his, to say the least ungenerous, allocation of a 'dozen or so poems' on which he perceived Hardy's 'rank as a major poet' to rest. Many critics have echoed them so I must hope not to appear merely perverse if I enter a few caveats to the inclusion of *Neutral Tones* – fine poem as it undoubtedly is – in the ranks of Hardy's major masterpieces.

It is pointless to speculate on the identity of the woman involved; the location on the other hand is very probably the pond on the heath near Puddletown which gives its name to another poem *At Rushy Pond* (680/D/*). Though less successful, this exhibits some interesting thematic correspondences with *Neutral Tones*, and its second stanza is quite as brilliantly visual as the first of what was probably a companion piece. (*At Rushy Pond* is undated and was published much later.)

The intensely realised setting is, of course, what first takes the reader's eye, a feature aptly compared by J. O. Bailey to 'an etching in steel'. For the poem is wholly devoid of colour and movement; its wintry stillness and silence an integral part of its mood, the inanition which succeeds a once passionate love gone irrevocably sour. The lovers have nothing significant to say to each other, the landscape has nothing to say to them of spring or summer. We cannot usefully talk about 'background' here; *where it happened* is as important as what took place in the anguished impression which memory holds.

The stanza form is simple; rhymed quatrains with an internal couplet, but there are some subtle variations in stress and rhythmic pattern which can best be seen by comparing the last lines of each stanza. Apart from the rather mannered *chidden of God*, the language is similarly unaffected for the most part. There are certainly some reminiscences of D. G. Rossetti (especially of *Willowwood III* and, thematically perhaps, of *The*

Woodspurge), but the echoes are quite faint and probably unconscious.

It is difficult to fault the first two stanzas either for economy or clarity of expression; I am, however, a little less happy with the third. The trope on *deadest* and *die* has an ingenuity foreign to Hardy at his best; such verbal sleights-of-hand, impressive at a first reading, come to feel meretricious on further acquaintance. Nor is it quite clear to what the conjuction *thereby* refers. Again, the closing simile – aside from the fact that the *ominous bird* has a whiff of cliché about it – is not altogether convincing. Does a *grin* in fact suggest a bird in flight? I think the whole stanza is something of an elaboration, and the return in the last to the directness and precision of the first two reinforces this impression. The adjective *keen* with its double sense of 'eager' and 'painful', the assured word-play of *wrings with wrong* (where the homophone 'rings' gives 'surrounds' as well as 'twists') and the telling return to the opening, with the brilliant 'turn' of *God-curst sun*, perverting that primal source of warmth and light into a malign presence; all these are impressive aspects of a poem which, one might say, gives a voice to mute despair and disillusion. Overall, *Neutral Tones* displays a dimaond-hard, if cold, brilliance. But it is monochromatic; to place it beside one of the *Poems of 1912–13* is to see that there is a precociousness, an inevitable immaturity in it, which precludes our rating it with Hardy's greatest verse.

MATURE LOVE POEMS

This is nearly, but not quite, the same categorisation as would be covered by the heading 'Later Love Poems'. Not everything Hardy wrote in the way of love poetry was rewarding; there are pieces which can only be called trivial and conventional among the numerous poems which are not addressed to Emma, though there are remarkably few of them, and hardly any which quite descend to the banalities of *I Said and Sang Her Excellence* (399) with its unalluring sub-title *Fickle Lover's Song* and its bathetic refrain ('Have your way, my heart O!'). Ignoring these, we are left with the fairly small number of poems which can, with some degree of confidence, be ascribed to particular women, and the larger number which cannot, either because Hardy gave no clue, or because they are written about some 'not impossible she' who is either a composite of his acquaintaince or a figment of his imagination. It should not be supposed that there is anything odd about this; even where the nominal subject of a love poem is known the poet may play fast and loose with her physical and mental characteristics. It is improbable that Robert Herrick, as a parson of a remote Devonshire village, had the superfluity of mistresses that the numerous beautiful names in his *Hesperides* suggest, and though Fanny Brawne was real enough she was never the demi-goddess Keats made of her. Perhaps neither love nor love poetry can bear too much reality.

There is only one poem that can be attributed to Hardy's equivalent of the girl next door, his cousin Tryphena Sparks, with complete certainty. this is *Thoughts of [Try]Phena at News of Her Death* (38/C/D/W/H/*), though we have some others, two or three of high quality, that are very probably to be associated with their engagement and its unhappy ending.

The memorial poem itself, Hardy tells us, 'was a curious instance of sympathetic telepathy'. He began it, in the train, only six days before Tryphena's death, though he was 'quite in ignorance' of her illness. The MS title is *T----a. At news of her death*, which he slightly obscured for publication, also deleting the year of her death. Such reticence, in Emma's lifetime, is hardly as surprising as some have supposed. There can be no doubt, however, that Hardy's feelings were deeply engaged, and the language of the first verse – 'lost prize', 'dreams upbrimming with light.//And with laughter her eyes' suggest the gaiety and vivacity Hardy remembered. The movement of the verse, light and swift, is in contrast with the poem's elegiac purpose; the lament is perhaps more for young love than Tryphena, whom he had not seen for some twenty years. He can only speculate on her 'last days', resisting the obvious temptation to envisage an 'aureate nimb' (i.e. nimbus) encompassing them, when it is just as likely they were dominated by 'mischances'. The opposition between these possibilities is particularly well brought out by the light imagery Hardy employs in lines 10–15. The last verse, with its poignant, melancholy realisation that his disposal of her letters, of a lock of her hair may, ironically, have made his vision of the 'best of her//Fined in my brain' all the sharper, ends with a most subtle, telling, and technically assured variation on the first. It is a graceful, gentle farewell; 'all passion spent'.

Two associated poems, both evidently retrospective, seem to be about Tryphena. The first, *In A Ewe-Leaze [i.e. sheep-pasture] Near Weatherbury* (47/G/H/*), is set, as Hardy's own illustration (in *Wessex Poems*) shows, midway between his own home and Tryphena's. It contains a notably Donne-like image in its second verse, 'Yet I note the little chisel//Of never-napping Time//Defacing . . . // . . . my prime.' Despite the opening line's acceptance that 'The years have gathered grayly', Hardy asserts that 'Still, I'd go the world with Beauty,' but that, now – and the poem is significantly dated 1890 –

> She would not balm the breeze
> By murmuring 'Thine for ever!'
> As she did upon this leaze.

There is a certain ambiguity about the subject of the poem; it is not quite clear whether Hardy is addressing Love or the woman he once loved. But it states, though much less tragically, the age-old theme of Love versus Time which was to resonate through so many later love poems.

A Spot (104/H/*), if it *is* autobiographical, seems to me to be most likely to be set in Dorset again, to judge from its 'lonely shepherd souls', whose divinatory powers are part of Wessex folk-lore. It is both more profound and more accomplished than the preceding poem; but it shares its retrospective sadness. It is as if we were looking through the wrong end of a telescope; everything is remote but also crystal clear. I print it in full.

> In years defaced and lost,
> Two sat here, transport-tossed,
> Lit by a living love
> The wilted world knew nothing of:
> Scared momently
> By gaingivings,
> Then hoping things
> That could not be . . .

> Of love and us no trace
> Abides upon the place;
> The sun and shadows wheel
> Season and season sereward steal;
> Foul days and fair
> Here too, prevail,
> And gust and gale
> As everywhere.
>
> But lonely shepherd souls
> Who bask amid these knolls
> May catch a faery sound
> On sleepy noontides from the ground:
> 'O not again
> Till Earth outwears
> Shall love like theirs
> Suffuse this glen!'

It is, of course, the old enemy Time, who has 'defaced' the years which Hardy pictures as the leaves of a book. Though 'transport-tossed' is not one of his happier coinages it does, with 'wilted world' suggest an essentially youthful state, a kind of ecstatic pride, while 'hoping things//That could not be . . .' may well refer to their abortive engagement. This merely serves to show how little biography really matters; what is truly remarkable here is the wonderful economy of statement in the second verse; the feeling of vacancy in the first couplet, and of the indifferent progress of weather and seasons succeeding, conveyed in such bare, simple, yet telling phrases. Hardy employs, as so often elsewhere, a hymn-stanza, slightly modified, which gives an appropriate dignity to his verses. But he does not end on as dark a note as might have been expected, 'turning' the poem with a charming, somewhat Keatsian fancy, back to the summery weather of the first verse and softening the bleakness of the second, by offering us the idea that the very intensity of love can confer upon it a kind of immortality, 'Till Earth outwears', thus stating another of his recurrent themes.

There are a number of other poems that may, with varying degrees of plausibility, be claimed for Hardy's relationship with Tryphena. One, *The End of the Episode* (178/*) is, in my opinion, an undervalued lyric of great force and I analyse it fully later. *The Wind's Prophecy* (440) – which is only marginally relevant – has been considered in Chapter 5. Of the remainder, disregarding the quite numerous poems for which tenuous claims have been advanced on scanty evidence or on pure supposition, *In the Vaulted Way* (176/D/W), though dated 1870 in the MS, seems unlikely to refer to Emma, as its central concern is rejection and parting, after 'words that burned//My fond frail happiness out of me'. In it Hardy offers us a sharp insight into the painful contradictions love can occasion; asking why 'you again//As of old kissed me?' He ends with three lines that touch upon the inherent mysteriousness of love

> Do you cleave to me after that light-tongued blow?
> If you scorned me at eventide, how love then?
> The thing is dark, Dear, I do not know,

That last line with its stark monosyllables is particularly memorable, encapsulating much of Hardy's later musings on the subject. *Singing Lovers* (686/H/*), a Weymouth poem of 1869, has a fine descriptive opening, and explores the feelings of a lover, alone in the company of others very much in love. *She Did Not Turn* (582/*) displays a sharp brevity which lives up to its tersely suggestive title. Two more poems which may possibly look back to Hardy's courtship of Tryphena occur in *Moments of Vision* (1917). *On a Heath* (406/C/D) if, as seems likely, the heath is Puddletown Heath (Egdon Heath in *The Return of the Native*) then appears to refer to that painful period when Hardy hesitated between his old love in Dorset and his new one in Cornwall. We never *see* the woman, only 'hear a gown-shirt rustling' on an 'evening of dark weather' and a 'voice' saying 'Dear is't you? I fear the night'. The method, an initial sharply designated scene, a random moment in time only later seen to have been of profound significance; the backward glance followed by a retrospective probing of its meaning, was to become one of Hardy's most common approaches, not confined to love poetry. The last stanza is obliquely foreboding – re-enacting the inexplicable shadow that can fall between lovers. Here perhaps the 'shade entombing//All that was bright of me,' is Hardy's guilty awareness of his divided loyalties, but the poem's impact does not depend upon the reader's awareness of this. This is equally true of *By the Runic Stone [Two who became a story]* (408) where some claim the only 'Runic Stone' that fills the bill is on Puddletown Heath, but the (later) sub-title appears to imply Hardy and Emma who 'became a story' in *A Pair of Blue Eyes*. The last verse is enigmatic,

> It might have strown
> Their zest with qualms to see,
> As in a glass, Time toss their history
> From zone to zone!

yet what is has to say about the unpredictability of love is universal, and serves to reinforce the fact that it is seldom very material to the appreciation of a love poem for the reader to know of whom it is speaking. Such knowledge may now and then able us better to grasp the weight of what is left unsaid or only implied in a particular context: more often than not the combination of wishful thinking and wafer-thin speculation hinders rather than helps us to a full understanding of the words on the page. This contention may be supported by citing two further fine poems, of which the biographical significance is hotly disputed. The first, *In Death Divided* (262/C/D/W/H), is manifestly *not* about Emma, though plainly personal and deeply felt. It is notable for its 'shock' opening 'I shall rot here . . . ', the macabre intensity of its graveyard imagery, and Hardy's vivid image of the invisible yet 'eternal tie which binds us twain in one', all strongly reminiscent of John Donne. Hardy's use of 'the miles that sever you and me' is said to echo the dividing 'hundred miles' of *The Division* (169/ALL/H/*) which is about Mrs Henniker and discussed later. *Per contra* his speculations about the differing 'form' that their memorials may take is urged in favour of Tryphena Sparks since she was buried (next to, not under) a tombstone of 'stately make' which he visited at Topsham. In the face of such intensely projected feeling as that of stanza II such niggling fades into insignificance,

> No shade of pinnacle or tree or tower,
> While earth endures,

> Will fall on my mound and within the hour
>> Steal on to yours;
> One robin never haunt our two green covertures.

Those three words 'While earth endures', simultaneously homespun and resonant, the silent, ineluctable passage of time in 'shade', in the poignant vignette of the robin, come home to the heart quite unassisted by annotation. Similarly, the graceful, song-like *I say 'I'll seek her'* (172/H/*) has been equally vehemently claimed for both Emma and Tryphena. Yet its true origin is much more likely to lie in a somewhat melodramatic and certainly memorable incident which Hardy witnessed, and in the sequel to which he was unhappily involved, when he and Emma were living in Sturminster Newton, early in their married life. On 29 June 1877 their maidservant aroused them as she crept out to a midnight assignation. Hardy looked out and saw her with 'only her night-gown on . . . . Beside her slight white figure in the moonlight his form looked dark and gigantic.' After Emma had run down and ordered the girl in (she later escaped through a window and ran off with her lover) Hardy 'found that the bolts of the back-door had been *oiled*.' He had the painful task of informing the girl's parents. In his poem Hardy makes the woman complain of the man's 'indecision', a role-reversal which is hinted at in his prose account. She continues, 'The creaking hinge is oiled,//I have unbarred the backway', clearly indicating the significant detail which is the genesis of the poem, and the poem's last verse comes close to distilling the essence of folk-song,

> 'Far cock-crows echo shrill,
> The shadows are abating,
> And I am waiting, waiting,
> But O, you tarry still!'

But the graceful movement and lyrical phrasing do not disguise the poem's insight into the fallacy of seeing love in terms of romantic stereotypes. It is not a fiction, but neither is it a personal poem. The same may be said about the elegiac love lyric, *I Need Not Go* (102/W/H), in which Hardy, for once, appears more concerned with expression than with content. It begins, using a verse-form borrowed without alteration from Sir Thomas Wyatt,

> I need not go
> Through sleet and snow
> To where I know
> She waits for me;
> She will tarry me there
> Till I find it fair,
> And have time to spare
> From company.

This musical lucidity is much more difficult to do than it looks. Everything is implied: Hardy's grief, the grave in winter, the powerlessness of the dead. The tone is dry, what has been called 'shrugging' in Wyatt, whose influence may be detected in this too, but Hardy cannot quite sustain it. His third verse is padded out with a frail parenthesis – '(Though ample measure/ /Of fitting leisure//Await my pleasure)'. The 'pure lyric' wasn't really Hardy's *métier*: like the mythical giant Antaeus he needs to sustain contact with Earth to put forth his full strength.

This generalisation is borne out by the miscellaneous group of 25 poems sub-titled '*More Love Lyrics*', which he assembled in *Time's Laughing Stocks*. These vary widely in subject, treatment and date. Though rarely happy in mood, the later ones are less prone to the theatrical and self-regarding manner of some of the 1860s vintage (a few more of which appear in this group). Some, certainly, are more subtle and probing than any Hardy had written hitherto. Though Emma can scarcely have been delighted to find that only one could plausibly be associated with her, Hardy generally took care to leave the ascriptions vague. External evidence, however, quite strongly supports the view that one at least deals with Hardy's long friendship with the beautiful Mrs Arthur Henniker, who was a not unaccomplished writer (with whom Hardy actually collaborated in a story). There is little doubt that Hardy's feelings for Mrs Henniker were warmer than hers for him, and the date of the poem (1893), taken together with her quotation, unascribed and unacknowledged, of two stanzas from *The Division* (169/ALL/ H/*) in her novel *Second Fiddle* makes it pretty clear that *she* thought the poem was about their relationship.

This poem is written in the folk-song mode of Robert Burns's best-known love lyric, *My Love is Like a Red, Red Rose*; though the theme could hardly be more different. It begins with a simple statement of the 'severance' that distance and unkindly weather have imposed – Hardy's 'hundred miles' may perhaps be an unconscious echo of Burns's more extravagant 'ten thousand mile'. The second verse is lighter in tone, conceding that, if distance were the sole obstacle, 'There might be room for smiles'. But the last verse has a sombre power and finality which makes the whole poem memorable

> But that thwart thing betwixt us twain,
>   Which nothing cleaves or clears
> Is more than distance, Dear, or rain,
>   And longer than the years!

So much emotion is injected into the poem by the intrusion of the single word 'Dear', one Hardy employs sparingly in his verse, but always to great effect. It was for many years supposed that this poem was about the breakdown in the relationship between Hardy and Emma, as, in a sense, it is. But we must accept, sadly, that the 'thwart [i.e. thwarting] thing' was really the barrier that Hardy's marriage imposed on a closer friendship. Two other poems about Mrs Henniker are *A Broken Appointment* (99/ALL/H/*) in which Hardy coins the striking epiethet 'a time-torn man' for himself, but which seems to me, *pace* the high praise of some critics, a trifle high-flown in manner, and the altogether delightful *A Thunderstorm in Town* (255/C/D/W/*) later analysed.

There are three poems about Florence Emily, Hardy's second wife, whom he first met in 1904. Of these, *On the Departure Platform* (170/C/D/W/H/*) is an elegant, light-hearted poem, in which only one line conveys Hardy's feelings directly. He portrays Florence's 'flexible form, that nebulous white' as she 'down the diminishing platform bore' until she was lost in the 'hustling crowds' finally 'to disappear'. The visual emphasis is very strong indeed; one might compare the overall effect with that of an Impressionist painting. The intellectual hinge of the poem is that this joyous moment may be re-enacted, 'But never as then', at which point Hardy assumes the persona of a 'young man' to answer his own question as to why such 'joy . . . must eternally fly.' The experience of seventy years replies, in the last two terse lines, with 'O friend, nought happens twice thus; why,//I cannot tell!'

There are two further interesting and significant poems about Hardy's second wife, printed together in *Satires of Circumstance* after their marriage. The first, *After the Visit* (250/C/D/W/H/*) was printed separately in 1910, but without the dedication 'To F[lorence] E[mily[D[ugdale]. Hardy was attracted to Florence's physical delicacy and grace – she was not beautiful in a conventional way, but Emma had grown dumpy and drab in her dress by this juncture. He deftly compares her movements to those of 'a leaf that skims//Down a drouthy way'; he sees her feet as 'light on the green as a thistle-down ball.' But in her 'large, luminous, living yes' he discerned, or at least believed he did, a nature that, like his own, was meditative, intrigued by 'The eternal question of what life was//And why we were there'. The poem is couched in terms of fluent compliment; its successor takes up their shared perception of life as governed by 'strange laws' and develops the title's question *To Meet Or Otherwise* (251/W/H), conceding that life is a predicament 'from whose thorns we ache' as we struggle to make 'frail, faltering progress' in our quest for 'some path or plan'. The first two and the last verses are certainly accomplished, if at times somewhat mannered and almost Tennysonian in style. But the third strikes a deep, resounding chord, to be heard in much of Hardy's finest later love poetry.

> By briefest meeting something sure is won;
> It will have been:
> Nor God nor Demon can undo the done,
> Unsight the seen,
> Make muted music be as unbegun,
> Though things terrene
> Groan in their bondage till oblivion supervene.

Already quoted in this chapter, where I noted the affinity with Dryden's version of Horace, there is also a remarkably close correspondence with John Milton's *Paradise Lost* Book IX, where Adam tells Eve, who has eaten the fatal apple, 'But past who can recall, or done undo?//Not God omnipotent, nor Fate.' This is one of the few poems which we *know* Hardy valued highly. He actually chose it to illustrate, for Edward Thomas's benefit, what he called his 'idiosyncrasy' as a 'writer'. It is no crude advocacy of the ultimately self-regarding *Carpe diem* ('Seize the moment') credo, but a dignified plea for human love notwithstanding that it can, in the 'long-sweeping symphony' of human history, only 'Supply one note//Small and untraced, yet that will ever be//Somewhere afloat//Amid the spheres', an idea much more humorously touched on in *The Kiss* (401) a *jeu d'esprit* based on the then fairly recent scientific thesis that sounds continue in space forever, so that the 'particular kiss . . . pursues its flight//Travelling aethereal rounds//Far from earth's bounds//In the infinite.'

Hardy is often thought to have been incapable of a light touch. This is not the only poem which refutes the charge but it is hardly typical. The scientific emphasis of *The Kiss*, however, reminds us that Hardy was a child of the industrial revolution, which impinges, in the shape of the railways, on two more love poems, *After a Romantic Day* (599/D/W/*), already discussed in Chapter 5, though perhaps only a love poem by implication, and *Faintheart in a Railway Train* (516/ALL/*) in which the narrator, very possibly Hardy himself, glimpses a 'radiant stranger' at a halt, is inspired to speak to her, but procrastinates too long in his mental 'search for a plea', and is carried away by the train out of her life forever. In his futile lament 'O could it but be//That I had alighted there/' we have Hardy's statement of the theme that Robert Frost was later to label 'The Road Not Taken'. The infinite possibilities of happiness or misery that chance and choice lead us to leave unexplored fascinated Hardy; here the train is an image of the extreme brevity of life's opportunities, the poem painfully reminds us that we are more apt to regret what we did not do than what we did!

If the last poem perhaps qualifies as romantic it is certainly not sentimental; a description which, though not necessarily pejorative, can be applied to very few of Hardy's love poems indeed. But, as usual with him, there are exceptions, taking the form of distant retrospects of childhood's fond attachments, touching in their evocation of innocent idealisation, free from sexual passion. A typical example, *To Lizbie Brown* (D/G/W/H/*) was probably written in the 1890s. It is an assured, elegant, airy poem, to which the word 'song' might aptly be applied. (Gerald Finzi set it delightfully in his *Earth and Air and Rain*.) Hardy playfully, but with marked technical virtuosity, deploys the name 'Lizbie Brown' in the opening and closing lines of each verse. There is nothing weighty about it, indeed the *Life* tells us that its heroine 'despised [Hardy] as being two or three years her junior', but it is both attractive and accomplished, like a Minuet by Mozart. The poems written about Louisa Harding, the pretty farmer's daughter (for whom, the *Life* tells us, Hardy aged fifteen, once cherished an unavailing infatuation, re-warded with a solitary 'shy smile'), are more serious. All are late; the first, *The Passer-By* (627), adds, in the MS, to the sub-title 'To L[ouisa] H[arding]' the words *In Memoriam* and 'She speaks'. It is a slight and fanciful treatment of the idea that Louisa, who never married, reciprocated the feeling of the shy, 'blushing youth . . . of bounding gait' but was as incapable as he of saying so. *Louie* (739/D/W/*) is of more interest. Her death, in 1913, coincided with Emma Hardy's and they were both buried in Stinsford churchyard; the girl he might have loved and the woman he married, as the slow, sad, last line has it, 'Long two strangers and far apart; such neighbours now!' Time, Hardy implies, thus plays ironic tricks. The latest and best, one of the last love poems Hardy wrote, is *To Louisa in the Lane* (822/W/*), which appeared posthumously, in *Winter Words*. Hardy, now in his eighties, allows us to envisage him as momentarily forgetful of the present when he begins, 'Meet me again as at that time//In the hollow of the lane'. Then he recalls her death, that to meet him she 'will have to see/Anew this sorry scene where you have ceased to be'; where the elongated last line, as in all three verses, gives a sad, resigned tone to the whole verse, dispersing the illusion. His summoning up of her as a revenant is delicately achieved, with her 'aspen form', her 'gaze wondering round' and her speech in tones of 'spectral frail alarm', as if she had recaptured her long-lost youth. But Hardy's gentle concluding verse disavows any wish to summon her spirit back; to seek her 'Wait must I, till with flung-off flesh I follow you.' Her return is, of course, and is acknowledged to be, illusory, nor had Hardy any evidence that his belief that she reciprocated his feeling was anything but illusion too. But such dreams of the might-have-been are universal and the tactful poise with which he handles a poem with such a large potential for mawkishness is notable.

But in his old age love had become, inevitably, something of a spectator sport for Hardy. When he was younger the detachment and relative serenity of the poem just considered was not much in evidence. There are indeed a number of poems which view love with a decidedly jaundiced, occasionally cynical eye, though few of these rank with his best. Some have a vinegary sharpness; *In the Night She Came* (180), for example. Here Hardy takes Tom Moore's famous song, 'Believe me, if all those endearing young charms' and turns it inside out. Hardy's lover protests, like Moore's, 'that whatsoever weight of care//Might strain our love, Time's mere assault//Would work no changes there.' But, the first verse continues,

> And in the night she came to me,
>   Toothless, and wan, and old,
> With leaden concaves round her eyes,
>   And wrinkles manifold.

Faced with this evidence of what 'dull, defacing Time' will do, the lover in a sourly authentic exchange, 'faltered', and the last verse concludes with an acrid vignette, 'And when next day I paid//My due caress, we seemed to be//Divided by some shade.' There is a bitter precision about the diction in 'paid' and 'due caress'. *Misconception* (185) somewhat more sardonically examines a lover's attempt to 'preserve my Love secure//From the world's rage'. His efforts are rewarded by a 'pitying smile': what he fears for her, she says coolly, 'I find most pleasure in.' Such disillusioning insights form the subject of various other poems, mostly early. They can, when less surgically handled, be rather wearisome. That cannot be said about two particularly striking and sombre poems, one of which forms the dark conclusion to More Love Lyrics. Since *He Abjures Love* (192/C/D/W/H/*) written in 1883, and *Shut Out That Moon* (164/ALL/H/*) written in 1904, appeared together in 1909, though the second, for no apparent reason, is not included in *More Love Lyrics*, it is difficult not to read them as personal statements, published only after he had ceased much to care what Emma might make of them. *Shut Out That Moon* is fully analysed later; *He Abjures Love* forms a natural postscript to this section, as it also does to Hardy's own grouping of poems which treat of love from many different viewpoints. The word 'abjure' in the title is interesting; it is a legal term meaning to 'renounce on oath' some error, and most commonly applied to heresy. The lover's abdication opens briskly, 'At last I put off love,//For twice ten years//The daysman of my thought,// [daysman means arbitrator, controller] And hope, and doing.' His devotion to Love's 'pursuing', his 'heart-enslavement' has been total.

> But lo, Love beckoned me,
>   And I was bare,
> And poor, and starved and dry.
>   And fever-stricken.

The eight-line stanzas, strongly stressed and rhymed cumulatively ABCD/ABCD suggest a lute-song, as does some of the diction 'kith and kind', 'fatuous fires' 'comelier hue' etc. But Sir Thomas Wyatt comes most to mind in the theme, which he made so much his own, of the 'Lover's Complaint'. It is the traditional topos of Mediaeval Courtly Love that Hardy has reworked here, complete with the lover as enslaved to Love (seen here as Eros, hence 'his' and 'him'), forfeiting everything 'to give him glory', 'enkindled by his wiles', heedless of his friends' concern. But this is no pastiche; in the fifth verse there is a characteristic Hardeian volte-face. In the act of abjuring Love's 'desolations' once and for all, he seems to cry out for them in an ecstasy of longing. For it is surely a deliberate ambiguity to clothe what purports to be a rejection of romance in language so incandescently romantic as this:

> No more will now rate I
>   The common rare,
> The midnight drizzle dew,
>   The gray hour golden,
> The wind a yearning cry,
>   The faulty fair,
> Things dreamt, of comelier hue
>   Than things beholden! . . .

And this impression is confirmed by the last verse, in which despite its ratiocinative opening claiming to 'sound//Clear views and certain', Hardy finally returns upon himself to ask ' – after love what comes?' and to answer, in three desolating lines 'A scene that lours//A few sad vacant hours,//And then, the Curtain.' When in 1920 this poem was cited as evidence of Hardy's general pessimism, he jestingly replied that this was a love poem and 'Lovers are chartered irresponsibles.' But the truth is that *He Abjures Love* enunciates a theme to which Hardy often reverts; the perpetual debate between what we might call the arithmetic of thought and the music of feeling which are here held in equipoise in so far as the argument is concerned: Hardy will never fudge the issue or cook the evidence. But what the poetry *imparts* to us is another matter altogether.

Analyses

A Thunderstorm in Town (255/C/D/W/H/*)
(*A Reminiscence: 1893*)

She wore a new 'terra-cotta' dress,
And we stayed, because of the pelting storm,
Within the hansom's dry recess,
Though the horse had stopped; yea, motionless
    We sat on, snug and warm.

Then the downpour ceased, to my sharp sad pain,
And the glass that had screened our forms before
Flew up, and out she sprang to her door:
I should have kissed her if the rain
    Had lasted a minute more.

This brief lyric, a product of Hardy's mild flirtation with Mrs Henniker in the 1890s, follows nevertheless a typical Hardeian pattern, in that an unremarkable moment retrospectively acquires significance – as in *Beyond the Last Lamp* (257) – in this instance because of its unrealised potential, as in *Faintheart in a Railway Train* (516). The location, unusually for him, is London and the poem is – appropriately – urbane in mood, and elegantly controlled in form, somewhat in the manner of Robert

Browning. The first stanza sets the tone economically with its glancing reference to the world of fashionable society in *terra-cotta dress* and its dry indication of the *hansom,* a form of conveyance where the cabby could not see his fares because he was perched on the roof, conveniently for some. The *pelting storm* and later *downpour* suggests a sudden irruption of feeling, the *snug and warm* interior is subtly sensual; the world of convention momentarily suspended, as if time, like the horse, were motionless.

But it is a momentary illusion, of course, giving way at once in stanza 2 where a deftly chosen series of verbs – *ceased, flew up, out she sprang* – shatters the fragile equilibrium; an effect which Hardy's change to *sharp, sad pain* (from his MS 'lasting pain') accentuates. There is a flurry of action and the poem ends with Hardy sitting alone with his regret. But the poem is like a clip from a film; it will not do to read too much into it. There is irony and wry self-mockery here too, and society, in the shape of the cabby (who would have released the *glass that . . . screened them*) re-asserts itself. Though it is not without an undertone of sadness for another 'road not taken' it is a poised, controlled performance, as near perhaps as Hardy ever came to *vers de société,* which is to say not very near. But, given that it is not a profound poem, it is hard to imagine it better done.

Shut Out That Moon (164/ALL/H/*)

It has been questioned whether, remarkable as it is, this can properly be considered as a love poem. Some commentators see in it a threnody for a happier past, others as a more specific lament for lost love. The first interpretation refers stanza 1 to Hardy's dead father and their shared delight in music, stanza 2 to his mother (who died in 1904) and shared her son's pleasure in star gazing. Only stanza 3 would then refer to someone, presumably Emma, with whom he experienced another kind of love. In both, the concluding stanza is an apparent renunciation of romance and its attendant illusions. I incline to the second view: the *moon* and the *lute* have exceptionally strong traditional associations with love while the use of the plural (*we read, we were drawn,* and *you and me*) in all three stanzas, implies shared experiences both now and then, which would add poignancy to the solitary *my* of stanza 4, a significant change, obviously calculated.

Hardy uses a simple form, allowing himself the freedom to omit some of the rhymes in stanzas 1 (*blind/wore/read*) and 3, while employing a six-line variant of the 'common metre' hymn-stanza he so frequently resorted to. The strongly rhythmic impulse this imposes adds to the charged atmosphere; the language is of an unashamedly romantic bent. Albeit the two superb compound epithets, *years-deep dust* and *dew-dashed lawn* are characteristic of Hardy, one feels Tennyson would have been proud to own them. But there are anti-romantic undertones. The *moon* may be beautiful but it is nearly always a bad augury in Hardy. Moreover the epithet *stealing* (a telling emendation for the MS 'sad-shaped') suggests not only the moon's apparent fleeting movement but also its ability to 'steal' man's wits (as in 'moon-struck') while to view the moon through glass was an unlucky omen in folk-belief. Again, lovely as the stars may be they are, for Hardy, often the epitome of inhuman coldness and indifference. Even the richly evocative image which opens stanza 3 – probably Hardy was referring to a feature of the lilac – is offset by the qualifying *seemed a laugh*, and *said to be*. Nevertheless the overall impression remains, in contrast to the negative injunctions; full of enchantment, redolent of past happiness, so that the reader is taken aback by the vehemence with which the final stanza appears to reject all this. It is grim in thought and grey in language, its spirit of negation and retreat shown in the bleak adjectives and adverbs, *common*, *dingy*, *crudely*, *mechanic*; and the dour verbs, *prison*, *loom* and *wrought*. The world of suburban convention, of middle-aged caution, has obtruded upon the world of natural feeling. But can we believe in Hardy as an advocate of reason as against passion; does the poem mean what it says? For myself I think not, there is too much implicit contempt for the merely utilitarian and complacent attitude set out in stanza 4, too little conviction in the commands to *Shut out*, *Close up*, *Step not out*, *Stay in*, *Brush not* for us to accept them as serious advice. Considered purely as an argument *Shut Out That Moon* comes down glumly enough on the side of the head. But all the emotional weight inclines us towards the promptings of the heart, the smelly oil lamp has no chance against the moon, the stars, the fragrance *of life's early bloom*, however *tart* its fruit.

The End of the Episode (178/*)

Indulge no more may we
In this sweet-bitter pastime:
The love-light shines the last time
Between you, Dear, and me.

There shall remain no trace
Of what so closely tied us,
And blank as ere love eyed us
Will be our meeting-place.

The flowers and thymy air,
Will they now miss our coming?
The dumbles thin their humming
To find we haunt not there?

Though fervent was our vow,
Though ruddily ran our pleasure,
Bliss has fulfilled its measure,
And sees its sentence now.

Ache deep; but make no moans:
Smile out; but stilly suffer:
The paths of love are rougher
Than thoroughfares of stones.

There is no overt indication of the woman to whom this poem refers. If I incline to think it was Tryphena Sparks it is because Hardy's life with Emma could hardly be regarded as an *episode*. Technically, in Greek drama, with which Hardy was familiar, 'episode' meant an interpolating passage between two choric songs, and in the older tradition of the novel it was a self-contained narrative within the larger novel. Hardy may well have thought of his affair with Tryphena in that light, and the homely countryside setting is that of Dorset rather than Cornwall. It does not matter much, however; the poem is not about a personality but a state of mind.

We may begin by noticing the simple, song-like verse pattern, the even unhurried flow of which is assisted by Hardy's use of what are termed 'feminine' or 'double' rhymes in the internal couplet of each verse (for example, *pastime//last time*). Because in Victorian verse it was so often used for comic purposes it had become a 'dangerous' device and most serious poets shunned it. But neither Sir Thomas Wyatt nor John Donne feared to employ it and nor did Hardy, who effortlessly avoids any hint of a jingle. The diction is similarly plain; only the inverted compound in the second line (where we *expect* 'bitter-sweet' which would give a false stress) and the slightly archaic *stilly*, sign it as Hardy's. There is, however, an extremely subtle and pervasive use of alliteration throughout which helps counterbalance the sometimes heavily stressed phrases. See, for example, the sequences *more may . . . me* and *love-light . . . last* in stanza 1. Thus, though each verse has an almost epigrammatic pungency and concentration which could almost permit it to stand on its own, each also contributes to the cumulative effect.

The mood is gentle, the tone quite free from rancour or reproach, a point exemplified in the solitary word about the beloved, *Dear* (which was an inspired replacement for Hardy's MS 'sweet' and one we have seen him place to great effect elsewhere). But this is not a soft-centred poem: Hardy evades nothing. Bit by bit, stanzas 2, 3 and 4 demolish any grounds the lovers may find for consolation. Their 'Time is up'; nothing can prevail over that implacable adversary, whose malign presence is also suggested in the brilliant 'pun' on the double sense of *measure* (as 'a dance' and 'an allocated share').

Yet notwithstanding its iron honesty, this is far from a cold or cynical assessment of love. For while the sounds and scents, the harmless *dumbles' humming*, the *flowers and thymy air* suggest the pastoral happiness of their meetings, the richness and warmth of diction in stanza 4, in *fervent, ruddily ran our pleasure* (*ruddily* here has implications of healthy, rosy, fresh) and the tellingly stressed *Bliss*, imparts something of lost ecstasy, a passion deeply felt even in retrospect, and thus all the more effectively preparing us for the painful conclusion.

And then we have the last stanza. If Hardy wrote better poems, he wrote no better lines than these. How easy it seems, yet how difficult it is, that heroic plainness of diction. Like nearly all the finest love poetry this lies only a hairsbreadth away from the banal: it says nothing new, nothing we might not have thought of ourselves. Some might object to *stilly suffer* perhaps, but the word has a long ancestry; moreover it implies both silence and immobility, while its *sound* suggests 'steely' also. As for the last two lines they have that simple, proverbial ring that persuades us something has been said once and for all, like Shakespeare's 'Youth's a stuff will not endure.' Nevertheless, the lasting impression is not one of love as ultimately futile and transitory but of a mind capable of re-entering the past with joy while still able to view it dispassionately. Here again is that equipoise between cool head and warm heart which gives Hardy's love poetry its peculiar intensity.

8

Love Poems II: Poems about Emma

Thomas Hardy wrote about a hundred poems about Emma Lavinia, his first wife; over a tenth of his entire lyric *oeuvre*. At least 80 of these are avowedly about their courtship and marriage; 20 or so more may, with reasonable certitude, be ascribed to the same creative origin. Of all this passionate outpouring Emma herself – and it is a truly terrible irony – can have seen scarcely a trace. Only four poems, two certainly and two very probably about her, were published in her lifetime, and it is most unlikely that she saw more than a few others in manuscript. In fact, almost every line Hardy traced upon his tremendous map of love was posthumous, and though several great poets, Donne and Milton among them, have left individual tributes to their dead wives, there is nothing in all literature to compare with Hardy's elegiac commemoration of Emma, of which what is now the most celebrated part appeared, as *Poems of 1912–13*, not long after her death; to be supplemented by a steady stream of others until Hardy's own death in 1928.

In terms of subject, these poems may be divided into two broad categories; those which treat of Hardy's brief but happy time with Emma in Cornwall, and those dealing with aspects of their subsequent, far from idyllic, marriage. But, because virtually all the poems are retrospective, I shall ignore their dates of composition and arrange the poems in an order which, to a very limited degree, allows a narrative element to appear. I therefore begin with what, following Hardy's own practice, I shall call the *Lyonnesse Poems*; those set in a country which, however minutely observed its topography, had always some element of the visionary about it. Next, because their arrangement was deliberate, I shall look at the *Poems of 1912–13* as a group, and finally I shall more briefly consider the *Poems of*

Marriage. Numerically speaking this last category is more or less equal to the poems set in Cornwall or Lyonnesse (where some of the finest of the *1912–13 Poems* are also located). But, qualitatively speaking, as will appear, it is another matter. Still, before commencing our study of those poems in which Hardy's art is most triumphantly manifested – as even critics who seem to have been weaned on a pickle concede – it may be helpful to attempt a brief summary of the love poetry's leading character- istics as they have emerged from the examples already consi- dered. Briefly, these are: the endless conflict between Time and Memory, the clash between what the heart feels and the intellect perceives, the acceptance of love as both infinitely valuable and infinitely fragile, the finely held poise between a pervasive tenderness and a ruthless honesty, with a final sad recognition of the unbridgeable gulf between Love's appea- rance and its reality.

LYONNESSE POEMS

> She opened the door of the West to me,
> > With its loud sea-lashings,
> > And cliff-side clashings,
> Of water rife with revelry.
>
> She opened the door of Romance to me, . . .
> > > *She Opened the Door* (740/D/W/*)

On 7 March 1870 – the date still set on his old desk-calendar in Dorchester Museum – Thomas Hardy was up well before dawn to hump his surveyor's paraphernalia into Dorchester and there – probably alone – board an early train. This, after va- rious changes and a long cross-country peregrination, set him down at Launceston, there to continue his by now tiring journey for seventeen miles by pony-trap to St Juliot, where he was due to ply his trade as architect's assistant by surveying the dilapidated church. Travelling through it in the twilight Corn- wall seemed to him then – as it was always to seem – another country; his destination an all-but-inaccessible hamlet near to the 'wild, weird Western shore' of the Atlantic was indeed 'a

spot few see'. Even today the twentieth century has not much
marked or marred those 'haunted heights'. His long journey
came to seem fraught with significance, so momentous indeed
that it gave rise to four poems. One, *The Wind's Prophecy*
(440/C/D/W/*), has already been considered in Chapter 5. It
may well date from close to the visit but its superb glimpses of
the coast from the speeding train are unrivalled, as in

> From tides the lofty coastlands screen
> Come smitings like the slam of doors,

and

> Yonder the headland vulturine,
> Snores like old Skrymer in his sleep,

though, as a love poem, it is slight. *The Discovery* (271/W/*) has
a fine opening verse – in which Hardy, having 'wandered to a
crude coast . . . heard breaking//Waves like distant cannonades
that set the land shaking', but the second stanza sags after
Hardy's ill-judged use of 'love-nest' in line 2. In *A Man Was
Drawing Near to Me* (536/C/D/*) which derives, like so many of
these poems, in part from Emma's *Some Recollections*, Hardy
imagines Emma, as she put it, 'on the *qui vive*' for his arrival,
playing upon the names of the tiny hamlets that marked his
route, like 'Otterham' and 'Tresparrett Posts', to stress the swift,
dramatic quality of his arrival when 'There was a rumble at the
door,//A draught disturbed the drapery,' and 'With gaze that
bore//My destiny,//A man revealed himself to me', a scene
memorably recreated in *A Pair of Blue Eyes* also. But the best of
these poems is *When I Set Out for Lyonnesse* (254/ALL/H/*). This
is a gay, lilting poem, charged with the spirit of romance and
young love. Each six-line stanza repeats its opening two lines as
its conclusion, adding to the intensity of feeling, and there is
one particularly fine emendation. The last stanza, when first
published, ran

> When I came back from Lyonnesse
> With magic in my eyes,
> *None managed to surmise*

> *What meant my godlike gloriousness*
> When I came back from Lyonnesse
> With magic in my eyes.

Some years later Hardy altered the over-opulent third and fourth lines to the far more unusual and compelling text we have: 'All marked with mute surmise//My radiance rare and fathomless.' Hardy thought this his 'sweetest lyric' and it is no surprise to find that it has been set to music by more than a dozen composers.

It is not easy to distinguish between poems deriving from that first visit and his subsequent trips that summer, though two fine lyrics later analysed – *At the Word Farewell* (360/C/D/W/H*) and *The Frozen Greenhouse* (706/G/W/*) – both probably relate to those few days in March. Twenty or so more bear on later periods at the Rectory. Some are general rather than particular; the experimental and perhaps not quite successful *Lines to a Movement [MS Minuet] in Mozart's E-Flat Symphony* (388/D/W), for example, which, apart from the manifest technical skill with which it follows Mozart's lead, offers some charming vignettes. The second stanza begins

> Show me again the day
> When from the sandy bay
> We looked together upon the pestered sea! –

where the strikingly apt 'pestered' replaced the MS 'capricious' which had in turn replaced 'burnished', a word nine poets out of ten would have been happy to leave! But the music's sustained phrasing prompted Hardy to a long, elaborately alliterated, fourth line in each stanza. Here he ends

> Yea to such surging, swaying, sighing, swelling, shrinking
> Love lures life on.

I confess to an affectionate regard for this poem because, like Hardy's, my feelings for Mozart are only just 'this side idolatry'. But, gallant though the attempt is, I do not think the two arts quite cohere. The poem Hardy placed next to it, *In the Seventies* (389/D/*), is again about the 'vision' . . . 'delicate as lamp-worm's lucency', which Hardy then held, as he says. 'In my breast//Penned tight.' This, too, has its moments but it is a trifle too repetitive; the notion is stretched thinly over four verses. It lacks that contact with the specific which is almost always a vital ingredient in Hardy's success, and nowhere more so than in the love poetry.

This is borne out by several poems in this grouping; most notably by the superb retrospect of *Under the Waterfall* (276/C/ D/W/*), which is later analysed in full. But often hardly more than a breath of actuality is enough. Thus Hardy's imagination fastened on what must have been little more than a guess that *The Young Churchwarden* (386/W/*) who gave its title to a poem (subscribed in the MS 'At an Evening Service, August 14th 1870) had cherished an unavailing fondness for Emma. It gave him an entry into the young man's mind, to feel and enable us to feel, what he felt

> When he lit the candles there,
> And the light fell on his hand,
> And it trembled . . .

Hardy pities his 'rival's' 'vanquished air' as he notes that he has 'begun to understand', and how sharply that moment of quiet suffering comes back to us across the years. But the second stanza shifts its stance to a subdued irony, for later, 'When Love's viol was unstrung' – when illusion has given way to reality – Hardy could have wished their roles reversed, that 'the hand that shook//Had been mine that shared her book' – Emma's *Service Book* that is. But ultimately there are no winners or losers in Love;

> Now her dust lies listless there,
> His afar from tending hand,
> What avails the victory scanned?

It is a grimly perceptive poem. *The Face at the Casement* (258/*) treats a similar situation in the guise of a fictitious narrative. But the setting suggests it is based upon Hardy's memory of a former suitor of Emma's who was dying. The incident on which the poem hangs may well be invented; the narrator and his fiancée visit 'St Clether' 'to enquire//If but to cheer him' about the housebound young man's health. He glimpses 'as we drove away' a 'white face' at an upstairs 'lattice' and instantly 'deigned a deed of hell', embracing his fiancée, thus cruelly asserting his triumph. The 'pale face vanished quick//As if blasted', but the pitiless gesture carries its own curse, the narrator cannot escape the endless 'prick' of 'shame and self-abasement' for 'That stab of Love's fierce fashion'. The poem ends, most poignantly, with a blend of the folk-song 'O Waly. Waly' and the Bible's Song of Songs,

> Love is long-suffering, brave,
> Sweet, prompt precious as a jewel;
> But jealousy is cruel,
> Cruel as the grave!

What might at first seem a slight, ballad-like anecdote has become a penetrating insight into the subtle cruelties that love can give rise to, the close affinity between love and hate.

Two juxtaposed poems about the same incident, both good in themselves, also introduce a theme of the first importance in some of the greatest lyrics of *Poems of 1912–13*: the 'immutable past' one might call it. They are *The Figure in the Scene* (416/D/W/*) and *Why Did I Sketch?* (417/*) and both refer to an excursion to Beeny Cliff on 22 August 1870. The first poem tells us that Hardy 'had stood back that I might pencil it' [i.e. the cliff] while Emma had chosen to 'sit amid the scene' when suddenly 'it gloomed and rained'. But Hardy completed his sketch despite the 'drifting wet' so that it had all 'the blots engrained.' It is a moving experience to see what T. S. Eliot would have termed the 'objective correlative' of this poem in the Dorchester Museum. Probably Hardy turned up the sketch when going through other mementoes of his days in Lyonnesse, perhaps with the 'old notes' on which he tells us he based these poems, albeit both in their present form are plainly subsequent to Emma's death. The loving exactitude with which Hardy conjures up that fragment from the past, and the intensity with which he endows what was evidently then a negligible occurrence with portentousness are both notable; rather more so in *The Figure in the Scene*. *Why Did I Sketch?* argues indeed that it would have been better to 'Let no soft curves intrude' but 'Show the escarpments stark and stiff//As in utter solitude;//So shall you half forget.' The second stanza of the first poem however, after perfectly capturing the hazy, one might say ghostly, quality of Emma 'alone//Seated amid the gauze//Of moisture, hooded, . . . ' rises in its last four magniloquent lines to a remarkable assertion,

> Yet her rainy form is the Genius still of the spot,
>   Immutable, yea
> Though the place now knows her no more and has known
>   her not
>   Ever since that day.

While Hardy survives to remember it – in spite of the monosyl-labic hammer-blows of the penultimate line – that remains true; when he is dead his words – this poem – will continue to validate that 'Immutable, yea'. And how crucial a single word may be is demonstrated by the adjective 'immutable', which now seems such an inevitable choice. For Hardy went from the innocuous 'As pictured' to 'There permanent' with its over--physical connotations, and to 'Inseparable', which is inexact, before he hit on the one word which combines all those shades of meaning and adds the sense of inviolable, and indestructible, as well.

   The prevailing temper of these poems, while not unsha-dowed, is usually happy enough, a point further borne out by some others like *Green Slates* (678/W/*) and *The West of Wessex Girl* (526/W). But Hardy learned, as we all do, that life rarely lives up to our exotic expectations. Hindsight enabled him to read a premonitory shadow into some occurrences, one of which provided the catalyst for *Where Three Roads Joined* (544/*) which the MS locates as 'Near Tresparrett Posts', roughly equidistant from St Juliot and Beeny Cliff. Here Hardy must have walked to a prearranged meeting with Emma, no doubt *en route* to Beeny and

> Where three roads joined it was green and fair,
> And over a gate was the sun-glazed sea,
> And life laughed sweet when I halted there;
> Yet there I never again would be.

The simple charm and clarity of the opening vista is deceptive, the place is at once seen 'now' as 'brooding' and 'spectre-ridden', redolent of despair. Hardy, who as a rule avoids the so-called 'pathetic fallacy', here allows the 'spot', metaphorically at least, to 'grieve' over the pair' who 'in bliss for a spell',

> Not far from thence, should have let it roll
> Away from them down a plumbless well.

The word 'spell' is effectively ambiguous here; the surface meaning of 'brief space' does not conceal the 'magical' implications; and the image of 'bliss' as something tangible that can 'roll away' perhaps links it with the 'wormwood cup' of the next stanza, which the 'ghosts' are doomed to drink from. It is certainly a subdued reference to the enchanted cup which brought both 'bale and bliss' to Tristram and Iseult in the Arthurian romance, a love potion that destroyed them both. (Hardy retells the story in his verse play *The Queen of Cornwall*.) 'Wormwood' may literally be both an intoxicating stimulant and intolerably bitter in its aftertaste. The implication is that Hardy and Emma drank, figuratively, from the fateful cup (in the Tristram story it was meant for someone else), giving up their individuality 'when their sky was clear' in exchange for an ill-fated passion. The illusion now dispersed by time and death, Hardy envisages the same spot in the last stanza, where, with minute verbal changes, he contrives to make it as bleak as it was formerly beautiful, the last line tailing away into a flat despondency, 'It is where I never again would be.' This is a subtle exploration of the division between heart and mind which affects all these poems about Emma. Hardy longs passionately to reach back across the gulf of time to the 'green and fair' landscape, the 'sun-glazed sea', but he cannot discard his awareness of what the intervening years had brought; like a dark cloud they shadow the summery prospect and the 'branch-ways' – the 'three roads' perhaps symbolise those 'not taken' – become 'rutted and bare', impassable and without their former beauty. This is an under-rated poem, unlike *Near Lanivet* (366/C/D/W/H/*), which it resembles closely in mood, and which I shall analyse shortly. It remains only to say that several of the *Poems of 1912–13*, to be discussed in the next section, share both themes and settings with the Lyonnesse

poems just considered and should always be considered alongside them.

Analyses

At the Word Farewell (360/C/D/W/H/*)

> She looked like a bird from a cloud
>   On the clammy lawn,
> Moving alone, bare-browed
>   In the dim of dawn.
> The candles alight in the room
>   For my parting meal
> Made all things withoutdoors loom
>   Strange, ghostly, unreal.
>
> The hour itself was a ghost,
>   And it seemed to me then
> As of chances the chance furthermost
>   I should see her again.
> I beheld not where all was so fleet
>   That a Plan of the past
> Which had ruled us from birthtime to meet
>   Was in working at last:
>
> No prelude did I there perceive
>   To a drama at all,
> Or foreshadow what fortune might weave
>   From beginnings so small;
> But I rose as if quicked by a spur
>   I was bound to obey,
> And stepped through the casement to her
>   Still alone in the gray.
>
> 'I am leaving you . . . Farewell!' I said,
>   As I followed her on
> By an alley bare boughs overspread;
>   'I soon must be gone!'
> Even then the scale might have been turned
>   Against love by a feather,
> – But crimson one cheek of hers burned
>   When we came in together.

If the *bare boughs* of stanza 4 are anything to go by this delightful poem is set in the Rectory garden at St Juliot, on 11 March 1870. *The Life* quotes Hardy's journal for the day, 'Dawn. Adieu. E. L. G. has struck a light six times in her anxiety to call the servants early enough for me.' and Hardy told Mrs Henniker in 1918 that this poem was among those of his he 'liked best' because (like *Why Did I Sketch?* and *Near Lanivet*) it was 'literally true.' He also employed the incident in *A Pair of Blue Eyes*, though without the implied kiss. What one might call the narrative element therefore scarcely needs comment. The mood of the poem is much more complex, far removed from mere sentimental reminiscence. The verse-form is simple enough, indeed the alternately rhymed eight-line stanzas could just as well be set out in four lines verses. The movement is light, but sometimes hesitant, suggesting tension and anxiety. Initially, Hardy is concerned to summon up the charged, nervous anticipation generated by feelings so far unexpressed overtly – Hardy and Emma had only met four days before. This he does by creating the strange, otherwordly quality of the *dim of dawn* by a series of images, incidentally emphasising the effect by altering his MS 'sloping' lawn to *clammy*. Similarly the vision of Emma as *a bird from a cloud* brings her to mind as not only delicate and graceful but also remote and perhaps inaccessible. The second stanza moves us further into the *strange, ghostly, unreal* atmosphere which ends the first and adds the dimension of inevitability; a *Plan of the past* which, however fanciful it may seem in the cold light of reason, is such a potent ingredient in romance. Then, by the neat inversion which drives home *of chances the chance furthermost*, and the phrase *all was so fleet*, the fragile thread on which the future hangs is introduced. The tension is suspended by the musing first quatrain of stanza 4, insisting on Hardy's unawareness of the moment as critical, so that the next four lines come as a surprise, with their sudden increase in pace, their sharply sensual image of the *spur*. Action has replaced the hazy inertia and the open garden the *ghost house*. The last stanza imparts, with admirable delicacy and sensitivity, both love's extreme fragility, like a *feather* in the *scale*, and, with a sudden, brilliant turn of phrase, its fiery impulsiveness. For the penultimate line *But crimson one cheek of hers burned*, is the solitary moment of colour and warmth in a poem otherwise uniformly *gray, clammy* and cold. It is technical *tour de force* quietly complemented by the last line, so full of implication.

The Frozen Greenhouse (706/G/W/*)

'There was a frost
Last night!' she said,
'And the stove was forgot
When we went to bed,
And the greenhouse plants
Are frozen dead!'

By the breakfast blaze
Blank-faced spoke she,
Her scared young look
Seeming to be the very symbol
Of tragedy.

The frost is fiercer
Than then to-day,
As I pass the place
Of her once dismay,
But the greenhouse stands
Warm, tight, and gay,

While she who grieved
At the sad lot
Of her pretty plants –
Cold, iced, forgot –
Herself is colder,
And knows it not.

Hardy's addition of the words 'St. Juliot' makes it virtually certain that this poem derives from his revisitation, in January 1913, of the scenes he associated with his courtship of Emma in 1870. With no firm evidence of another visit at a time when frost *might* have occurred we must assume that the original event took place on Hardy's first visit, or perhaps early 1873.

The verse-form with its exceptionally short lines and minimal rhymes is a very simple-seeming one indeed, perhaps ultimately deriving from Hardy's admiration for Sir Thomas Wyatt, though not identical with any of his. But it is much more demanding than a superficial glance suggests; if the metre were adhered to strictly as in lines 1 and 2, with four equal trochaic beats to each line, it would soon become over-emphatic and monotonous. As it is, Hardy loosens and frees it by inserting disyllabic words such as *forgot*, *breakfast* and *pretty*, avoiding any risk of metronomic uniformity. The mood displays a savage contrast between the first and second halves of the poem; it is a particularly clear example of Hynes's 'antinomian' idea; life here repeats its musical pattern but with a cruelly discordant change of key.

Hardy, in the first stanza catches, with unerring authenticity, the child-like quality of Emma's speech. It is a touching vignette and in the next stanza he seems to be smiling gently at her naive over-reaction, though there is a subdued irony in Emma's *young look* as a *symbol of tragedy*. The third stanza presents compactly, almost curtly, the re-enactment forty years later, with the *fiercer frost* – as always in Hardy – a foreboding symbol, and the epithets *warm, tight and gay*, though perfectly apt for the flower-filled greenhouse, also suggesting a human presence.

This prepares us for the excoriating brevity of the last stanza, which is, like all the rest, a single, self-contained sentence, pure statement, not so much as implying Hardy's sorrow. The words too are of the plainest kind, yet chosen with a profound sense of their connotations, their undertones. How tellingly the adjectives *Cold, iced, forgot* apply both backwards to the plants in the past and forwards to the planter in the present. And nothing could be more desolate than the last lines: their raw, harsh plangency recalling Lear's hopeless grief over the dead Cordelia: 'She'll come no more. Never, never, never'.

Near Lanivet, 1872 (366/C/D/W/H/*)

There was a stunted handpost just on the crest,
  Only a few feet high:
She was tired, and we stopped in the twilight-time for her
    rest,
  At the crossways close thereby.

She leant back, being so weary, against its stem,
  And laid her arms on its own,
Each open palm stretched out to each end of them,
  Her sad face sideways thrown.

Her white-clothed form at this dim-lit cease of day
  Made her look as one crucified
In my gaze at her from the midst of the dusty way,
  And hurriedly 'Don't,' I cried.

I do not think she heard. Loosing thence she said,
  As she stepped forth ready to go,
'I am rested now. – Something strange came into my head;
  I wish I had not leant so!'

And wordless we moved onward down from the hill
  In the west cloud's murked obscure,
And looking back we could see the handpost still
  In the solitude of the moor.

'It struck her too,' I thought, for as if afraid
  She heavily breathed as we trailed;
Till she said, 'I did not think how 'twould look in the shade,
  When I leant there like one nailed.'

I, lightly: 'There's nothing in it. For *you*, anyhow!'
  – 'O I know there is not,' said she . . .
'Yet I wonder . . . If no one is bodily crucified now,
  In spirit one may be!'

And we dragged on and on, while we seemed to see
  In the running of Time's far glass
Her crucified, as she had wondered if she might be
  Some day. – Alas, alas!

This poem has been the subject of much discussion, most of it
biographical. It is another of those Hardy said were 'literally
true' and it, too, the MS tells us is 'From an old note.' It certainly
casts some doubts upon *The Life's* sanguine account of Hardy's
courtship as proceeding 'without a hitch . . . with encourage-
ment from all parties.' The date, 1872, suggests that it may, if it
was drafted at the time, derive some of its premonitory gloom
from Hardy's bitter resentment, which is obliquely touched on

in *I Rose and Went to Routor* (468), at his treatment by Emma's father, an arrant snob. He once, according to Florence Hardy, actually addressed his would-be son-in-law as 'a low-born churl' in a letter, during 1872. But it is probable that most of the poem we have was written when the marriage had ended and the incident, perhaps recalled by the 'old note', re-assumed a prophetic significance.

The narrative strand is much more prominent here than it is in most of the Lyonnesse poems, and this insistence on detail is perhaps overdone. The dialogue is also a little forced in places. Something may *be* authentic and yet not appear so, but this is the reverse side of Hardy's insistence on 'literal truth'; art may sometimes be sacrificed to authenticity.

So much conceded, this remains a remarkable poem, not least because it is so 'modern' in its sensibility, so un-Victorian in both form and content. For though the stanzas do use rhyme and the second and fourth lines are fairly, if not completely, regular, the first and third are no more than tenuously so. Hardy seems to be experimenting with a free stress-pattern which enables him to play very fast and loose with the metrical beat. Not only do the long, slow, broken-up lines contrast with the short and generally more concentrated ones which succeed them, they also impose a mood of exhaustion and enervation, not merely physical, upon the whole poem, as if love itself were fatigued, like the lovers. The stress-pattern can also, as in line 7, break up the movement of the poem, here throwing a strong emphasis on *each open palm stretched out*, and so hinting at the crucifixion motif of the next stanza. There is an all-pervading, weird, dreamlike quality about the whole incident which is emphasised by the trance-like rhythms. And this shadowy unreality is made even more evident in the diction; repeated words and phrases like *twilight-time, dim-lit, murked obscure, solitude* and *shade* add their cumulative weight of inference to the atmosphere. All the glimmering colour which elsewhere marks the Lyonnesse poems is absent from this dim, *dusty* world. Similarly the lovers' mood is conveyed in such heavily suggestive terms as *tired, weary, sad, strange, dragged* and *trailed on and on*. The night which is encompassing them is a more than physical darkness.

It all adds up to an overwhelming impression of a love that has lost its vital impetus; as the light goes out of the day we are reminded how, at the original crucifixion, 'darkness covered the whole earth', and foresee, in a scene described only by the loaded word *dusty*, an augury of the drab, defeated future the whole poem leans towards. One brilliant phrase – *In the running of Time's far glass* – sums it all up; as sand, in the hour-glass which Hardy envisages future Time holding up runs out, so what their dark 'moment of vision' foretold will be re-enacted. And the ending, with its full stop and pause after *Some day*, brings us suddenly face to face with Hardy, at 73, unable to say more of the intervening half-century than the helpless '*Alas, Alas!*'

Under the Waterfall (276/C/D/W/*)

'Whenever I plunge my arm, like this,
In a basin of water, I never miss
The sweet sharp sense of a fugitive day
Fetched back from its thickening shroud of gray,
   Hence the only prime
   And real love-rhyme
   That I know by heart
   And that leaves no smart,
Is the purl of a little valley fall
About three spans wide and two spans tall
Over a table of solid rock,
And into a scoop of the self-same block;
The purl of a runlet that never ceases
In stir of kingdoms, in wars, in peaces;
With a hollow boiling voice it speaks
And has spoken since hills were turfless peaks.'

'And why gives this the only prime
Idea to you of a real love-rhyme?
And why does plunging your arm in a bowl
Full of spring water, bring throbs to your soul?'

'Well, under the fall, in a crease of the stone,
Though where precisely none ever has known,

Jammed darkly, nothing to show how prized,
And by now with its smoothness opalized,
   Is a drinking-glass:
   For, down that pass
   My lover and I
   Walked under a sky
Of blue with a leaf-wove awning of green,
In the burn of August, to paint the scene,
And we placed our basket of fruit and wine
By the runlet's rim, where we sat to dine;
And when we had drunk from the glass together,
Arched by the oak-copse from the weather,
I held the vessel to rinse in the fall,
Where it slipped, and sank, and was past recall,
Though we stooped and plumbed the little abyss
With long bared arms. There the glass still is.
And, as said, if I thrust my arm below
Cold water in basin or bowl, a throe
From the past awakens a sense of that time,
And the glass we used, and the cascade's rhyme.
The basin seems the pool, and its edge
The hard smooth face of the brook-side ledge,
And the leafy pattern of china-ware
The hanging plants that were bathing there.

'By night, by day, when it shines or lours,
There lies intact that chalice of ours,
And its presence adds to the rhyme of love
Persistently sung by the fall above.
No lip has touched it since his and mine
In turns therefrom sipped lovers' wine.'

Of all those poems which Hardy did not include with *Poems of 1912–13* the palm must be awarded to *Under the Waterfall*, which he placed immediately before them in his final arrangement. It derives directly, as he acknowledged himself, from an episode in Emma's *Some Recollections*, where he read of 'a sparkling little brook . . . into which we once lost a tiny picnic tumbler, and there it is to this day no doubt between two small boulders.' Hardy's own pencil sketch of her 'Searching for the

Glass', dated 19 August 1870, survives, and there is something curiously moving in the contrast between the rather clumsy drawing, precise but amateurish, and the commanding sweep of this great poem.

The form he chose is common in English verse, though less so with Hardy. The rhymed couplets are written in iambic metre, with four feet to a line making them, technically, tetrameters. Here, in what is, of course, a monologue, Hardy varies the stress-pattern with consummate skill to give a very close approximation to actual speech rhythms, well illustrated by lines 21–24. (What look like inserted quatrains (lines 5–8 and 25–28) are really the standard tetrameters halved, with additional rhymes, so as to mark transitions.)

At first reading the predominant impression is pictorial, and we do indeed have here some of Hardy's most dazzling evocations of the Cornish landscape in high summer, in lines 9–13 and 29–34 especially. The opening is notable for its swift immediacy, *Whenever I plunge my arm, like this,//In a basin of water* . . . but this 'attack' is not sustained. It is displaced by a mood of dreamy, reminiscent happiness, which remains the dominant note throughout, in spite of the faint shadow cast by the ambiguous phrase *thickening shroud of gray*, symbolising the intervening years. Although we have to wait till the penultimate line to be certain, Hardy gives the whole poem to Emma, no doubt because of its origin in her work. (The interlocutor – whose four lines are the thinnest in the poem – we could happily dispense with altogether!). This decision naturally affected the tone, and perhaps to some extent the diction of the poem. There is often an innocent gaiety about it which is entirely appropriate to what we know of Emma at the time. Indeed, *Some Recollections* at this juncture, speaks of 'dawdling, enjoyable, slow' excursions, 'sketching and talking of books [along] the beautiful Valency valley,' giving off something of the same timelessness and peace which the poem itself exudes so markedly. Though it is no mere pastoral idyll, we are not to be jolted back into a raw awareness of loss and loneliness as so frequently happens in the *Poems of 1912–13*. It may be that this is why Hardy kept this poem apart. It is a celebration rather than an elegy, something of an answer to his own request, in *Lines to a Movement in Mozart's E-Flat Symphony* (388) 'Show me again the hour'. It shares, with John Donne's famous *The Ecstasy* a semi-mystical conviction that 'Lovers' hours be full eternity.'

Nevertheless, Hardy's truthfulness will not permit him to manipulate the facts, nor is the day's pervading *sweet, sharp sense*, conveyed in that exquisitely simple narrative beginning *My lover and I///Walked under a sky*, wholly unqualified. First is the word *fugitive*, an epithet of genius. For though at one level of meaning it is undeniable that the day was 'ephemeral' and 'fleeting' as the dictionary has it, yet in another and more crucial sense the day has 'escaped', has run free from the bondage of Time; so long as it is held fast in memory it will not fade. We also have *the purl of a runlet that never ceases* as a symbol of love made manifest. The *turfless peaks* may remind the lovers 'How small a part of time they share', for Hardy was the first English poet to convey the immensity of geological time, as the famous cliff scene in *A Pair of Blue Eyes* (Chapter XXI) demonstrates, but the *stir of kingdoms, of wars and peaces* cannot silence the voice of the stream.

Finally there is the symbol of the *glass*, which initially seems to stand for love lost, for an irrecoverable past, *jammed darkly, opalised* and *past recall* as it is. The phrase *little abyss* perhaps even hints at Shakespeare's 'dark backward and abysm of Time'. But after the flat, apparently conclusive, admission, *'There the glass still is'*, comes a remarkable transmutation. We return to the beginning, a *throe from the past* dissolves the barrier between it and the present, the *basin seems the pool* and the commonplace 'picnic tumbler' is transformed into a *chalice*, a magical cup preserved and preserving inviolate the moment in time when – the phrase is an echo of Donne – it held *'lovers' wine'*. As Dylan Thomas, another admirer of Hardy, wrote, 'Though lovers be lost, love shall not.'

POEMS OF 1912–13

Though he often put quotations at the head of chapters in his novels, Hardy was not much given to using epigraphs in his verse. The Virgilian phrase *Veteris vestigiae flammae* which precedes *Poems of 1912–13*, and may be freely translated as 'Last

flickerings from a dying fire', is an exception and, with characteristic modesty, perhaps not untouched by a gentle irony, it
gives the reader no indication whatever of the passionate
intensity with which these elegiac love-poems are ablaze. In the
fine sonnet, *Thoughts From Sophocles* (924) Hardy, paraphrasing
his favourite Greek dramatist, wrote,

> Gaunt age is as some grey upstanding beak
> Chafed by the billows of a northern shore
> And facing friendless cold calamity . . .
> Where sunshine bird and bloom frequent no more.

It is as if, from some such grim mountain as this, a long
dammed-up spring were to burst out, full of force and beauty,
to turn the parched and rocky hillside green again.

He made a lonely pilgrimage to St Juliot on 6 March 1913,
'almost to a day, forty-three years after his first journey,' as he
records in *The Life* and some of these poems derive directly
from that enkindling experience. Others grew out of his reading, only after her death, of Emma' artless record in *Some
Reminiscences*, of their courtship. He looked at the sketches they
had each made at that time. I think he also re-read the opening
chapters of *A Pair of Blue Eyes*, and then he must have
meditated on the slow widening of that spiritual gulf which
time, radical differences of taste, temperament and belief,
Emma's endemic snobbery and increasingly neurotic behaviour, with his own growing absorption in his work, had
combined to open up between them until it became unbridgeable. So, in essence, these poems are the record of his haunting
by two ghosts, one the spectre of remorse now made futile by
death, the other the phantom of lost love. Out of this complex of
grief and regret, past happiness recalled and old haunts revisited, out of his own magical faculty for re-entering the past as
if it were the present, he created a series of poems which
express, better than any others I have read, both the searing
anguish of loss and the sudden ecstasy of recapturing joy long
gone out of mind. Hardy was 72; the poems are the product, one
might say the apotheosis, of half a century's unremitting toil at
his chosen art. Everyone who attempts to write about them
must share Douglas Brown's conviction that this is 'Hardy's

deepest theme . . . speaking with a quiet voice in the tradition of our poetry but leaving a permanent accent upon its language'. Hardy's only recorded comment upon them was made in conversation with his friend A. C. Benson to whom he said 'The verses came; it was quite natural. One looked back through the years and saw some pictures; a loss like that makes one's old brain vocal.'

Something must be said about the arrangement since it was plainly quite deliberate. As it first appeared in *Satires of Circumstance* (1914) the sequence comprised only seventeen poems (CP 277–294 inclusive). After 1919 three more were added (CP 295–297) and it is debatable whether this decision was altogether wise; I certainly feel that *The Phantom Horsewoman* (294/C/D/W/*) makes a more resonant and appropriate conclusion, while of the three additions *The Spell of the Rose* (295/C/W/*) and *St. Launce's Revisited* (296/C/*) – which were formerly placed *before* the series and immediately after *Under the Waterfall* – are not quite in the first class as poetry, and *Where the Picnic Was* (297/C/D/W/H/*) though very good, has a more tenuous link with the others, and, unless it is realised that it does *not* refer to Cornwall in the 1870s, can be confusing. In addition there are at least a dozen more poems which, from the evidence of their dates and subjects, have a good claim to be considered alongside the series too. However, with one or two possible exceptions, it is evident that Hardy was right to judge them somewhat inferior in quality and defer their piecemeal publication until later. I shall look at a few of these at the end of this section.

With the *Poems of 1912–13* the arrangement matters, since the order in which they stand was clearly the product of deliberate thought. There is no need to mount elaborate theories about the minutiae of Hardy's placings; the essential point is that they derive from a natural progression in his mind modified by the sequence of events which he drew on for inspiration. He starts with Emma's death in *The Going* (277/ALL/H/*) which amounts to an overture for the whole sequence, announcing, verse by verse, those themes he was subsequently to elaborate or vary. Thus, the second verse shows us Emma at Max Gate and the third shifts to a more distant retrospect of St Juliot, the fourth glances at the unhappiness of their later married life, and the last ends with Hardy's acceptance of his own unavailing grief and imminent mortality. The movement within this poem, like that of several others, is cyclic; Hardy escapes in imagination from the grim reality of Emma's death only to be driven back upon himself and his bereft condition before the end; a cycle which the entire series may be seen as repeating. The first ten poems are all located in and around Hardy's home, in the fairly recent past. All are primarily concerned with aspects of Emma's nature: she speaks in three of them and one is given over entirely to her 'voice' – *The Haunter* (284/ALL/*). Only two glimpses of Cornwall occur, one fleeting but crucial in *The Voice* (285/ALL/H/*) the other as part of a contrast between the 'there' of 1870 and the 'here' of 1912. *A Dream or No* (288/C/D/W/*) is evidently a transitional poem, possibly designed as such (it is not one of the best). It explores Hardy's reasons for his return to a St Juliot which, as he admits, may no longer 'exist'.

The ensuing six poems (289–94) are all located in Cornwall; five certainly and one very probably date from 1913 (most of the earlier ones are from 1912), and in all of them Hardy himself and his reactions to his return tend to loom larger than in the preceding group, though not by any means to the exclusion of Emma whose presence is invariably felt. Individually and as a group they all return to the dark lodestone of Emma's death, and the last, *The Phantom Horsewoman* (294/C/D/W/H/*), leaves the reader with Hardy frail, bereft and alone as he was at the outset. The three supplementary poems appear to me in the nature of an interesting postscript but not an integral part of the structure, which, though far from a rigid framework, does contribute significantly to the impact of the series on the reader, who, if at all possible, should read them all, in sequence, at a sitting. For this reason, instead of grouping my close analyses at the end of this section, I shall intersperse them in the general commentary.

The Going (277/ALL/H/*)

This is the first and only poem to treat circumstantially of Emma's sudden and unexpected death, though it does not dwell on it. After the first stanza it moves out and away in space and time, returning only at the end to the inescapable fact. The seven-line stanzas with their unusual rhyme-scheme A/B/A/B/ CC/B and feminine rhymes in the truncated couplet seem to be of Hardy's own invention, and this is the moment to point out the extraordinary technical virtuosity of the *Poems of 1912–13* as a whole. No two use identical verse-forms and all display a wealth of metrical resource and verse-patterning.

Because *The Going* addresses Emma's 'spirit' directly (like five others of the series) the tone is conversational in the opening four lines, the manner light, almost casual. *You would close your term up here* is not the language of bereavement, but there is a dramatic and harrowing change of tone in the final three lines, made even more poignant by the airy rhymes *follow/swallow*. This emotional transmutation, a light touch masking deeper feeling until the fourth line triggers realisation and the rawness of the wound is exposed, is repeated in stanzas 3 and 4.

There are many small verbal felicities in all these poems which invite comment; I can only select a few. Thus, in stanza 2, the tenderness implicit in Hardy's use of *lip* as a verb in the second line is the result of a typically exacting revision from MS 'give'. How telling too is his use of *harden* of the morning. Daylight is not ordinarily seen as harsh and cruel; here, perhaps, taken with *Unmoved, unknowing*, it may hint at Hardy's own hardness towards Emma: self-reproach is certainly implied in the stanza. In stanza 3 *a breath*, which suggests surprise as well as brevity, replaced MS 'an instant', and the line also introduces the 'haunting' theme which is to recur frequently. The sullen weight of the four descriptive words in the couplet is also striking, *yawning* is especially apt with its double sense of 'gaping' and 'wearying'.

In stanza 4 Hardy moves further off into the distant past with an evocation of Lyonnesse like a brilliantly coloured miniature. But it is an insecure, momentary escape, instantly offset by stanza 5 with its sombre reminders that regret, remorse and even retrospective tenderness are all alike useless. The phrase 'That time's renewal' – something of a leitmotif for the series – and the extreme fragility of love implied in *days long dead and vanishing*, are themes we shall meet again.

As the poem progresses we see Hardy seeking, as we all do, to sublimate his loss, to evade what reminds him of it by speculating on what might have been. But his heart was at odds with his head over this: truth is not compatible with self-deception. It is, of course, this opposition – which we all acknowledge in ourselves – that makes these poems so heart-rending. And so in the last stanza, unwillingly, draggingly and painfully, he contemplates the fact of death once more, at first in broken, groping, all but incoherent phrases so authentic that we are surprised to see them fit so easily into the verse-framework. There follows the appalling image of himself as an inverted corpse, *held on end* like a marionette perhaps or possibly the Hanged Man (who is depicted in the Tarot Pack as suspended by his ankle). But this mood of self-pity, which is rare in these poems, is subsumed in a final tender return to Emma, her *swift fleeing* echoing the *swallow* metaphor in stanza 1, and a muted, resigned close which finally answers the question posed at the outset, absolving Emma from blame, asserting his renewed awareness of her centrality to his life now it is too late to matter. Only a great poet could have made poetry out of the fumbling speech of a man whom grief has stripped naked of pretence.

The next poem, *Your Last Drive* (278/C/D/W/*) follows the structural pattern of the first: an escape from the imprisonment of grief into a false dawn of remembered happiness, only to relapse into an even deeper trough of desolation. The context is anecdotal; only eight days before her death Emma had been driven 'to pay a visit six miles off' according to *The Life* and returned, passing Stinsford Churchyard where she was to lie, after dark. The narrative is counterpointed with continual reminders of Emma's death, but Emma's and Hardy's unaware-ness of its approach is also stressed and the tone is relatively cool and detached until what begins with a purely suppositious remark *I go hence soon*, turns quite unexpectedly into a dialogue with Hardy's 'dear ghost'. Emma speaks without resentment, her dispassionate assessment of their situation is all the more poignant as it points up *know*, *care*, *heed* and *need* only to show how abortive such emotions have become. Hardy is, of course, arguing with himself and he now tries, with tender delicacy, to set aside what he knows the silent dead would say if she could, preferring to trust in feeling rather than calculation. The two lines beginning *Dear ghost* which encapsulate this thought include one of his most perceptive strokes of revision; for the second as first printed ran, much more ostentatiously, 'Me one

whom consequence influenced much?' But even as he is drawn
into this 'argument', defying, for a moment, both time and
intellectual conviction, he accepts that it is all illusion. Few lines
are bleaker than the last two with their remorseless iteration.
But their truthfulness is warranty for Hardy's despair. Next
comes *The Walk* (279/ALL/*) which is succinct, even clipped, in
its reminiscence of walks to Culliford Hill. But the last two lines
in answer to the question 'What difference then?' in reference
to Emma's absence, are a marvel of compressed suggestiveness,

> Only that underlying sense
> Of the look of a room on returning thence.

More simple, more lyrical in expression, and perhaps the
tenderest of all the series is *Rain on a Grave* (280/ALL/*). It first
conjures up the grave in Stinsford Churchyard during a downpour, which prompts Hardy to recall Emma as 'One who to
shelter//Her delicate head//Would quicken and quicken//Each
tentative tread'. But that was in summertime, no doubt in
Cornwall; this was written on 30 January 1913 and neither love
nor memory can shield her from the elements, 'Clouds spout
upon her//Their waters amain//In ruthless disdain.' These are
cold, hard words, suggesting, like 'arrows of rain' a wintry
malevolence and Hardy, recalling how he and Emma would
walk in the churchyard when 'evening was clear//At the prime
of the year' feels he would be content to be 'folded
away . . . together' with Emma, an admission of weariness as
well as grief. Yet the poem ends in gentle resignation and
affectionate recall. Life continues, the spring will come and

> Soon will be growing
> Green blades from her mound,
> And daisies be showing
> Like stars on the ground,
> Till she form part of them –
> Ay – the sweet heart of them,
> Loved beyond measure
> With child's pleasure
> All her life's round.

That something of the clarity and purity of a hymn by Isaac Watts and is obviously among those poems Hardy was referring to in a letter he sent, with a copy of *Satires of Circumstance*, to Emma's cousin Kate. In it he says she will 'perceive some of [Emma's] characteristics in the poems about her', mentioning her 'childlike and trusting [nature] formerly'. Emma's own *Some Recollections* on its first page speaks of her 'surprise and joy' being 'very great when I saw a whole field of [daisies]' at the age of three. A group of four poems (280–83 and, with a difference, 284) all celebrate, at the same time as they mourn its loss, Emma's essential simplicity of response; her one-time openness to experience which had so captivated Hardy when, for example, with quick sympathy and a touching faith in his talents, she had urged him to go on with his writing as a career, and had made the fair copy of a whole novel to help him.

The shadow of those years when 'wasted were two souls in their prime' as the poem *We Sat At the Window* (355/ALL/*) bleakly puts it, does not fall upon *I Found Her Out There* (281/ALL/H/*) nor do Hardy's own feelings of regret intrude except in the gentlest of hints, where he acknowledges that Emma might have preferred burial where 'she once domiciled'. As mentioned in Chapter 3 this poem is notable for its purity and plainness of diction, and this is surely meant to mirror those qualities in Emma herself. The theme could hardly be less elaborate, the extent to which Hardy's diction is confined to words of the most everyday kind is remarkable, only *loamy* and *thought-bound*, *salt-edged* and *domiciled* show his hand. Yet he manages the strong rhythms, the marked alliteration, with an ease Tennyson would have applauded, in, for example the fourth verse,

> And would sigh at the tale
> Of sunk Lyonnesse,
> As a wind-tugged tress
> Flapped her cheek like a flail;

Without Ceremony (282/C/D/W/*), shorter and slighter, nevertheless neatly catches Emma's volatility, in contrast with *Lament* (283/C/W/*) where her ingenuous delight in 'junketings' is set against her 'infinite rest'. Each verse, except the last, opens with a snapshot of Emma alive, 'How she would have loved//A party today!' – 'And she would have sought//With a child's eager glance//The shy snowdrops . . . '. The tone is almost chatty, the movement too is eager and light as thistledown. Every seventh line, however, stops short, three times with the harsh monosyllable 'But'; to be followed by a tolling, dirge-like refrain, using shorter more heavily stressed lines: 'She is shut, she is shut// From friendship's spell//In the jailing shell//Of her tiny cell.' and the last verse places Hardy alone amid 'These stale things' – the socialising which bored and still bores him but 'used so to joy her' – leaving him more darkly aware than ever that Emma is 'dead//To all done and said//In her yew-arched bed.' Memory opens the door, only for truth to 'shut' it again, the lilt of the opening lines arrested by the grim, tolling beat of the refrain, signed off by the unmistakably Hardeian touch of 'yew-arched bed.' It is intimate, almost private indeed, and reminds us, as many of the series do, the next in particular, of John Stuart Mill's remark that 'Eloquence is heard; poetry is overhead' which Arthur McDowall so appositely applied to Hardy's poetry.

In *The Haunter* (284/ALL/*) Emma, whose nature has been explored in several poems, appears as a revenant, as does the occupant of *The Unquiet Grave* and other ballads Hardy knew well. The metre of *The Unquiet Grave* is not dissimilar to that of *The Haunter*, nor is the idea, a topos of Hardy's verse, that the dead live on as long as we remember them. This is a more wistful and fanciful poem than the others, depicting an Emma returned after death to her youthful gentleness and gaiety, evoking in four lines their shared love of the lonelier parts of the country,

> Yes, I companion him to places
> Only dreamers know,
> Where the shy hares print long paces,
> Where the night-rooks go;

It would have been easy to stray into whimsy here but Hardy's sure touch preserves him, for the ghost must remain 'Always lacking the power to call to him,//Near as I reach thereto.' Had she spoken directly the fragile equipoise of the poem would have been lost; their shared inability to communicate remains, just as it was in Emma's lifetime, an ineluctable barrier to happiness, as it also is, for Hardy, to a full acceptance of Emma's death. For though his tribute here to his wife's inherent generosity of spirit is perfectly sincere it is no sort of expiation. We cannot atone to the dead; he is as dumb to tell her of *his* feelings as his 'faithful phantom' is to tell of hers. Finally, evidence of the mature judgement and impeccable taste that was applied to virtually every line of these poems is evident in the radical revision of the second quatrain of the final stanza. This, when first published, read,

> And if it be that at night I am stronger,
>   Little harm day can do:
> Please, then, keep him in gloom no longer,
>   Even ghosts tend thereto.

There is no need to detail how much weaker in sense, sicklier in sentiment and strained in diction those lines are than the text we have. The only aspect where one might wish he had had third thoughts too is the muffled 'thereto' which ends every stanza, a word whose legalistic overtones are perhaps too intrusive for it to occupy such a key position more than adequately.

The next poem is one of the four which are generally acknowledged to stand at the summit of Hardy's achievement, in this series and in his work as a whole.

The Voice (285/ALL/H/*)

This poem has frequently been singled out for praise even by those critics whose general assessment of Hardy's verse is lukewarm. F. R. Leavis, as early as 1932, very justly spoke of it as evoking 'utter loss . . . the poignancy of love and its helplessness, and the cruelty of time,' though we may view with more reserve his categorisation of it as primarily 'a triumph of character'. It is the last poem dated, in the MS, 1912 and – perhaps designedly – marks the precise mid-point of the seventeen which constituted the original series. Certainly it is to some degree a bridge between the winter landscape of Dorset *now*, and the other country of Lyonnesse, which we glimpse in stanza 3 by implication, as it were. But, more importantly, it unites three of the central motifs of the series; the themes of 'haunting', the 'inviolate past' and the 'false dawn' as I have called them, are here fused into a single, compressed statement, which Leavis's formula eloquently states.

The verse-form demands notice; though hardly Leavis's 'crude popular lilt' it has, even for Hardy, some startling features. It is not that the alternately rhymed four-line verses are unusual in themselves, but the extended first and third lines, with their rippling, wave-like flow pointed up by the rare triple-rhymes: *call to me//all to me*, certainly are. Bearing in mind the serious subject, they seem to set up an inappropriately casual, colloquial tone. And the abrupt, indeed curt, opening address *Woman much missed* is equally surprising, so different from the 'Dear ghost' of *Your Last Drive* (albeit a vast improvement on the MS 'O woman weird'!)

But the tone derives from Hardy's wish to shut out the *Voice* of the title; the hard carapace of resentment deriving from *when you had changed* is at first impervious to Emma's repeated call to remember. Yet in the second verse with its sudden, willed movement from verbal to visual imagery we have one of the most moving transitions anywhere in English poetry. To me at least, nothing so tears at the heart as that tiny, brilliant vignette from St Juliot, nor is there any revision, even by Hardy, more telling than his change from the MS's entirely innocuous 'hat and gown' to the seemingly inevitable *air-blue*. For, of course, it is not just the gown but the young Emma herself who is characterised by that *air-blue*: her (and Hardy's) carefree gaiety, their delight in the summery weather, a whole complex of warmth and happiness are all caught up in that one compound epithet.

Then, like a sullen physical ache returns the thought that this is all illusory, the vision fades, the landscape resumes its *listlessness* – a telling word – and the ghost dissolves to *wan wistlessness*. Now, for once comes a decidedly questionable emendation. Hardy only changed his original rhyme 'existlessness' to *wan wistlessness* in the second edition of his *Collected*

Poems. While I think *wan* enhances the mood, I have to agree
with Leavis that 'existlessness', though itself odd, is less eccen-
trically so than *wistlessness*. On the other hand *wistless* perhaps
suggests 'wistful' as well as 'unwitting', a subtle paradox.
Readers may like to decide for themselves, though Hardy's
intentions were clear.

Then we have what Leavis so aptly calls the 'exquisite
modulation' into the last stanza. This is the apotheosis of
desolation: the verse, like its author, now falters and slows. The
dead landscape and the heart's winter are together imparted by
the masterly third line, long-drawn-out and dying away into
despair. (Try substituting 'howling fierce' – my phrase not
Hardy's – for *oozing thin* to assess the significance of a single
phrase.) And Hardy's return upon himself at the end is all but
unbearable, for though his sharp sceptical intellect has rejected
the pleading, reproachful *voice* as only *the wind*, he cannot shut
his heart to *the woman calling*.

The next two poems are less personal and passionate. *His
Visitor* (286/C/W/*) tells impressionistically of Emma's ghostly
return from Mellstock to Max Gate 'in the gray, at the passing of
the mail-train' – a typical life-giving detail, and her uneasy
perception of the contrasts she now encounters in this dream-
visit, before her return to 'the roomy silence and the mute and
manifold//Souls of old.' Neither it, nor the next, *A Circular*
(287/C/W/*) is particularly memorable, and the first of the St
Juliot poems, *A Dream or No* (288/C/D/W) seems to me, for once,
to exhibit both technical and thematic weaknesses. The rhythm
often flags into a jog-trot, as in *And other than nigh things
uncaring to know*; the feminine rhymes are sometimes forced in
necromancy/fancy or *been here/sheen here* and sometimes feeble,
found her/around her, for example. As to the theme it is really
encapsulated in the last stanza, a small triumph of expression,
well worth waiting for even if it cannot quite redeem the rest of
the poem from mediocrity,

> Does there even a place like St. Juliot exist?
>   Or a Vallency valley
>   With stream and leafed alley
> Or Beeny, or Bos with its flounce flinging mist?

Setting aside for the moment the marvellous *After a Journey* (289/ALL/H/*) to be analysed alongside *Beeny Cliff* (291/ALL/ H/*) and *At Castle Boterel* (292/ALL/H/*), the next poem *A Deathday Recalled* (290/C/W/*) seems to derive from what was, for Hardy, an aberrant impulse. Normally he had no patience with the 'pathetic fallacy', frequently deriding the notion that Nature can 'feel' for Man. Accordingly his complaint that those places which, 'in her flower', Emma had 'sought and loved' did not utter 'dimmest note of dirge' for her passing' does not ring true, even though the swift lyrical movement and light touch do suggest a deliberate fancifulness. The conventions of the classical elegy are not Hardy's *métier*, as, in their different ways, the next three great poems demonstrate; though tradition might fructify his verse, he had no need of it as a crutch.

After a Journey (289/ALL/H/*)

This was written after, perhaps drafted immediately after, a visit to Pentargan Bay, as the subscription shows, in January 1913. The cliff path to it is now dangerous but it remains a spot of unspoiled and breathtaking beauty of which there is a fine prose account in *A Pair of Blue Eyes* (Chapter XXI), 'The small stream . . . running over the precipice . . . was dispersed in spray before it was half-way down.' A hundred and twenty years later this feature, like all the other components of the scene in the poem, remains unchanged. In some ways this poem summarises the themes variously stated and explored in earlier ones. Thus, in stanza 1, we meet the *ghost* again, in stanza 2 *the dark space* of the years between, clinched by *Time's derision*; stanza 3 presents the 'past involate', only for stanza 4 to reveal that as an apparent delusion. But there is a new dimension in *After a Journey*, as will appear.

This is, of course, another instance of Hardy's 'haunting', and the ghost, as before, is voiceless. Indeed, until 1920, the first line ran 'interview a ghost' which is much weaker in that 'interview' has an inappropriate flavour of journalism about it while *voiceless* is crucial to the sense. Yet, despite Emma's silence, Hardy, very subtly, contrives to 'speak' for her; her questions and statements are all implied, though there is no sense of contrivance in the assured ease with which this one-sided

conversation is handled. The verse-form is original and effective, the feminine rhymes in this poem are not subjected to the,
sometimes over-emphatic, proximity of couplets, and the variation in form between the first and second quatrains of each
stanza adds variety. It would take far too long to go into every
detail of Hardy's craftsmanship here; his resourcefulness is
endless. But there is the way in which Hardy suggests his
lonely, lost state of mind by the flitting, hesitant movement of
the first verse, the stresses cutting across the metrical beat to
hold up its forward impetus. Then *ejaculations* in line 4 of stanza
1 is a startlingly apt replacement of 'soliloquies', its extra
syllable rectifying the metre, its sound and its associations both
enacting the sound and suggesting the strangeness of the
invisible sea under the cliff-edge. This sense of bewilderment,
of puzzled groping, is resolved in a clear and lovely picture of
Emma; the last two lines are one of Hardy's rare glimpses of
sensuous and glowing phyical beauty. It seems to me that
Emma has a dual role in this poem, both as herself and as a kind
of goddess, representing an ideal once, but no longer, attain-
able; perhaps Aphrodite herself.

But the warmth of that last line is soon dispersed by the
sombre questionings of stanza 2, with its slower, dragging
tempo. Here reiterations serve to show us Hardy's own weariness and misery: *years, dead scenes, past, dark space, lacked,
division,* even the ambiguous *twain* all add to the cumulative
effect of disillusion. Emma's implied, gentle rebukes bring him
face to face with *Time's derision,* and the stanza ends harshly on
this image of the Old Enemy, apparently triumphant.

In stanza 3 Memory replies by summoning up the 'inviolate
past' again, where in Hardy's own phrase, once more 'Everything glowed with a gleam'. Here too is that awareness of love's
precariousness, like a walk on a razor-edge, which is omnipresent in Hardy's love poetry. *At the then fair hour in the then fair
weather,* he writes, with what would be clumsy insistence if it
did not so immediately convey his impassioned belief that
those moments were enchanted, outside time. But the bleak last
line extinguishes, at a stroke, all the warmth and light, leaving
Hardy with only the mocking echo from the *cave,* so well
suggested by the repeated alliteration in 1 from *hollow* to *call, all
aglow* and the concluding phrase *frailly follow.* Hardy's age, the

perceived futility of his quest, the waning of his vision are all implied in it. The heart's journey seems to end in frustration.

The next stanza offers no immediate consolation; full as the scene is of natural beauty it is *ignorant*, indifferent. With daylight and when *Life lours* the revenant must return to her grave, the 'Unquiet Ghost' be stilled as in the folk-song, and Hardy acknowledges the fact. But feelings are facts too and in these splendid lines with their solemn music, their symbolic dwelling on the borderland between night and day, and above all their intimacy, their gentleness seen in that stress on *Dear*, and their quiet humour even – for who but Hardy would have put *seals flop* and *stars close their shutters* – it ceases to matter any more what logic preaches. Love's adversaries, Time, Reason and Reality are disempowered, not by argument, but by the sheer force of conviction with which Hardy communicates his renewed vision. With our heads we may deny but with our hearts we assent to another kind of truth, to Hardy's: *I am just the same as when//Our days were a joy and our paths through flowers*. The *Journey* of the title has come to an end, it is seen now as a journey, not just into Cornwall but into love, life and time. It is John Donne's great paradox restated,

> Only our love hath no decay;
> This no tomorrow hath nor yesterday,
> Running, it never runs from us away,
> But truly keeps his first, last, everlasting day.
>
> John Donne, *The Anniversary*

Beeny Cliff (291/ALL/H/*)

Here Hardy takes off from where *After a Journey* ended, evoking a *clear-sunned March day* exactly 43 years later, as the double dates make clear. The first visit is recorded in one of the few pages that survive from Hardy's early journals. On 10 March 1870 he wrote, 'Went with E. L. G. to Beeny Cliff. She on horseback . . . On the cliff . . . 'The tender grace of a day,' etc.' The cliff is the setting of *Why Did I Sketch* (417) and *The Figure in the Scene* (416) both already discussed, and features prominently in *A Pair of Blue Eyes* too. Hardy listed it among 'The Best Scenery I know' and it is undoubtedly dramatic and impressive, but its beauty is severe and sometimes forbidding; 'green towards the land – blue-black towards the sea . . . dark-grey ocean, pale-green sky . . . sea full of motion internally, but still as a whole', as he described it in 1872. More than most natural features it is capable, even in summer, of chameleonic changes of aspect; in a matter of moments the weather can turn it from a gay, welcoming vista into a grim, foreboding presence. It is thus a particularly potent image: its double-nature mirroring symbolically Hardy's own divided feelings, towards it and his own revisitation as a whole.

I have already discussed Hardy's technique here towards the end of Chapter 3, and Donald Davie followed by Tom Paulin has very thoroughly analysed the verse-form and metre. It is enough to say that the metre is basically *septenary* (i.e. having seven feet) and closely resembles what Tennyson used in one of his most famous poems *Locksley Hall*. But though it suits Hardy to employ the same long, flowing lines and wave-like rhythms, his rhymes are in triplets instead of Tennyson's couplets, and, by varying the stress pattern he avoids the Poet Laureate's slightly hypnotic regularity. None the less, this is meant to be a musical, lyrical even opulent poem, re-enacting the lovers' heightened awareness of the scene around them, just as the lilting alliteration in *l* points up the mood in *laughed light-heartedly aloft*. Hardy indeed deploys alliteration to great effect throughout the poem, more subtly in *d* and *l* to suggest the shadow which overcasts the sea – and the poem – in stanza 3 line 2, more strongly to stress the massive grandeur in *beauty bulks old Beeny*, or to emphasise the strangeness of Lyonnesse in *wild weird western shore*.

Despite the ominous implications succinctly implied in *dull misfeatured stain*, the 1870 visit ends as joyously as it began, with an effulgent final line, and a characteristically Hardeian verb *prinked* of which the basic meaning is to 'spruce or dress up', suggesting the ocean's beauty as feminine, perhaps even coquettish, and so treacherous perhaps.

The pause and the change to the present tense returns us to 1913; the one word *chasmal*, an epithet which goes far beyond mere aptness, signals a radical change of temper, though the calculated simplicity of language and diction in the next two lines is disarming, counterpointing the hard logic that under-lies the actual question. The extraordinarily prolonged and rapid sequence of monosyllables (26 out of 28 words) imparts to us a sudden upsurge of feeling, an anguished appeal against reason which can have only one answer. But the last stanza, which as first printed began, bluntly 'Nay. Though . . . ' turns this futile petition aside with another question, which still clings to the beauty of the scene, and then – with an agonised reluctance realised by the emphatic pause and the evasive anodyne of *elsewhere* – finally answers it with the last line, with its hollow, echoing sounds, so empty of hope. *Beeny Cliff* enacts the whole swing of Hardy's emotional pendulum, from the apogee of the first line, redolent of colour, light and desire, summed up in the simple phrase *laughed light-heartedly*, down to the harrowing nadir of the conclusion, where the poignant echo of that carefree delight was a revision of genius from the original flat 'see it', replaced by *laugh there* as late as 1920. Even at 80 no trouble was too great for Hardy in his quest for the last refinements of expression and meaning; as he drily observed 'Criticism is so easy and art so hard.'

At Castle Boterel (292/ALL/H/*)

The evidence of this poem's greatness is that it was a prime favourite of two such diverse poets as Philip Larkin and Dylan Thomas. It stems from an excursion of 9 March 1870 to Tintagel by pony-trap, noted by Hardy in his journal. The old road home from Boscastle harbour (i.e. from *Castle Boterel*) is precipitous and rock-lined. Emma's sister must have driven the burdened pony up the hill, leaving the – as yet undeclared – lovers to walk. But I believe the true genesis of this poem was Hardy's re-reading of his novel *A Pair of Blue Eyes* after Emma's death. The steep hill and pony-trap appear in Chapter VI, but it was surely the fine passage near the end of Chapter XXVII which was the catalyst. It relates an emotional crisis involving Elfride (the heroine, whose physical appearance Hardy altered in compliment to Emma) and the rival heroes Stephen Smith and Henry Knight (who embody differing aspects of Hardy's own nature). It states the central theme of one the finest love poems in English as follows

Their eyes met. Measurement of life should be proportioned rather to the intensity of the experience than to its actual length. Their glance, but a moment chronologically, was a season in their history.

The resemblance is striking; even the words 'but a moment' are apparently echoed in stanza 4's phrase *but a minute*. This is not an original idea, John Donne used it quite often, as in, for example, these lines

> Love, all alike, no season knows, nor clime,
> Nor hours, days, months, which are the rags of time.

Nor is Hardy's treatment of this topos at all elaborate or obscure; this is anything but a complex poem thematically; an incident is recalled, its significance examined, and Hardy turns away from his contemplation of the past to the present: that is all; though all the motifs which we have seen in earlier poems are touched on, as in a musical recapitulation, one by one. Hardy adopts, it would seem invented, a verse-form of dig-nified sobriety. Each five-line stanza, though given a rhythmic 'life' by the feminine rhymes of lines 1 and 3, ends in a heavily stressed final couplet, made yet more weighty by the clipped last line, which (with one exception) makes some statement crucial to Hardy's intention, though his skilful control of the poem's syntax, as between stanzas 1 and 2 for instance, pre-vents any jerkiness in the transitions; both the narrative and the argument sustain the pressure on the reader throughout.

The simple-seeming diction of *At Castle Boterel* is frequently deceptive. In stanza 1, for example, *look behind* applies both to direction (now) and to time (past) so that the *byway* is fading both to sight and to memory, while the repeated *shrinking* of stanza 7 is a good instance of multiple connotations. For not only is Emma's phantom shrinking as the light fades and as Hardy draws away from her, she is also shrinking into the past and the grave, perhaps even from the rain she disliked so much (see above, *Rain on a Grave*/280), – and – most chilling of all the implications – shrinking away from Hardy's desire to reassert their love, to atone for his indifference, as if to reproach him for his failure to return until it is too late. Meticulous as ever the neat opposition between *foot-swift*, *foot-sore* (stanza 4) was Hardy's final resolution of MS attempts, 'of late and yore' and 'in sun, rain, hoar', while the cruel vigour of *rude reason* replaced the MS's stodgy 'sore pressure'.

The first two verses carry the narrative economically to that vital *minute* which is the emotional and intellectual fulcrum of the poem. Love, the *something that life will not be balked of,* was then declared, or possibly only apprehended (the word *love* is held back until it appears, with tragic inevitability, in the penultimate line). The rest of the poem comprises a debate, conducted by Hardy's heart versus his head, into the question whether love really is 'A preface without any book,' as *A Two year's Idyll* (587) glumly concludes, or whether [Emma's] rainy form is the 'Genius still of that spot//Immutable . . . ' as *The Figure in the Scene* (416) defiantly asserts.

Traditionally, 'passion' is opposed to 'reason', so Hardy implies that it is, in this situation, *rude* in the sense of 'rough, crude, primitive' and hence unreliable as a preceptor. Logic has nothing to say to love; so far so good.

Yet Love is subject to Time, and though he now triumphantly produces the contention that, as the sentence from *A Pair of Blue Eyes* asserted, it is the *quality* of time that matters ultimately, he is much too honest to suppose this satisfies all intellectual objections. His even-handedness is shown in the image of the *primaeval rocks* than which nothing could better show, in Shakespeare's phrase, 'How small a part of time [we] share'. But he then sets the dizzying geological implications aside as irrelevant, dumb to him except in so far as they testify that *we two passed*. Only man endows a place with significance, without his presence there is a void. So, paradoxically, Hardy's unbelief, his scientific outlook, while it helps him in coming to terms with his own insignificance, makes love more, not less, meaningful.

Now *Time*, accorded personified status, is granted his full due. Hardy concedes that the *substance* (i.e. the actual events, as opposed to the 'essence') of the unique *minute* has been ruled from sight by – and this has all the resonance of Shakespeare's Sonnets – *Time's unflinching rigour*. Yet the Old Enemy is disarmed by a brilliant and subtle device. For Hardy portrays him, implicitly, in the words *mindless rote* and *ruled from sight*, not as the remorseless wielder of the scythe, but as some sort of pen-pushing ledger-clerk, casting up and ruling off his accounts by rote. This 'turn' has an almost Donne-like arrogance but it is immediately dissipated by the fleeting glimpse of the *phantom figure* that was once a *girlish form* and is now, like it, *benighted* in another sense altogether. Hardy's moment of vision is profoundly affecting: it is as if the very intensity of his desire could lend it something of infinity, just as long as he can look back in time and *see it there*. But the waggonette drives on, dusk and the rain fall together and Hardy's ultimate return upon himself is excoriating in its poignancy. For with whatever stoicism or serenity he accepts that his *sand is sinking* – and here perhaps is the 'running of time's far glass' foretold in *Near Lanivet* (366) – the receding of the vision brings with it the knowledge that his own death will also bring *old love's domain* to an end. And his two last words may accordingly seem almost dangerously commonplace. But we do not feel that *Never again* as a cliché: rather it is as if the words had been recharged with the emotive power they must have generated when someone first put them together. Nowhere is Hardy's ability to renew the roots of English poetry, to re-endow it with that directness and plangency which it exudes in medieval lyric or the songs from Shakespeare's plays, better exemplified than it is in *At Castle Boterel*. If I had to choose one poem to speak for him, this would be it!

In comparison with its predecessor, *Places* (293/C/D/W/*), for all its vivid evocations of Emma's childhood and youth when riding, 'free of fear//She cantered down as if she must fall// (Though she never did' verges on the nostalgic, though it gives a sharp insight into the mind of an old man 'To whom today is beneaped and stale,//And its urgent clack//But a vapid tale'; three lines as crisply definitive as any he wrote. But he ends the original sequence on a high note with *The Phantom Horsewoman* (294/ALL/H/*). This poem differs from its predecessors in that Hardy distances himself from its protagonist, writing of a 'queer', 'careworn' man of whom 'They say he sees as an instant thing//More clear than today,// . . . //A phantom of his own figuring.' He concedes that to the looker-on his 'vision' may appear the product of obsessive, 'crazed' behaviour. But, to him, it seems 'drawn rose-bright' on his mind. The function of the poem is both to recapitulate the themes of the series and, in a sense, to defend himself against the charge that his grief is disproportionate. But this is not a ratiocinative poem; the 'argument' is in the poetry, and because critics should know when to be quiet, I am content simply to quote the superb final stanza where his 'vision of heretofore', up to this moment only obiquely touched on, suddenly opens out as

> A ghost-girl-rider. And though, toil-tried
>   He withers daily,
>   Time touches her not,
>   But she still rides gaily
>   In his rapt thought
>   On that shagged and shaly
>   Atlantic spot,
>   And as when first eyed
> Draws rein and sings to the swing of the tide.

Of the three added poems *The Spell of the Rose* (295/C/W/*) is intriguing. It has Emma's ghost speaking again, but Hardy has thought fit to equip the opening verses with a Max Gate *à la* William Morris, with 'turrets' and a 'newelled stair' together with some medieval rose-symbolism which never quite gets assimilated into the 'heart-bane' theme. *St. Launce's Revisited* (296/C/W/*) is pleasant but lightweight and though *Where the Picnic Was* (297/C/D/W/H/*) is the best of the three, its link with the series is rather tenuous. There are, however, several other poems, mostly dated 1912 and 1913 and plainly stemming from the period when, as Hardy said, '[he] was in flower . . . but the flower was sad-coloured.' With most of them it is not too hard to understand why, whatever their incidental felicities, he judged them to be unsuited or unequal to the series. *The Change* (384/W/*), for example, is patchy, and *The Curtains Now Are Drawn* (523/D/W/H/*), though it opens most impressively, does not quite stand up to Hardy's introduction, as a refrain, of Emma singing what seem like (and perhaps are, judging by Hardy's use of quotation marks), lines from a Victorian ballad. But several appear to me comparable in quality with those of the *Poems of 1912–13* which are not quite in the first rank. Thus, *The Dream Is Which?* (611/D/W/*) of March 1913 develops a theme very similar to that of *A Dream Or No* (288) much more adeptly. Its three verses each show a 'harsh change' impinging on such joyous moments as 'We danced in heys around the hall//Weightless as thistleball', and starkly oppose illusion and reality. *On a Discovered Curl of Hair* (630/G/*) may verge on sentimentality perhaps, to begin with, but the change of key in 'Where are its fellows now? Ah they//For brightest brown have donned a gray', is very telling. *The Prospect* (735/W/*) of December 1912, probably the poem written most recently after Emma's death makes use of some of Hardy's most masterly visual imagery to contrast the 'summertime, yea, of last July' and a garden party, with an aural impression of Max Gate garden in winter, when, 'Icicled airs wheeze through the skeletoned hedge from the north,//With steady snores . . . '. Both *She Opened the Door* (740/D/W/*) and *He Prefers Her Earthly* (442/C/D/W/*) deserve careful reading also. One brief poem *A Night in November* (542/C/D/G/H/*) is, however, so outstanding that I propose to end this chapter with it.

POEMS OF MARRIAGE

For fairly obvious reasons this is nothing like as homogenous a group as the last: the poems, like the events they touch on, are scattered over many years, and one cannot always be sure that they do refer to the Hardys' marriage because some are plainly fictionalised in varying degrees. Broadly speaking, for all the often fascinating biographical insights they offer, they do not – as poetry – reach the level of the best of those already discussed. Nevertheless, from the forty-odd which fall into this category, a number stand out from those which, because they deal more or less explicitly with the unhappier aspects of their marriage, Hardy had naturally felt unable to publish until after Emma's death, even if, as may be true of a few of them, he had *written* them before 1912. Thus, *Alike and Unlike* (762/C/D/W/*), with its cryptic title, its location 'Great Orme's Head', and its note, 'She Speaks' on the MS, refers to a visit of 1893 to Llandudno, and the way in which the 'magnificent purples' of the scene in stormy weather, though their 'eye-records' of them were identical, left only a 'slight' impression on Emma, but on Hardy's mind 'gravings' . . . 'tragic, gruesome, gray', which tended 'to sever us thenceforth alway'. What exactly occurred

Hardy does not tell us, but the lasting involvement of a place with an emotion experienced there is seen here on its dark face. *Had You Wept* (313/D/W/*) is not certainly about Emma, but it identifies as a prime cause of 'our deep division, and our dark undying pain' that inarticulate reticence leading to what Hardy, in his notebook, called 'Misapprehension' where 'shrinking soul[s] show by constraint' fear that their 'weak place is going to be laid bare . . . withdraw . . . and misunderstand.' That dates from 1886 but Hardy does not seem to have been able to apply its sharp insight to his own predicament, and many of these poems revolve around that failure of empathy, some very painfully indeed. *On the Tune Called the Old 104th* (576/*) is one in which Hardy reflects on 'Ravenscroft's terse old tune' which Emma and he both loved but 'never sang together' in life. Now they may, in 'Sheol' (the Hebrew afterworld) 'sing it in desolation' when they might have done so 'With love and exultation// Before our sands had run.' It is a simple, poignant treatment of a 'road not taken'. The use of a music as a motif occurs also in *The Strange House* (537/W/*), a compelling dialogue between later occupants of Max Gate in AD 2000. The wife hears 'a piano playing//Just as a ghost might play', but the husband is unresponsive to 'her vision//Of showings beyond our sphere' and indifferent to the 'love-thralls' and their 'joy or despair'. This parallels, surely deliberately, Hardy's own attitude to Emma's intuitiveness. *The Musical Box* (425/C/D/W), one of the best of these, is set at Sturminster Newton which had far happier associations. This offers a glowing picture of Hardy coming home at evening, in 'the fair colour of the time', hearing the 'mindless lyre' playing as Emma 'white-muslined, waiting there//With high-expectant heart,' stands to welcome him, but in his 'dull soul-swoon' not apprehending the 'spirit' of the 'gentle chime'; 'O value what the nonce outpours//This best of life . . . '. It is an appropriately lyrical and melodious poem. That cannot be said of *The Interloper* (432/D/W/*), which is significantly subscribed, 'And I saw the figure and visage of Madness seeking for a home'. Structurally and in terms of diction this resembles *During Wind and Rain* (441); snapshots, innocuous in themselves, from the past are given tragic weight by the refrain which intrudes a presence, never overtly identified and consequently the more menacing, except as 'One who ought not to be there.' The degree to which Emma's instability could be construed as 'madness' is disputable, but the poem's sometimes clumsily colloquial manner does not mask its grim sincerity. It might have been more effective if Hardy had not written an 'explanatory' fifth verse which, in its attempts to define 'that under which best lives corrode' rather muffles the sinsister suggestiveness of the first four.

Finally, there are a few posthumous poems which relate to events or places different from those of the 1912–13 series. *If You Had Known* (592/W/*) relates a visit to Emma's grave 'Fifty years thence to an hour' after 'listening with her to the far-down moan//Of the white-selvaged and empurpled sea,' – a marvellous line – in Cornwall. It is a very simple poem, compactly and elegantly expressing the universal lament 'If only?' and quite without comment. *The Marble Tablet* (617/D/W) in contrast, is about the memorial Hardy had erected, to his own design, in St Juliot Church (its twin now commemorates him). This is not so much an epitaph as a poem about the ultimate futility of epitaphs, a twist altogether typical of Hardy. The 'cold white look' of the memorial can show us nothing of Emma at all – 'Not her glance, glide or smile; not a tittle of her// Voice . . . '. But, paradoxically, this is exactly what the poem can do, and does, going on to compress her life into a few lines and then to admit that, for both kinds of memorial, there is 'Nothing more.' But that bleakness is softened by the conclusion, remarkable for its stillness and sobriety, like that of the marble tablet, which tells

> That one has at length found the haven
> Which every one other will find;
> With silence on what shone behind.

In its treatment of such a sensitive subject, so open to facile emotion, it is restrained but not at all dispassionate: stone may be dumb to tell us Emma's worth or Hardy's grief, but print is capable of a more durable eloquence. This was a quality to which, in his modesty, he laid no claim. But he was not unaware of the quality of his poetry, unerringly selecting the best of the *Poems of 1912–13* for his own selection from his verse and, indeed, as the codings demonstrate, together with his emendations, showing himself generally as far shrewder than those of his critics who supposed him to be a rustic naïf.

He included in *Chosen Poems* one not in the 1912–13 series. It is hard to guess why he withheld *A Night in November* for it is a small triumph, succinct, perceptive, deceptively subtle, ineffably sad.

A Night in November (542/C/D/G/H/*)

I marked when the weather changed,
And the panes began to quake,
And the winds rose up and ranged,
That night, lying half-awake.

Dead leaves blew into my room,
And alighted upon my bed,
And a tree declared to the gloom,
Its sorrow that they were shed.

One leaf of them touched my hand,
And I thought that it was you
There stood as you used to stand,
And saying at last you knew!

This seems (Hardy put a question mark by the date of 1913) to have been written on or about the first anniversary of Emma's death in 1912. It can scarcely be said to embody a thought at all, merely a momentary sense-impression, the fleeting illusion that a dead leaf's touch was that of a living woman. But much of Hardy's finest poetry occupies that debatable territory between his 'five and country senses' so acute even in old age, and the emotions that stem from them. Here, things are animated in both senses; the *panes quake*, (and how easy it would have been to put 'shake') the winds *range*, even the leaf *alights* – like a live thing, like a bird, rather than 'falls' – and the tree *declares* its *sorrow*. So Hardy holds in perfect equipoise the 'scientific fact' that nature is indifferent to man, and the emotional conviction that it can feel. And there is the same blend of truth and fancy in the conclusion; the delicate touch of the leaf calls up the Emma of Lyonnesse, of which she once wrote, quoting Coleridge, of how 'Lightly then I flashed along'. That poem, like Hardy's, is about the 'sad' change 'twixt now and then.' But Hardy's firm stress on *thought* qualifies his last two lines; whether Emma 'knew' is left for us to judge, as always he offers 'impression not conviction'.

It is fitting that we should end with a tree symbolising Hardy's bereavement, for he loved trees all his life, planting many with his own hands, and they appear repeatedly in both his prose and his verse. And indeed his poetry resembles an ancient oak; seen close it may appear rugged and earthbound, lacking in grace and delicacy. But the flaws in both arise from a massive strength and an enduring vigour; we lose sight of them if we draw back to contemplate the splendour of the whole achievement; an achievement rooted in truth, wisdom and humility; a vision that in Matthew Arnold's lapidary phrase, 'saw life steadily and saw it whole.'

Matthew Arnold was actually writing of Sophocles, whose work Hardy revered, and the phrases he employs to characterise the Greek poet's achievement also identify, very precisely, what I think of as the salient characteristics of Hardy's. In 'saw life steadily' Arnold refers to that cool truthfulness which is surely Hardy's greatest asset. As he once told the novelist Meade Faulkner, all his work had been ' – just what I could not help doing even if [it] had led to poverty and ruin.' Of his 'sincerity', as Edward Thomas pointed out, there can be no doubt. Other poets may be more spectacular, more cerebral, more complex, more witty or more lyrical; Hardy's first loyalty is always to the integrity of his vision. He will neither palliate nor denigrate the human condition as he sees it, and if that leads him, as it sometimes does, into the seemingly banal or bathetic, yet it also assures us of a bedrock of truth which underpins all his verse and also empowers him to deliver sentiments of an heroic plainness with utter conviction. When he writes, 'The paths of love are rougher//Than thoroughfares of stones', we do not feel, simple as the thought and image may be, that this is any kind of platitude. Rather it has that air of something said once and for all that Shakespeare can command in, say, 'Youth's a stuff will not endure.' Like Wordsworth's his is a 'Truth not standing upon external testimony but carried alive into the heart by passion.' And, because fealty to the truth cannot be reconciled with rose-coloured spectacles, Hardy became, as Middleton Murry observed, of all English poets the one who has 'most steadfastly refused to be comforted'. But that steadfastness also encompasses a refusal to rush into emotional or intellectual panaceas. If he owes to his rural forbears one thing more than another it is that tough, down-to-earth commensensicality which his Wessex labourers bring to bear upon the follies and fantasies of his heroes and heroines in the novels. Yet, in him, the hard-headedness is always tempered by a compassionate heart. Though he could not believe that God sees the sparrow fall, no living thing was too insignificant for him to pity its fate.

Mention of Hardy's powers of empathy leads naturally to a consideration of his range, which was, in terms of both theme and form, exceptionally wide. Though 'to see life whole' is doubtless beyond the capacity of any artist, many fine poets have only been able to make full creative use of a fairly constricted frame of experience. Hardy, on the other hand, could fashion a poem out of anything and everything – not invariably a good poem be it said – and this Protean appetite, coupled with his architect's eye for significant detail and his prodigiously retentive memory, endows him with his second claim upon our minds, that immense breadth and variety which, as Philip Larkin said, mean that 'One can read him for years and years and still be surprised.'

While Arnold naturally takes for granted Sophocles' mastery of poetic form Hardy's technique was, for many years, the score on which critics found it easiest to denigrate him for his 'uncelestial music of marrowbones and cleavers', as Lytton Strachey put it. Significantly, practising poets have never shared this view. Walter de la Mare in 1919 remarked that 'Difficulty, seeming impossibility, is the breath of [Hardy's] nostrils as a craftsman.' W. H. Auden and Philip Larkin among many other poets have since echoed him, and – now that stanzas and rhymes are back with us again – it is possible to see Hardy for what he really is, the last great master of traditional verse-form (the inventor indeed of hundreds), rather than as some antediluvian survival from the liberating deluge of 'free verse'. Hardy himself wrote of Sophocles as one of those who 'burnt brightlier towards their setting-day' and that was equally true of him. There was no failure, either of nerve or creative vigour; the panoramic vision, the blend of pity and irony continued unabated into his eighties; 'Tasting years of moderate gladness//Mellowed by sundry days of sadness,' as he wrote in a late poem *A Private Man on Public Men* (916/C/G/ W/*). But the last word may be left with another poet. Edmund Blunden's *Thoughts of Thomas Hardy* has always seemed to me the best of the many poems about him. In it Blunden's ear is caught by the rustle of a stray dead leaf. It seems wholly lacking in significance to him until he envisages how Hardy would have contemplated it, and memorably pictures him as one who

> . . . in that sound
> Looked aware of a vaster threne of decline,
> And considering a law of all life.
> Yet he lingered, one lovingly regarding
> Your particular fate and experience, poor leaf.

Further Reading

This a selective reading list. Nearly everything it contains is available in book form (and thus via public libraries). My few comments are descriptive, not evaluative, but, where I think a book likely to be helpful to a beginner in Hardy studies, I add an asterisk to its title (thus *). The following abbreviations are used: H (Hardy's), TH (Thomas Hardy's), OUP (Oxford University Press), CUP (Cambridge University Press). Except where indicated all books are, or were, published by Macmillan. PB indicates that it is available in paperback edition.

I TEXTS OF HARDY'S VERSE

The eight successive volumes first appeared as follows: 1988, *Wessex Poems* and Other Verses (with H's illustrations); 1901, *Poems of the Past and the Present*; 1909, *Time's Laughingstocks* and Other Verses; 1914, *Satires of Circumstances*, Lyrics and Reveries; 1917, *Moments of Vision* and Miscellaneous Verses; 1922, *Late Lyrics and Earlier* with Many Other Verses (inc. H's Apology); 1925, *Human Shows*, Far Fantasies, Songs and Trifles; 1928, *Winter Words* (posthumously published).

All were first printed together as *The Collected Poems of TH* in 1930, often reprinted but never re-edited until J. Gibson's *The Complete Poems of TH* (1976) (the same editor's *Variorum Complete Poems* (1979) gives all printed and all significant MS variants). S. Hynes's *The Complete Poetical Works of TH* (OUP, 1982) *et seq.*) includes *The Dynasts* as Vols 4 and 5. NB. The italicised words in the titles of the separate volumes above are the usual 'short forms' employed.

Selections from Hardy's verse

Hardy himself chose 120 poems from his first four volumes as his *Selected Poems of TH* (1916), adding to them from the next three to make his *Chosen Poems of TH* (1929). Later selections by Young (1940); Ransom (USA, 1961) and Wain (1966) contain interesting and substantial introductions. See Chapter 1 for others.

II BIBLIOGRAPHIES AND COMMENTARIES

J. L. Purdy, *TH, A Bibliographical Study* (OUP, 1954). Definitive, lists all H's work.

R. P. Draper and M. Ray, *An Annotated Bibliography of TH* (Harvester Press, 1989).

J. O. Bailey, *The Poems of TH, A Handbook and a Commentary* (Chapel Hill, USA, 1970).

F. B. Pinion, *A Commentary on the Poems of TH* (1976).

Bailey and Pinion annotate virtually all the poems between them.

III BIOGRAPHIES OF HARDY, LETTERS ETC.

F. E. Hardy, *The Life of TH** (originally 2 volumes 1928–30) in one volume 1962, re-edited, some deletions restored by M. Millgate as *The Life and Work of TH by TH* 1985*. Despite evasions and omissions remains essential. See index for H's comments on many of his own poems. PB.

M. Millgate, *TH, A Biography* (OUP, 1983). Full, judicious and authoritative. PB.

T. O'Sullivan, *TH, A Pictorial Biography* (1977). Good short life, fine illustrations.

E. Hardy, *Some Recollections** (OUP, 1961). Emma's lively account of her early life and first meeting with H in Cornwall. PB.

R. L. Purdy and M. Millgate (eds), *The Collected Letters of TH*, Vols I–VII (OUP, 1975–88) – much trivia but some valuable insights – and *Selected Letters* (OUP, 1990).
R. H. Taylor, *The Personal Notebooks of TH* (1978).

IV   CONTEMPORARY REVIEWS OF HARDY'S POETRY

J. Gibson and T. Johnson (eds), *TH Poems** (Macmillans 'Casebook' series, 1979). Gives full selection of reviews 1898–1928 as its second section. PB.

V   BOOKS ABOUT HARDY'S POETRY (LISTED IN ORDER OF PUBLICATION)

J. G. Southworth, *The Poetry of TH* (Columbia University, USA, 1947).
S. Hynes, *The Pattern of H's Poetry** (Chapel Hill, USA, 1956).
K. Marsden, *The Poems of TH** (Athlone Press, London University, 1970).
D. Davie, *TH and British Poetry* (Routledge, 1972).
P. Zietlow, *Moments of Vision: The Poetry of H* (Harvard University, USA, 1974).
T. Paulin, *TH, The Poetry of Perception** (1977). PB.
J. C. Richardson, *TH, The Poetry of Necessity* (Chicago University, USA, 1977).
P. Clement and J. Grindle (eds), *The Poetry of TH* (Vision Press, 1980). A collection of essays by various hands.
D. Taylor, *H's Poetry 1860–1928* (1981). PB.
M. Mukul Das, *H, Poet of Tragic Vision* (Macmillan, India, 1983).
W. E. Buckler, *The Poetry of TH* (New York, University Press, USA, 1983).
D. Taylor, *TH and Victorian Prosody* (OUP, 1989).
J. Cullen Brown,* *A Journey into H's Poetry* (W.H. Allen, 1989).

VI GENERAL BOOKS ABOUT HARDY

Note. These are very numerous. Only those with significant content on H's poems are listed below.

A. McDowall, *TH, A Critical Study** (Faber, 1931).

E. Blunden, *TH* (1940).

D. Brown, *TH** (Longman, 1954). PB.

T. Johnson, *TH* (Evans, 1968). PB.

F. B. Pinion, *TH, Art and Thought* (1971). A collection of his essays.

J. Brooks, *H, The Poetic Structure** (Elek, 1971). PB.

H. Orel, *H, the Final Years* 1912–28 (1976).

N. Page, *TH* (Routledge, 1977). PB.

J. Bayley, *An Essay on H* (CUP, 1978).

VII ESSAYS, ARTICLES ETC. ABOUT HARDY'S POETRY

There are hundreds of these; with few exceptions I have only listed those that may be consulted *in books* because the original periodical publications are often inaccessible except in academic libraries. Three *collections* of essays will be found useful:

R. G. Cox (ed), *TH, The Critical Heritage* (Routledge, 1970) cited as COX.

A. J. Guerard (ed), *H. A Collection of Critical Essays* (Prentice Hall, USA, 1963). In the 'Twentieth Century Views' series, PB, cited as C20 VIEWS.

J. Gibson and T. Johnson (eds), *TH Poems*, A Casebook (1979, in Macmillan's 'Casebook' series) PB, cited as CASE.

There are three specialist periodicals on Hardy which must be mentioned.

The TH Annual, ed. N. Page, 1983–.

The TH Yearbook, ed. G. Stevens Cox, Toucan Press, Guernsey, 1970–, cited as THYB.

The TH Journal, ed. J. Gibson, The Thomas Hardy Society, 1975–, cited as THJ.

Three special issues of periodicals are of particular importance also:

The Southern Review (USA), The 'TH Centennial' edtion 1940. This contains eight fine essays on H's poetry. Reprinted by Kraus, 1961.

Agenda (UK), 'TH Special Issue', 1972, ed. D. Davie. 8 essays on H's poems.

Victorian Poetry (USA), 'Special H Issue' 1979, ed. Giordano. 8 essays on H's poems.

The listing below is in alphabetical order of authors.

W. H. Auden, *H, A Literary Transference** in *Southern Review* (1940) and C20 VIEWS.

H. Baker, *H's Poetic Certitude* in *Southern Review* (1940) and CASE.

J. Barzun, *Truth and Poetry in H* in *Southern Review* (1940).

M. Bowra, *The Lyrical Poetry of H* in his *Inspiration and Poetry* (1955).

C. Cox and A. Dyson, *H's 'After a Journey'** in their *Modern Poetry* (Arnold, 1963) and CASE.

D. Davie, *H's Virgilian Purples* in *Agenda* 'TH Special Issue' (1972).

C. Day Lewis, *The Lyrical Poetry of TH**, Warton Lecture (OUP, 1951) and CASE.

W. de la Mare, *TH's Lyrics** in his *Private View* (Faber, 1953) and CASE.

J. Gibson, *Introduction* to his *Variorum Complete Poems* of TH (1979).

E. Gosse, *Mr. H's Lyrical Poems* in his *Selected Essays* (Cape, 1928) and COX.

T. Gunn, *H and the Ballads** in *Agenda* 'TH Special Issue' (1972) and CASE.

S. Hynes, *The H Tradition in Modern English Poetry*, THJ (Oct. 1986).

T. Johnson, *H and the Respectable Muse*, THYB 1, (1970).

T. Johnson, *'Despite Time's Derision' H, Donne and the 'Poems of 1912–13'* THYB VII (1979).

F. R. Leavis, *H the Poet** in *Southern Review* (1940).

F. R. Leavis, *New Bearings in English Poetry* (Chapter 1) (Chatto and Windus, 1932) PB.

J. M. Murry, *The Poetry of Mr. H* in his *Aspects of Literature* (Cape, 1920) and CASE.

D. Perkins, *H and the Poetry of Isolation* (1959) in C20 VIEWS.

V de Sola Pinto, *'H and Housman'* in his *Crisis in English Poetry* (Hutchinson, 1951).

I. A. Richards, *Notes on H's Poetry* in *Victorian Poetry* Special Issue (1979).

J. C. Ransom, *Honey and Gall* [H's poems] in *Southern Review* (1940).

D. Schwarz, *Poetry and Belief in TH* in *Southern Review* (1940).

C. H. Sisson, *H and Barnes* in *Agenda* 'TH Special Issue' (1971).

L. E. W. Smith, *'The Impercipient'* in THJ (May 1988) and CASE.

L. Strachey, *H's 'Satires of Circumstance'** in his *Literary Essays* (1948) and CASE.

A. Tate, *H's Philosophic Metaphors* in *Southern Review* (1940).

E. Thomas, *Three Dorset Poets** in his *In Pursuit of Spring* (Nelson, 1914). *'Hardy'* in his *A Literary Pilgrim in England** (Methuen, 1917). (Both are reprinted in THYB IV, 1976.)

A. Young, *Radical Tradition: TH and Dylan Thomas*, THYB VII (1979).

VIII HARDY ON POETRY

What Hardy himself wrote on poetry is scattered and mostly fragmentary. *The Complete Poems* contains his Prefaces and the important 'Apology' of 1922. The Creighton and the Hynes selections, like CASE, contain generous extracts from *The Life*, the Letters and the Notebooks. The *General Preface* to the 'Wessex Edition' is in H. Orel's useful compilation *H's Personal Writings*, 1966.

IX MISCELLANEOUS MATERIAL

J. Gibson's slide/tape programme *TH: The Making of Poetry* is available from Macmillan Education. There is a cassette recording by A. Chedzoy on 'Canto' cassettes from the Carcanet Press. The most handy guide for walking the Hardy country is A. M. Edward's *In the Steps of TH*, Countryside Books, 1989.

Index

Note: This is not a full index. Its main function is to help the reader to locate discussion of particular poems by Hardy in the text. Thus, in Section A, every poem by Hardy which is mentioned, however briefly, is indexed alphabetically by title. Because there are minor variations in the alphabetical conventions used in differing selections, I have here followed the order of the *Complete Poems*, adding its serial numbers in parenthesis after the titles. Page references for major entries (i.e. those giving substantial comment, normally of half a page or more) are set in **bold type**, as in the example which follows:

Beeny Cliff (291) 46, **50–51**, 228, **230–232**.

Section B is an alphabetical list of persons (authors, critics, family, friends and so on) who are mentioned and sometimes quoted in the text. Section C lists references and quotations from other works by Hardy, in order of composition. Note that no attempt is made to classify references to Hardy himself. The chapter headings will provide a rough guide as to where his views on particular subjects are likely to appear. Only the initial reference to a member of Hardy's immediate family is given, but virtually all of these occur in Chapters 1 and 2 of course, though there are quite numerous references to his wives in Chapter 7.

Index. Section A
Poems by Hardy

Index. Section B
Persons mentioned in the text